Jung and the New

Just as formal religion appears to dwindle to a minority interest, 'New Age' spirituality gathers increasing momentum and baffles us with its popular appeal. What is more, it has appropriated Jung as one of its spiritual leaders.

In his own trenchant style, David Tacey offers a theoretical and philosophical account of the New Age phenomenon and the archetypal imperatives that have brought it about. He also investigates the popular claim that Jung is a prophet or mystic, and argues that critics have been only too willing to concur with what the New Age has made of him, conspiring to turn Jung into a figure of ridicule.

Jung and the New Age redresses the balance, while offering a wide-ranging discussion about the state of consciousness in the New Age culture, and the future of spirituality versus formal religion.

David Tacey is Associate Professor at La Trobe University, Australia.

Jung and the New Age

David Tacey

Brunner-Routledge
Taylor & Francis Group

HOVE AND NEW YORK

First published 2001
by Brunner-Routledge
27 Church Road, Hove, East Sussex, BN3 2FA

Simultaneously published in the USA and Canada
by Brunner-Routledge
325 Chestnut Street, Suite 800, Philadelphia, PA 19106

Reprinted 2002 (three times)
by Brunner-Routledge
27 Church Road, Hove, East Sussex, BN3 2FA
29 West 35th Street, New York, NY 10001

Brunner-Routledge is an imprint of the Taylor & Francis Group

© 2001 David Tacey

Typeset in Times by Keystroke, Jacaranda Lodge, Wolverhampton
Printed and bound in Great Britain by TJ International Ltd,
Padstow, Cornwall

British Library Cataloguing in Publication Data
A catalogue record for this book is available from the British Library

Library of Congress Cataloging in Publication Data
A catalog record for this book is available from the Library of Congress

ISBN 1–58391–159–6 (hbk)
ISBN 1–58391–160–X (pbk)

This book is dedicated to my students
and to all who are looking toward the future.

The New Age says,
'it's easy',
The Old Age says,
'it can't be done',
But the prophetic voice says:
'it can be done,
but it's not easy'.

May we work together to build a new spirituality.

We are living in what the Greeks called the *kairos*, the right moment, for a 'metamorphosis of the gods', of the fundamental principles and symbols. This peculiarity of our time, which is certainly not of our conscious choosing, is the expression of the unconscious man within us who is changing.

Jung (1957: 585)

Everything old in our unconscious hints at something coming.

Jung (1921: 630)

We moderns are faced with the necessity of rediscovering the life of the spirit; we must experience it anew for ourselves.

Jung (1929b: 780)

Every analysand starts by unconsciously misusing his newly won knowledge.

Jung (1928: 223)

The myth of the new was always beckoning to us. In America we love new religions, new ways of life, new heavens, and new techniques for reaching these heavens, all summed up in the phrase 'New Age'.

Rollo May (1991: 101)

Man today, stripped of myth, stands famished among all his pasts and must dig frantically for roots, be it among the most remote antiquities.

Nietzsche (1872: 136)

Contents

Acknowledgements

The Collected Works of C.G. Jung 1953–1992, by C.G. Jung, translated by Hull, edited by Fordham. © 1997 Princeton University Press.

Blake – Complete Writings, edited by Geoffrey Keynes. © 1966 Oxford University Press.

The Second Coming and *Selected Poetry* by W.B. Yeats extracts used with the permission of A.P. Watt Ltd. on behalf of Michael B. Yeats.

Every effort has been made to contact authors and copyright holders, but if proper acknowledgement has not been made, the copyright holder should contact the publishers.

Preface

The New Age movement is a significant spiritual phenomenon, and Jungians should be more interested in it than they appear to be, especially because the movement has appropriated Jung as one of its spiritual leaders. The New Age is generally frowned upon by the religious, academic and psychological institutions of our time, but it is 'there' and it has to be taken into account. Although its expressions may be crude or untutored, it is able to tell us much about the spirit of the time, about what is being left out of Western consciousness and what needs to be reconsidered or regarded with greater respect.

The New Age compensates our consciousness in different ways. It compensates our secular, materialist society by nakedly displaying the powerful longings of the human spirit, even if this compensation is unsuccessful, i.e. unacceptable to mainstream secular attitudes. It also compensates our established religious traditions by forcing us to attend to what has been repressed or ignored by Western religion: the sacred feminine, the Earth Mother, the Goddess, the body, nature, instincts, ecstasy and mysticism. When our Western institutions have carefully considered these elements then the New Age will disappear, because it will no longer need to compensate the one-sidedness that currently exists. But our institutions appear to be in no hurry to change, which suggests that the New Age will be around for a long time, and will go through changes of its own.

The New Age, however, does not compensate our consumerist society but simply reproduces several of its features in its industry and enterprise, creating a spiritual consumerism. It turns the spiritual realm into a commodity, packaging ancient wisdoms, indigenous cosmologies and spiritual psychologies in order to satisfy our spiritual longing. But because the New Age operates in this consumerist mode, it rarely meets our spiritual needs, often providing a 'fast food' service, a kind of McSpirit that fails to satisfy. The human spirit calls for an authentic response, not simply for a symptomatic or artificial quick-fix. Therefore, the New Age itself is a kind of parody of the authentic spiritual life that longs to be realised in our time.

The New Age is largely a product of American popular culture, and in these chapters I explore several aspects of American psychology and spiritual aspiration. To some extent, the New Age production of Jung is also the Americanisation of Jung, and so I attempt to recover Jung from the American ideological interests that have so radically transformed his life and work for popular consumption. I almost doubt whether such recovery is possible, so thoroughly has Jung been processed by American popular culture. This book is vigorously critical of certain attempts to popularise Jung, but at the same time I am conscious that popularisation of Jung is necessary and inevitable. I offer a long overdue critique of the popularisation of Jungian ideas and aspirations.

I have sometimes been asked why I have spent so much time working on the topic of Jung and the New Age. Why do I bother? It matters to me, because most people in my country encounter Jung not directly or first-hand through his difficult writings, but indirectly through the simplistic and reductive creations of the New Age movement. In Australia, there is hardly any Jungian presence or influence in high culture, as Jung has been systematically dismissed or edited out from religion, theology, psychology, psychiatry, literature, journalism and tertiary education. As such, he falls into low or popular culture, where he is vigorously distorted and shape-shifted by commercial interests. The situation is fairly similar in other countries, with only a few variations. The way most people come into contact with Jung is through the popularised American versions of him. Therefore, clarifications, discernments and criticisms must be made as a matter of moral and intellectual responsibility.

I am not a psychoanalyst but an academic scholar interested in Jungian psychology, culture and authentic spirituality. However, I wish to strongly differentiate myself from other academics like Richard Noll and Frank McLynn who seem to harbour spite and resentment toward Jung. My agenda is not to debunk Jung or expose him as a fraud, but to redeem him from simplistic representations and distorted prejudices. In academia, a typical game is to identify Jung with the New Age representations of him, and to condemn both together. Scholars often engage in a deliberate falsification of Jung, only too willing to concur with what the New Age has made of him, as this serves to reinforce academic prejudices and resistances. High and low cultures have conspired to turn Jung into a figure of ridicule and contempt, and it is time this conspiracy was brought to light.

This is my fifth book on archetypes and culture, and although my writings to date have been on diverse subjects, they share the common interest of tracking the sacred in secular society (see Tacey 1988; 1995; 1997; 2000). My chief passion is to discover what happens to our longing for the sacred, and to our religious impulses, when we inhabit secular space and live in secular or non-religious culture. The major themes in my writings are the uprising of the sacred feminine, the awakening of the earth archetype, the failure of intellectual culture to grasp the reality of the sacred, and the demise of institutional faith through its incapacity to listen to the spirit of the time.

In writing about the New Age, I am in part trying to understand what attracted me to this movement as a young adult in the 1960s and early 1970s. As a teenager living in Alice Springs, central Australia, I was inducted into New Age popular culture by groups of Californian students, whose parents were stationed at the joint Australian–American space research and defence facility at Pine Gap. At long distance, thousands of miles from California, I lived through the late stages of the 'Age of Aquarius', and watched this movement flower and disintegrate, only to reappear a few years later as the 'New Age'. The New Age had shops, businesses and centres of awareness on main city streets, whereas the Age of Aquarius was largely nascent and underground, except in the music industry. Although far more tame and commercial, the New Age of the 1980s and 1990s contained essentially the same spiritual ideas that had come out of the previous hippy era. Today, generations later, I see young people going through a similar process of counter-cultural identification, although now the movement has become more interested in spiritual power, occultism, shamanism and witchcraft. The spirituality operates in a slightly darker light.

A few years after I graduated from the Age of Aquarius, I became interested in post-Jungian archetypal psychology, which I now see as a more intellectual version of the same values and attitudes that were apparent in the Aquarian Conspiracy. This American movement aspires toward egolessness and relaxation, viewing the unconscious as a stream of sacred images that entertain and dazzle us, without making any claims on us, or asking us to become morally involved in what we are experiencing. Although operating under Jung's name, this movement is not Jungian at all, since it fails to understand the need for consciousness to respond ethically to its encounter with archetypes. The desire to be entertained, without the hassle of having to be transformed, is precisely the problem of the New Age. In today's postmodern world we find parodies of everything: spiritual technologies that are not spiritual, Jungian movements that are not Jungian, and theories of personality that are not ethical. But turning the unconscious into entertainment and ourselves into tourists is a very real and grave problem that faces our civilisation, a problem as great as its corollary and opposite number, fundamentalism. Irresponsible soul-tourism and fanatical fundamentalism seem to be growing as fast as each other.

My task here is not to give a detailed account of any New Age field of activity (such as ufology, past lives, shamanistic ritual, astrology, or near death experience), but to offer a theoretical or philosophical account of the New Age phenomenon and the archetypal imperatives that have brought it to birth. I read the New Age as a sort of 'dream' of the Christian West, a dream in which all the repressed aspects of our culture come into view. I respond to the movement as if Western culture were on the couch, and I were trying to interpret its disturbances. Following Jung, I believe that disturbances only go away if we integrate their underlying cause. Other books give more detailed information about New Age groups and activities from a psychodynamic perspective, including Jungian analyst John Haule's *Perils of the Soul: Ancient Wisdom and the New Age* (1999), and Freudian analyst Mel Faber's *New Age Thinking: A Psychoanalytic Critique* (1996). Here I am speaking more broadly about the state of consciousness in New Age culture, its psychodynamic drives and directions, its oceanic spirituality, its spiritual materialism, its struggle with narcissism and grandiosity, and its new kind of fundamentalism. Its appropriation of Jungian terms, language and concepts is always in the foreground of this work.

I teach Jung and literature at La Trobe University in Melbourne, and large numbers of my students belong to the New Age movement, and enter my courses in the expectation and hope of developing their interests in New Age spirituality. Some are disillusioned or alarmed to discover that Jung is not what they had imagined, not what the New Age presents him to be. My courses on Jung are often *de facto* 'Jung and the New Age' seminars, because I am forced to explain Jung to students who come to the subject with New Age assumptions and expectations.

I am grateful to the C.G. Jung Institute of Kusnacht-Zurich, and in particular to John Granrose and Robert Hinshaw, for encouraging me to teach an intensive course on 'Jung and the New Age' during the summer semester of 2000. Several chapters of the present work had their first public airing in Zurich, and I am grateful to the students, faculty and administrative staff of the Zurich Institute for their feedback, constructive criticism and support. An earlier version of Chapter 4, 'American New Age Jungian Inflation', was first delivered in London at a conference on 'International Post-Jungian Perspectives', organised by the Society of Analytical Psychology and the University of Essex. I thank the organisers, and the chairperson Andrew Samuels, for this event, and its useful feedback and comment.

I thank Dolores Brien in Philadelphia for publishing and editing my essay 'Jung and the New Age: A Study in Contrasts', in *The Round Table Review of Contemporary Jungian Thought*, and I am grateful to Susan Greenberg in London for publishing my 'Why Jung would Doubt the New Age' in her book *Therapy on the Couch*. These essays have been incorporated into this work.

I am grateful to friends and colleagues for their continued discussions with me on these and related topics, especially Janine Burke, John Carroll, Trish Dutton, Michael Leunig, David Ranson, Peter Ross and Eve Steel. Finally, I am grateful to my publisher Kate Hawes at Brunner-Routledge, production editor Imogen Burch and copy editor David Sanders, for their discussions, advice and editorial support.

David Tacey, Associate Professor
School of Communication, Arts and Critical Enquiry
La Trobe University, Melbourne

Introduction

The need for an authentic New Age

Maybe we should just let the term 'New Age' drop. Certainly it rings all the wrong bells in the minds of mainstream Christians.

Thomas Matus

It's a pity, though, to leave this meaningful term to a historic period. The good news always calls for a New Age. In that sense, you can reintroduce this term.

David Steindl-Rast

(Capra and Steindl-Rast 1992: 180)

The rise of popular spirituality

Just as formal religion appears to dwindle to a minority interest, spirituality gathers increasing momentum and baffles us with its popular appeal. Many of us refer to ourselves as post-religious, and join in the modern protest against the authority of the faith institutions, yet the biblical injunction 'man does not live by bread alone' (Matthew 4.4) rings loudly in our ears. The unchurched secular mainstream are demanding a new kind of religious enchantment, and they are willing to spend considerable time and money exploring the enchantments which have become tagged as 'New Age'. Bookstores and publishers report huge sales of works on spirituality, and a thriving Mind/Body/Spirit market delivers workshops, tapes, books, music, meditation courses and insight seminars to the self-styled starving masses. Ten years ago, media commentators were saying that the New Age movement would not last; it was just a passing fad, and was destined for the rubbish heap of social fashions. But much to the anguish of media pundits, the alarm of social positivists, the disbelief of church leaders and the disdain of progressive intellectuals, the phenomenon of New Age spirituality looks like remaining with us for some time.

Far from being a minor fashion, in some countries the New Age, already a significant social force, is poised to rival the traditional institutions of faith for supremacy in religious and spiritual matters. In Britain and Australia, church attendance is down to an astonishingly low 7 per cent of the population, and yet far more than 7 per cent of people speak the language of astrology, horoscopes and spiritual journeys. The ascendancy of the New Age in California and in other American states is well known, even if these states sometimes reject the tag 'New Age'. In Canada, Australia and New Zealand, the presence of the New Age is clearly apparent for all to see. In the United Kingdom, the situation appears to be more complex. The UK prides itself on being a stable and level-headed society, relatively free from the suggestive influences of fashionable spirituality. But beneath its resistant and disbelieving persona, a thriving Mind/Body/Spirit market can be found, although these activities often take place under different headings, such as 'Druidic revival', 'Stonehenge festivals', 'British esotericism', or 'Findhorn mysticism'. But whatever it is called, the results are the same: a preference for revival-ist, mystical, unchurched or 'secular' spirituality. In Ireland, the New Age has a different complexion again; there it is called 'Celtic spirituality', and it has the wonderful advantage, at least over New World countries, of being historically related to the national character and cultural background, even if this background is being 'reinvented' by businesses and industries to suit New Age tastes.

Everywhere it is found, especially in youth cultures in most nations of the world, the New Age reveals itself as anti-church, oracular, prophetic and a serious contender for the role of dominant spiritual influence. When it first appeared, under the banner of the 'Aquarian Conspiracy', the New Age was anti-establishment and politically and socially radical. However, over recent years, as it has been incorporated into the mainstream and produced by commercial industries, it has lost its early radicalism and become extremely middle-class and a kind of mystical add-on to ordinary life. There is quite a difference between the original Aquarian Conspiracy of the 1960s and today's largely conservative and politically reactionary New Age movement. The only surviving hint of radicalism is found in the battle-line that continues to be drawn between the New Age and the establishment churches. When it enters into dialogue with the churches, a fighting spirit continues to be felt and a revolutionary current is still detected. Is this the result of California's ubiquitous influence upon the rest of the world? Or are we dealing with a spontaneous universal uprising of spiritual impulses that simply found their most recent expression on the western seaboard of the United States? Has the alternative, fringy, mystical explosion that occurred in the 1960s found its way back into mainstream society through the proliferation of New Age industries?

Christianity versus the New Age

In Australia, where I write, it is said that 'A struggle between two spiritual extremes, Christianity and the New Age, characterises the nation's spiritual state of play today' (Hope 2000: 2). But some predict that the New Age will emerge as the victor of this struggle. The churches are hoping that they can hold back the tides, but scholars in the sociology of religion are predicting that the New Age will gain further influence, and ultimately usurp the position once enjoyed by Christianity. Carole Cusack, a writer in religious studies, argues that,

> People are very stressed and anxious about change and global capitalism. When it comes to spirituality they want bite-sized chunks they can swallow, and New Age caters for it beautifully.
>
> (cited in Hope 2000: 3)

Philip Almond, professor of religious studies at the University of Queensland, comments:

> Replacing the notion that God is sacred is the belief that the self is sacred. In order to develop the sacred self, anything goes. In the New Age supermarket you can try out products off the shelf, as if they were brands of soap powder. It's a pragmatic spirituality, not a doctrinal one: the truth is what works for you.
>
> (cited in Hope 2000: 4)

The retired warden of Scotland's Iona Abbey, Peter Millar, concedes that 'People want some depth but they are not suddenly going to go back to church. The depth they discover does not have to say "God".' Millar reflects further:

> People can enter spiritual experiences by entering a charity or sitting with a dying neighbour. We are at a great turning point. We are not going back to the old expression. We have to move beyond narrow definitions to a broader view of faith.
>
> (cited in Hope 2000: 4)

Carole Cusack from Sydney University predicts that within a couple of decades the New Age movement will sweep the board:

Christianity is irrelevant. The secularisation of Australia is nearly complete; in 20 or 30 years, the New Age will have unseated Christianity as the mainstream form of spirituality. Mass migration is a wonderful thing. The religious marketplace is crowded, there's a climate of inquiry. We can see lots of old solutions have failed us. Australians are prepared to give new solutions a fair go.

(cited in Hope 2000: 4)

New World countries seem to be more prone to New Age influence. But we need to be cautious about such remarks. For a start, 'secularisation' can be very deceptive. On the surface, a society can appear to be secular, but underneath the official secular mask, levels of religious feeling can still be very high. For instance, while only 7 per cent of Australians attend places of worship on a regular basis, about 70 per cent say they continue to believe in God. Christianity may seem to have become 'irrelevant' if we are looking merely at externals, and observing things such as church attendance and outward conformity to doctrine. But although the Western world seems to be becoming less Christian, this may simply be a kind of optical illusion, whereby the externals of state religion are being discarded, while the true Christian message of hope and love of God sinks deeper into the human heart and culture, and is, in effect, more strongly placed than ever in its hold upon the soul.

It may be useful to compare our present religious situation with that of a different moment in recent history. In 1946, while a Fellow at Oxford University, C.S. Lewis reported:

In every class and every part of England the visible practice of Christianity has grown very much less in the last fifty years. This is often taken to show that the nation as a whole has passed from a Christian to a secular outlook. . . .

But the 'decline of religion' becomes a very ambiguous phenomenon. One way of putting the truth would be that the religion which has declined was not Christianity. It was a vague Theism with a strong and virile ethical code, which, far from standing over against the 'World', was absorbed into the whole fabric of English institutions and sentiment and therefore demanded churchgoing as a part of loyalty and good manners or a proof of respectability.

(Lewis 1946: 79–80)

Lewis's point is that the state religion of England has merely aped or imitated Christianity in its outward aspect, but state religion can hardly be said to represent a living or vibrant spirituality, because of its fusion with worldliness and its failure to express the distinct claims of the spirit and the radical mission of Jesus Christ. Following this line of reasoning, C.S. Lewis concludes that, 'The decline of "religion", thus understood, seems to me in some ways a blessing' (1946: 80). The same situation is put more humorously by the comedian Lenny Bruce: 'Every day people are straying away from the church and going back to God' (cited in Das 1999: 19).

Toward a new synthesis

Thus we need to be wary of external appearances, and to avoid outrageous or unfounded generalisations in this critical phase of cultural change and transition. It is a time where much discernment is required. Exactly what is dying and what is being born? What is the New Age and what is the Old Age?

The notion that Christianity could be swept aside saddens and alarms me, because I then have to ask: But if individualistic and feel-good spirituality is to replace it, from whence will the moral dimension and ethical aspect of human civilisation arise? Personally, I find the idea of an ongoing struggle between Christianity and the New Age to be very appealing. As I see it, in this struggle the New Age will supply the challenging new ideas about the individual experience of the spirit, the feminine face of God, and the resacralisation of nature and the earth, while the mainstream Western religious traditions – Christian, Jewish, Islamic – will contribute historical, moral and ethical counterpoints to the new rush toward personal and unhistorical experience of the sacred.

From the struggle between Christianity and the New Age an entirely new, third thing will be born, and my guess is that the third thing, as yet unknown, will hold the key to our religious future. But certainly the New Age remains a crucial element in the development of our religious civilisation. It represents the necessary cultural 'antithesis' to the 'thesis' of Judaeo-Christianity, and without that antithetical element the 'thesis' would not be propelled toward change, nor stimulated to produce a new synthesis to accommodate the warring elements. In Jung's model of psychic and cultural wholeness, it is not up to us to side with one warring party over the other, but to endure the conflict of the opposites and to look for signs of what may emerge from this epic battle of elements.

But certainly the New Age will not disappear just because some of us disapprove of it or find it embarrassing. The social commentators who dismiss the New Age as a joke and who are constantly hoping it will disappear had better revise their views and tone down their prejudices. Although it clearly does not accord with sophisticated intellectual or theological taste, there are many processes of the spirit going on in the New Age movement which are profoundly meaningful and must be taken seriously. The New Age is the 'scandalous corrective' to the excesses and one-sidedness of our advanced intellectual and scientific culture, and the scandalous corrective to the spiritual lifelessness and dogmatic pall of our official Judaeo-Christian culture.

A term with no meaning and huge meaning

What is the New Age? This question will be stated and restated in this book, because the term has almost lost all meaning, and is in urgent need of examination and exploration. We have to go in search of its meaning for us today and invent the term anew. One can hardly think of another term that has become more besieged by narrow clichés and constricting stereotypes. On the other hand, when we turn a new ear to the term it reveals new insights and cultural imperatives.

The term 'New Age' was originally an inspired and uplifting term, a term representing the human expectation of a new and better world. Historically, the New Age refers to the millennial hope that we might overcome our fallenness and corruption, and rise from present isolation and fear to regain our vital and original connection with the sacred. This is the sense in which William Blake, Jakob Boehme and other prophetic writers and mystics have used the term, linking it theologically to a post-lapsarian condition in which the 'fall' is overcome, and in which humanity recovers its awareness of itself as *homo religiosus* (Raine 1979). In this anticipated and longed-for state, humanity remembers who it is, revives its spiritual connection to its creator and realises that it must follow the divine will rather than its own wilfulness. All great religions point forward to the eventual reconnection between humanity and the creator, such as we find in the Judaeo-Christian idea of the coming of the Kingdom, as expressed in the prayer: 'Thy will be done on earth, as it is in heaven.'

In William Blake, the idea of the New Age is linked with the heavenly Jerusalem, and so represents the ultimate goal, the Omega, to which all human striving points. If this utopian state is never actually 'achieved' in historical terms, this does not make it any less valid as an important visionary goal or spiritual aspiration. In intellectual terms, it could be seen as an enabling fiction or guiding myth, a distant, shimmering point on the horizon; and while the critical intellect might wish to dismiss it as a mirage of little consequence, to the human spirit it remains a symbol of hope and future transcendence. How this once grand term has fallen into disrepute is one of our concerns here, and I would like to explore some of the social and psychological forces that have led to this massive decline and debasement.

Alternative spirituality

The New Age movement, it is claimed, grew out of the visionary impulses of the 1960s (the 'Age of Aquarius' movement), is influenced by Jung, theosophy (Madame Blavatsky, Annie Besant, Krishnamurti), and anthroposophy (Rudolph Steiner), has connections with Eastern philosophies and yoga, and is often enthusiastic about tribal or indigenous peoples and their earth-based religions. One can see from this brief sketch that there are indeed parallels between this popular, grassroots movement and the historical vision of a New Age of human civilisation. Both seek to overcome or transcend the gap between the sacred and the profane by experiencing the world and humanity not as fallen or sinful but as renewed and whole. The conflict that exists between historical Christianity and the New Age movement is partly due to the fact that historical Christianity is based on a fall and redemption theology, whereas the New Age is loosely based on a new creation theology, which some in the church find facile and overly optimistic, but which huge numbers of the unchurched are finding appealing, exciting and full of hope.

The New Age seeks to recover again the lost connection between time and eternity, humanity and nature, the individual and the group, and its definition of spirituality is often summed up in one word: *connectedness*. It finds historical Christianity too morbid and mournful, with too many negative attitudes toward the body, nature, matter, sexuality and women. If historical Christianity is dualistic in its separation of spirit and matter, and patriarchal in its privileging of spirit (viewed as 'male') over matter (seen as 'female'), the New Age is anti-dualistic, wholistic and integrative. However, as I will explain in the following chapters, the goal of 'wholeness' that is found at the heart of New Age aspiration is often lost sight of in practice. Wholeness is very difficult to attain, as anyone who has been through psychological analysis or self-examination will be able to affirm. Wholeness demands an active and dynamic consciousness, one that is capable of enduring great tensions between warring elements of the psyche. In the New Age movement, where relaxation and getting rid of tension is preferred to a dynamic management or balancing of tensions, the idea of wholeness frequently lapses into a nostalgic search for a lost unity or peacefulness which precedes the birth of consciousness and the epic human struggle for consciousness. In Erich Neumann's terms, the New Age tends to idealise the primal unity that is referred to in symbolism as the 'uroboros' or tail-biting snake, whereas Jungian psychology privileges a different, conscious unity which is symbolised by the 'mandala'.

Ancient, plural, feminine, earthly

In 1935, the great Irish poet W.B. Yeats wrote:

> Our civilisation was about to reverse itself, or some new civilisation about to be born from all that our age had rejected; because we had worshipped a single god it would worship many. The 2000-year cycle of Christianity was about to end, and to be replaced by a system antithetical to it.
>
> (cited in Allison 1983: 883n.)

Modern poets, philosophers and prophets have recognised the tremendous piling-up in the collective psyche of everything that Judaeo-Christianity had rejected. When Yeats reflected on the idea of a Second Coming, he saw rising up in the *Spiritus Mundi* or World Memory not an image of Jesus returning, but on the contrary, an image of the Beast or Anti-Christ slouching toward rebirth after 'twenty centuries of stony sleep'. The coming era and the new society would have to attempt to integrate the contents and forces that patriarchal monotheism had set aside or forcibly repressed. These would include the 'forbidden' realm of polytheistic experience and the plurality of the Gods; the 'banned' realm of eros, sexuality and the body; the 'immoral' realm of the shadow and evil; the 'suppressed' domain of women and the archetypal feminine; and the 'pagan' field of nature and the animated earth.

Christian culture tends to construct its opposite or counterpart as the Beast, Devil or Satan, and it often presents its antagonist in ways which are impossible for the human psyche to integrate, thus reinforcing a permanent rift in our psychic structure. But for the New Age movement, everything that has been rejected or despised by Christian culture is symbolised not by the Beast or Anti-Christ, but by the Great Goddess or the Earth Mother. And not only one Goddess, but many, a veritable archetypal pantheon of 'Lost Goddesses'. Also, where Christianity sees the Devil, the New Age tends to see Hermes, Mercurius or the Magician; these figures are interesting because they are more likely to be integrated by the mind, and they have redeeming features. The favoured Goddesses are usually accompanied by their phallic consorts, the son-lovers who represent the sexuality of nature and the fecundity of the earth in its seasonal cycles of birth, death and rebirth. The Great Goddess and her Son Lover are known by many names, and are found in all pre-Christian cosmologies in Old Europe and the ancient pagan world. Ironically, the New Age movement reaches back in time to ancient cosmologies that were outlawed, banned or defeated by the rise of Christianity and the subsequent political reign of Christendom. The notion is that 'twenty centuries of stony sleep' have not put these ancient forces to rest or sent them to oblivion. On the contrary, they have gained vigour and force in their cell of repression, and are now about to make their grand return to the cultural and human stage.

The New Age movement is constantly talking about the rise of the Great Goddess from her long slumber, or the reappearance of the Great Mother from the underworld. Taken literally or concretely, these claims can seem far-fetched or patently absurd, but regarded from a symbolic point of view, they are powerful, appropriate and apt. Western civilisation is already in the throes of an epic return of the repressed. In the last hundred years and more, we have witnessed the sexual revolution, the body revolution, the black revolution, the women's revolution and, most recently, the ecological and environmental revolution, and all of these are aspects of a colossal reversal or volte-face in Western society. These powerful revolutions have been induced partly by the rebellious strength of what has been repressed, and also by the weakening of Christianity, patriarchy and the hierarchical forces of cultural repression. Although political and social in their nature, and not consciously operating under a mythological banner or deity, the New Age nevertheless finds the Great Goddesses at work in these revolutions, and the next revolution will be a religious or spiritual revolution in which the face, name and nature of the uprising deity will be revealed.

Official Western religion will either have to face this mythic challenge or be destroyed. The New Age doesn't seem to care much about how the dice will roll, because it harbours considerable negative feeling toward Christianity, since it identifies almost exclusively with what has been banned and repressed. As stated, my own preference is for dialogue and interchange between the warring parties. I don't want to see the pagan world rise again triumphantly, but nor do I want to see the continued repression of the rejected or banned contents. Wholeness can never be achieved by replacing one form of one-sidedness with another form. Spirit has for centuries ruled over matter; and if matter now rebels and rules over spirit, will we be any better off? Highly unlikely, as we would see

one kind of tyranny replaced by another that could be worse – despite the
romantic illusions of neopagans, ecowarriors and postmodern witches.
For my money, I want to see spirit and matter conversing with each other
and sorting out a new cultural deal, and I agree with Jung that in this
endeavour the yin–yang symbol can be our guide. It matters very much
whether our official culture can rise to the challenge of the uprising
contents and learn to integrate them.

One world, magical connections

The New Age is fascinated, almost obsessed, by the pre-Christian
cosmological systems, whether these are from wicca, Celtic, Druidic,
Egyptian, hermetic, Nordic, ancient Chinese or Indian cultures. A core
feature of these cosmologies is the view that all reality is one, that spirit
infuses everything in the natural world, and that everything is bounded
by destiny and fate. Free will occurs but is at a minimum, and the
individual human being can always tune into the spiritual web of infinite
relations and ascertain what he or she must or should be doing, especially
if he or she feels alienated, isolated, or has otherwise lost touch with the
mystical unity of the universe. The New Age is particularly interested in
the means by which the individual in these ancient cosmologies found his
or her way back to the right way, to harmony, or to spiritual peace.

This is why the ancient divinatory systems are wildly popular today,
because the New Age sees them as holding out for us, even in our
fragmented and post-industrial condition, the possibility of recovering
a sense of harmony with the spiritual world and with nature. The New
Age is attracted to all divinatory techniques, whether they are found in
tarot, runes, astrology, Sufism, I Ching, magic or alchemy. The divinatory
systems are founded on a belief in an original unitary experience of the
world, one which knows no separation between spirit and nature. They
affirm that the individual who consults these systems with reverence and
respect can 'bind back to' (*religio*) the universal symbols and images, and
recover a lost relationship with the cosmos, its principles and rhythmic
meanings. Clearly, as modern society becomes more fragmented and
disconnected, the yearning for unity and connectedness becomes stronger
at a deeper, if somewhat irrational, level of experience. Jung wrote that,
'The wider and more numerous the fissures on the surface of the world,
the more the unity of the psyche is strengthened in the depths' (1933a:
306). The rational mind might find difficulty in understanding the
divinatory systems and why they work, but the heart's longing for
connectedness, and for a 're-placement' of the self in the cosmic totality,

is today stronger than the rational objections that might be made against such attempts at reconnection.

This is why many participants in the New Age have mixed responses to the divinatory systems and to the meanings they contain. The mind of the 'New Ager' might be rebelling and cursing, but his heart tells him to 'give it a try' because he 'has nothing to lose'. My own sense is that the alienation of the modern world is so intense, and the psyche is under such strain to splinter and fragment, that the soul will almost leap at any opportunity, whether astrology, tea-cup readings or white magic, to recover a sense of unity and to be relieved of the pressures of fragmentation. I don't think the soul cares if the mind or mental training finds it embarrassing, because the times are desperate and require desperate measures.

Thus, the New Age movement, which offers glimpses of lost unity and harmony, will prosper and grow, virtually in spite of us and not necessarily because we are 'willing' it to be so. In discussing the various phenomena of the New Age we are not necessarily talking about a consciously adopted ideology or an intellectual philosophy, but about very basic forms of spiritual longing, forms that are denied expression in the dominant secular culture and in the mainstream institutions of faith. In Jungian terms, the New Age movement carries for many people an image of the Self, that is, the 'greater' personality within us which moves toward unity, harmony and psychic integration.

On the other hand, our 'everyday' or secular reality, which is the opposite of enchanted and cosmic, is governed by the rational ego, which prefers separation to unity, distinction to harmony, and competition to integration. Today it seems that a great many people live in two worlds at once. In their 'normal' selves they are adjusted to social reality, competitive, tied to society by conventional bonds, and erstwhile participants in a secular world based on rationality and logic. But 'another' self within them longs for a larger and greater life, yearns for mystery, and often guiltily indulges that yearning, almost in the spirit of devouring a box of chocolates in private. It is this 'other' self that keeps the New Age the booming, burgeoning international industry that it is.

Separate reality, different geography

One reason why so many New Agers prefer Eastern to Western religious and mystical traditions could be that the East is more removed from Western consciousness, and therefore this exotic Other life best approximates to and carries the 'split off' hidden lives of their souls. There are, of course, many positive reasons for choosing East above West, but this could be one of the more covert, unconscious reasons. The soul that emerges in our time, and within ourselves, seems at first so unlike us, so foreign to our Western sensibility with its one-sided commitment to ego-values and proud ambition, that we prefer to link this soul to a wholly alien culture and a different historical tradition. The New Age habit of getting rid of the original so-called 'Christian' name and replacing it with an Indian or yogic name is itself symbolic of the intrusion of the buried cosmic Self that is rising to displace the normal ego identity. Some New Agers find their souls to be so unlike the West that they consider themselves to be reincarnated spirits from indigenous cultures. The Californian New Age contains many people who think of themselves as reincarnated American Indians, just as the Australian New Age movement includes people who claim that they are the reborn souls of ancient Aboriginal tribes, and similar situations are found in New Zealand and in South America.

Jung wrote, 'Everything old in our unconscious hints at something coming' (1921: 630). The New Age is, quite simply, the ancient world back again, or the primordial religious feeling stirring within and inspiring us again. In psychosocial terms, the New Age is the return of the repressed, where we find the sons and daughters of educated secular humanists, 'atheists', materialists and others who are desperately searching for a sense of soul and for the spiritual bonds that connect us to the cosmos and the wider world. 'New Age' is an umbrella term for all those contemporary social movements and spiritual expressions or cosmologies that indicate that the 'Old Age', or what has been called the 'modern period', is over. The New Age is a living reminder that the intellectual Enlightenment no longer delivers its promises of liberation and freedom, that the secular humanist experiment has been found wanting, and that people are demanding a newer, more profound kind of existence.

Where the wasteland ends: after the death of God

Finally, the New Age can also be conceived as a reaction-formation to the depressive psychosis of modernism and the existential gloom of the modern period. It is obvious to most observers that the New Age is optimistic and upbeat, and that it rejects the depressive mood and tempo of the modern and even late modern periods. Intellectuals are inclined to dismiss this as a defensive reaction against modernity, but I am not so sure about this. It could be the harbinger of something more profound:

the awakening of a genuine new confidence and optimism upon the realisation that there is, after all, treasure buried in the field, and that God is alive once again.

The modern period announced the death of the traditional concept of God, and this awareness subsequently gave rise to a series of mournful, depressive ideologies, including existentialism, in which the only 'meaning' was that which one invented for oneself, absurdism, in which no meaning at all was to be found, and ultimately nihilism, in which the very concept of meaning seemed ridiculous. In modern poetry, fiction, music, philosophy and the arts, a spirit of pessimism and gloom gave weight, gravity and seriousness to the *zeitgeist*. In the modern era, high culture inhabited a 'wasteland', and T.S. Eliot's poem of that name acted as the great icon and signifier of existential angst. But even Eliot could not stand to live long in that wasteland; he rapidly became involved in a revival of Christian spirit and religious meaning. Similarly, Yeats turned to Celtic revival, Joyce to the enchantments of language, and Lawrence to pagan vitality and aesthetic re-enchantment. Even Nietzsche, who announced the death of God, found himself identified at the end of his life with the God Dionysus and the enchantment of Greek culture and philosophy.

In other words, even the authors of modernity could not stand the modern condition, and actively sought to find ways out of its depressive hues and mournful tones. The human spirit naturally seeks its own edification and upliftment. The spirit is not always interested in the heavy, tragic mode of art and life, because one aspect of it is comical, light and optimistic. After all, if the spiritual reality is true, then the tragic realities of life and death are only relative, and do not represent the whole story of our existence.

At the level of popular culture, as distinct from high culture, we inevitably had to see a massive reaction to the depressive directions of modernity. There had to be a reaction to the absence of meaning caused by the death of God and the shaken edifice of the old values of Christendom and religious culture. One aspect of this reaction is clearly the rise of conservative evangelical religion at the popular and grassroots level, and here we would have to include the various cogent varieties of religious fundamentalism, as well as charismatic renewal, televangelism and the spiritualistic and apostolic churches. But the New Age spirituality movement is also part of this reaction to modernist gloom at the popular level.

After the sobering and shocking realisation that there is no God 'out there', no paternal figure in the heavens who cares for and nurtures us, the next phase of culture seems to be that God is to be rediscovered 'within'. This rediscovery or realisation will obviously give rise to a new optimism and a celebratory spirit. God did not die after all, this new dispensation will say; only our old image of God died, and it was an image which was archaic and superstitious anyway, couched in a medieval epistemology and a premodern worldview. After the death of our father in heaven, comes the rebirth of God in the human soul. At this level, not all the optimism of the New Age is unfounded or defensive, but some of it at least is genuine and authentic. Intellectuals who have been nurtured on the modernist brooding will be embarrassed by any sign of optimism, and regard it as artificial or fake, but although the New Age demonstrates excess and exaggeration in this new mood, we must not refute all of it because the discovery of the God within is indeed cause for celebration and joy.

Jung's reputation and the guru problem

Jung has been claimed by the New Age as one of its founding fathers and charismatic leaders. So we have to ask ourselves: Is Jung a New Age guru? This is one of the questions that prompted the present work, and at various stages of the project I have responded to it differently. My first response was a definite 'no', and at that stage my desire was to protect Jung's reputation against accusations of being lightweight, soft-centred, flaky, and 'mystical' in the negative or derogatory sense. But I shifted my position as I began to recognise the considerable impact that Jung has had on the New Age movement specifically, and on popular, global spirituality more generally. My protective strategies could not deny the fact that Jung's influence on the New Age has been significant, and that in some measure at least he has helped to bring a popular spirituality movement into existence.

Nevertheless, even in the later stages of this project, my intention has always been to rescue Jung's reputation from the quaking bog in which it is so often discovered. Although I could no longer deny his influence on the New Age, I was even more determined to expose the ways in which the New Age has packaged, invented and appropriated Jung to suit its own purposes. It is not simply that Jung has influenced the New Age, but that the New Age has influenced 'Jung', and especially our popular perceptions and understandings of his work. The whole matter of influence is not simple or straightforward, but is a matter of subtle and crude misapprehensions of his meanings and intentions. New Age advocates believe that their image of Jung is faithful to Jung, but those of us with greater knowledge of the field can see that his work and ideas have been significantly doctored, recast and refashioned by the movement.

There are considerable tensions and conflicts between the designs and purposes of Jung's psychology, and the aims and objectives of the New Age movement. These will be carefully examined in this book, and chief among these is Jung's belief that the human ego must voluntarily serve and attend a larger religious mystery, in contrast to the widespread popular belief that the spiritual mystery must serve and attend the needs of the ego and the personal self. Jung advocates renunciation and self-sacrifice as essential ingredients in the process of spiritual development, whereas the New Age relationship with religious realities is broadly narcissistic, producing states of being and attitudes that Jung would roundly condemn as inflationary and dangerously regressive.

One of the terrible ironies about the public reputation of Jung is that the popular New Age advocates of Jung, and the fierce denouncers of Jung, end up saying basically the same things about him. The popular New Age advocates see Jung as inviting us to inflation and grandiosity, and the hostile critics attack him precisely because they see him as encouraging these hubristic temptations. A kind of comedy of errors builds up around Jung and his reputation, a situation that would be hilarious if it were not so seriously distorting and harmful. Hostile academic opponents such as Richard Noll or Frank McLynn, and flattering admirers of Jung such as Marilyn Ferguson and Nevill Drury, end up using identical language to express their passionate admiration or fierce condemnation. Sometimes we wonder why academics have to attack Jung so viciously and relentlessly, but I think this is a compensatory corrective to the unthinking admiration that is found everywhere in our popular culture. In witnessing the 'Jung cult' in the wider community, intellectuals turn their nausea to spleen when they set to work on a major study of the man and his work.

But the point I am making is that both the New Age and the university are dealing with a straw man or stereotypal figure. Neither academia nor California reads Jung correctly. Nevill Drury and Marilyn Ferguson are building up a fantasy Jung, a permissive figure who encourages us to inflated visions, and Richard Noll and Frank McLynn are taking him down again. The debunking of the false guru is a necessary cultural task, and academics are only too willing to help out. But the danger is that they fail to distinguish between fantasy and reality. In *The Jung Cult*, Richard Noll allegedly believes that Jung is advocating that we adopt the likeness of the Gods, and he misreads Jung's mythological metaphors as literal assertions about human identity. I say 'allegedly' because it is hard to imagine that an educated person at Harvard University could make such stupid errors, unless, as I suspect, these errors are being made deliberately to cause an international sensation. When Jung makes links between his own work and the archetype of the horned God, Noll mischievously claims that Jung is abrogating God-like status for himself! This is the 'cult' that Noll feels obliged to blow out of the water. New Age writers read Jung in this same way, believing that he is displaying Gods for our pleasure, so we can choose which one we want to become. Literalism is the enemy of imagination and soul, and literalism is, on the one hand, an unconscious spiritual compulsion in the New Age, and on the other hand, a deceitful and conscious strategy adopted by certain academics.

Literalism in the perception of spirit is another vital difference between Jung and the New Age. For the New Age, spirit appears to be marvellous and miraculous, a kind of semi-tangible thing which can defy natural law, and which can pop in and out of human bodies like an astral presence. It can be commanded, directed and invoked by special people who work to develop occult skills, or who are gifted because they are prophets. Hence in the New Age, spirit is associated with extraordinary happenings such as altered states, astral travelling, shamanic visions, out of body experiences, spells and possessions. In this culture, spirituality degenerates into spiritualism, and religion dissolves into a power trip based on the siddhis or dangerous occult talents. As every true spiritual leader advises us, the siddhis or occult powers have nothing to do with authentic spirituality.

This problem is related to our perception of reality. If reality is seen as dull and boring, then 'spirit' must be superadded from above, a miraculous thing which is somehow apart from the real. For Jung, however, spirit exists inside the real and within the world. Spirit is the hidden essence or intelligent drive that works toward purpose, meaning, integration and wholeness. Spirit is organic and innate; if we cannot see it at work, it is only because the 'doors of perception' (William Blake) are obscured.

> If the doors of perception were cleansed, every thing would appear to man as it is, infinite.
>
> (Blake 1793: 154)

In other words, the failure to perceive spirit is a failure of imagination. For Jung, as for Blake, spirit is discovered through symbolic awareness and analogical thinking: by looking 'otherwise', metaphorically or poetically, at the images of psyche and the world. In the New Age, the world is ordinary and spirit is an extraordinary miracle from outside. In Jung, our common perception makes the world ordinary by its own limitation, while uncommon or intuitive perception releases spirit and adds a new dimension to the real. Spirit is not a power trip for a few manipulative tricksters, but a democratic reality which is the birthright of everyone. The New Age reveals itself to be a regression to premodern or superstitious thinking, whereas Jung's work looks forward to a post-modern interpretation of spirit. His sense of spirit is incarnational and historical, whereas the New Age version is magical and unhistorical.

Jung's radical and conservative vision

To be a suitable candidate for a New Age guru, Jung would have to be appropriately antagonistic to Western religion, anti-church, and in favour of personal mysticism. At first glance, he seems to meet these criteria, and for many in the New Age movement a 'first glance' is good enough. Jung is annexed, appropriated, colonised, and no further questions are asked. But Jung is far more complex than this populist perception will allow.

On the one hand, Jung can appear to be a religious radical, offering a psychological and cultural rationale for why Western religion and its old-style monotheism must be overturned by the new archetypal forces that have been unleashed in the modern era. Jung seems to champion all that has been forcibly repressed by Christianity, including polytheism and multiplicity; nature and the earth; the body, eros and sexuality; the shadow and the feminine. He has glimpsed a different guiding vision from Judaeo-Christianity, a vision that can be encapsulated by the word 'wholeness', and according to Jung the old ethic of 'perfection' stands in the way of the realisation of this new vision and so must be torn down. Jung is unsentimental toward the plight of our religious tradition if it is seen to be standing in the way of a new vision that has the full authority of the spirit behind it. In a radically Protestant temper, and true to his own Protestant roots, Jung is happy to make a complete separation between God and Church, and to stand the one over against the other. In his prophetic judgement, Christianity must either change or die, so that the new emergent vision can be born. If Western religion cannot expand its horizons to accommodate the emerging vision of wholeness, Jung is pleased to take sides with those who oppose Western religion and its narrow ethic based on the supremacy of transcendental spirit. This side of Jung is what the New Age movement adores, applauds and celebrates.

But on the other hand, Jung's religious vision is profoundly conservative, especially in his understanding of the *processes* of religious engagement and of the relations between humanity and the divine. This is a real sticking-point with the New Age philosophy and outlook, but the movement simply ignores this aspect of his work. The New Age is intensely humanistic and human-centred, always asking what we can 'get out of' the religious engagement, whereas Jung's vision is, as it were, through the human to the nonhuman, always trying to discern the hidden face of mystery that is the source and goal of our lives. As with Judaeo-Christianity, Jung's spiritual intention is not to bolster the status of mortal man but to challenge man to acquire a deeper and more abiding humility. The religious mystery does not exist to make us feel better or to enhance our personal power, as the New Age often asserts, but rather to compel us to serve a greater wholeness and a higher will that we can barely understand. New Age certainty, optimism and soaring confidence in human enterprise contrast markedly with Jung's sense of religious resignation, his emphasis on mystery, and on the need to have the personal will subsumed by a greater will.

In their giggling delight in Jung's challenge to the structure and content of Christian religion, New Agers completely overlook the fact that the dynamics, demands and claims of this religion have not been changed one bit by Jung's psychology of religion. The old strictures and demands remain in place as before. The human ego is not let off the hook; it cannot do what it likes or run amok, with everything justified under the glorious banner of self-development. The popular misreading of Jung is that, in the name of 'wholeness', all things are possible and everything we desire becomes psychologically and spiritually desirable. But this is not so. For Jung, Christ's passion and crucifixion remain the genuine and abiding symbols of our experience and of human suffering. We must still 'take up the Cross' and subordinate our lives to a greater life. The old-fashioned demands for sacrifice, limitation and renunciation – overlooking our own needs for the needs of the other – are just as important in Jung's psychology as they are in traditional religion.

The only difference is that today the greater life, the divine mystery, is more complex and broader than it was once perceived to be. According to Jung, we are no longer called to be goodie two-shoes or sweetness and perfection. We are called to experience both the light and the dark side of God. We are called to experience the highs and the lows, the realm of spirit and the realm of matter, and we are expected to bring the two sides of the Godhead, and of our own psychological nature, into some kind of reconciling vision. The element of imperative, of 'you ought' or 'you must do this', is still present as before. Jung has not debunked religion in favour of a new kind of feel-good humanism, or a dedication to human growth and potential. He has simply extended the Judaeo-Christian vision to include much more of reality, or expanded the horizons of spirit to include the depths of matter, instinct and eros. But the rules of the game of life remain the same as before. This is the paradoxical nature of his religious vision, and paradoxes fly out the window as soon as any religious philosophy goes popular and broadly public. Jung's psychology of religious experience is more profoundly conservative than the New Age movement is prepared to realise.

For Jung, the inner domain of the psyche is not some kind of personal resource centre designed to keep us entertained, plugged in and held in states of excited fascination, in much the same way as the Internet and the World Wide Web is viewed today by millions of consumers. The New Age betrays its essential worldliness and its kinship with business, commerce and entertainment industries, in its advocacy of a rather passive, consumerist approach to sacred experiences. When we feel bored, empty or isolated, we are encouraged to take a trip into an exotic sacred space. But for Jung, as for traditional religions, *the sacred makes claims on us*, and compels us into moral relationship and spiritual partnership. The sacred does not tolerate a casual or touristic approach, but asks us to be very serious about our involvement, and we cannot 'surf the spiritual web' in the way that we do the Internet.

Jung assumes, like the ancient monastic religious orders, that these sacred claims can never become 'popular', since the sacrifices are rigorous and the demands of the sacred are often considerable. If spirituality is authentic, it teaches us that the personal is not all-important, but is merely instrumental to larger goals and forces that work through the personal to achieve their transpersonal goals. The message of Jung is almost identical to 'unfashionable' traditional religion: not my will, but Thy will be done. The New Age imagines that, because Jung has located the mystery within the self, it must belong to the self and work toward its enhancement and glorification. What the New Age fails to understand is what Jung calls the 'objective psyche', namely, the idea that there is an objective reality within and beneath our subjectivity, which is far more important than subjectivity, and that subjectivity is entirely subordinate to this objective realm, not the other way around.

Hence, the New Age, true to its consumerist and late-modern context, adopts a selective, pick-and-mix approach to Jungian theory. It takes on board the bits that it likes, and it discards the rest. Those aspects of Jung's theory that are individualistic, mystical, developmental and inspirational to the personal spiritual journey are warmly embraced and endorsed. But the aspects that are not human-centred but God-centred, that are sacrificial, sacramental and broadly cosmological, are rejected, refuted or ignored. The New Age grasps only certain ego-syntonic aspects of Jung's theory, or reads him in a distorted way, with one eye shut.

But the New Age has taken on board many of Jung's insights, especially the important idea that if God is to be found anywhere at all, God is to be found within the recesses of the soul. The internal, inward location of the gods, goddesses, archetypes and ancient patterns, and the idea that the individual must journey through difficult, murky and often lonely terrain to make contact with these denizens of the deep; the New Age has incorporated all of this from Jung, and it has understood this well.

Flecks of gold in the rough ore

The New Age cannot be dismissed out of hand; it contains valuable new insights, though these are badly expressed and have to be sifted and refined. We have to moderate and control our responses to this movement and look for the flecks of gold in the dross and nonsense. The New Age has discovered the inner, subjective, psychological dimension of religious mystery, whereas Western religion is still officially battling against this dimension, declaring it to be wrong-headed, deluded, narcissistic, and so on. Western religion looks into the self and it sees only subjectivity, sinfulness and distance from God. It does not see what Jung sees, or not yet. Jung is obviously an epochal figure in the history of religious thought, and it may take some time for theology and religious understanding to catch up with him. The New Age has caught up with elements of his vision, and I suppose we should say this is better than nothing. However, the caution of Marie-Louise von Franz should be taken into account: 'A little Jung is worse than none at all.'

Entrenched negative attitudes toward the New Age in official religious cultures actually block the way to any new insights that the movement may have. Conservative religious people view the New Age as vulgar and inept, and for them, the movement seems to confirm their suspicion that the 'inner way' is a path which leads to narcissism and indulgence. Conservatives only see the negative, outward face of the movement, which blinds them to what is potentially valuable in it, and also excludes them from the popular vitality and interest which, if harnessed and utilised, could lead to a religious revival of Western institutions of faith. Our secular, professional cultures also frown upon the New Age, finding it to be negative, shallow, flaky and deluded by unreal fantasies of inner riches. The secular world of education, especially, fails to understand what its 'New Age' students are getting excited about, and so long as it persists in its condemnatory and judgemental attitude, it too will be excluded from the mystery of the inner world and the potential vitality and renewal that such discoveries can make to education, religion, health and society.

Chapter One

Jung in the New Age

The question of Jung's influence

Jung's name has been widely associated with New Age spirituality for about three decades, but his relationship to this movement is problematical. Advocates of the New Age often claim Jung as their ancestor and founding father, viewing the movement as the logical outcome of his public influence and social prophecy. On the other hand, Jungian analysts and professionals in the field frequently deny any connection between Jung and the New Age, dissociating Jung from the fashions and excesses of popular spirituality. The truth of the matter, I believe, lies somewhere between these extremes. It would be a gross exaggeration to assert that Jung has fathered the New Age, but to deny that he has played any part in this movement would be equally untrue. The New Age has seized hold of a clutch of his ideas, understanding some of them and misunderstanding others. As I will demonstrate in Chapter 3 the figure of 'Jung' has been annexed and appropriated by the movement. Rather than Jung influencing the movement, it could be turned around the other way: the movement has seized Jung, as a likely candidate or sitting duck for the role of spiritual guru, and put its own stamp upon him, using him as an authority to bolster its own interests.

Conflict between Jung and the New Age

It may be instructive to imagine a fictional dialogue between Jung and New Age culture. The New Age sees him as its founding father, but Jung is not sure that he wants to admit his paternity. Jung is not an adoring father of this movement, but he may be the worried uncle or distant relative who looks upon it with concern and some sense of moral responsibility. 'What am I to do about this narcissistic movement?' Jung might say to himself. 'How am I to set it right, or direct it upon a better course? How come the spiritual journey operating under my name has degenerated into an ego trip?' Meanwhile, the cheeky, nascent movement might retort: 'Well, you made us this way! We are only doing what you told us to do!' 'I am not your father,' Jung might reply sternly, 'and don't always use my name to justify all your new-fangled beliefs and supernormal activities!'

'But you are our most famous relative,' the New Age might protest in its defence. 'We have read your introductions to the I Ching, Chinese alchemy and Zen Buddhism. We have dipped into your writings on magic and astrology, on UFOs, and your Seven Sermons to the Dead. We read about your out-of-body experiences and your mystical visions in your spiritual autobiography. We agree with all of that, and naturally, since we have so much in common, we call upon your international reputation to promote our own cause. We are on the same side and playing for the same team: we both want spiritual revival in modern society. If you fail to see any similarities between us and what you have written, you need to look again'. The conversation might proceed in this manner for some time, with little sense of agreement or common resolve between the parties. The New Age would insist on its paternity and rightful heritage, and Jung would continue to withhold his acceptance or blessing.

There are points of connection and difference between Jung and the New Age, and whether we emphasise similarities or differences depends on our outlook and what we are trying to prove. But uppermost in Jung's mind during this fictional dialogue would be a sense of exasperation, bordering on desperation. Jung would quietly concede the similarities and family resemblances to his own ideas, but in public discussion he would be focused on the differences, not merely to protect his reputation from the vagaries of a feral movement, but to correct a popular spirituality that has got his message half right and about three-quarters wrong. The things that the New Age gets wrong are so fundamentally wrong that it makes the things that it gets right seem less important. It turns Jung's voyage of individuation and self-discovery into a pleasure-seeking, exotic mystery tour. Instead of transcending the ego, the human ego is grotesquely inflated and enlarged. There is precious little development of the higher Self in the New Age; instead, we find an almost systematic development of the ego, even though the New Age claims to be transcending the ego.

Jung's response to theosophy

Jung's response to the New Age can be ascertained by his response to theosophy in his own time. As Paul Heelas (1996) has argued, the roots of the New Age can be found in the theosophical ideas and practices of Annie Besant, Madame Blavatsky and Rudolph Steiner, all of whom were known to Jung by their reputation and influence. Jung kept a safe distance from theosophy and anthroposophy, while also recognising that these phenomena shared something in common with himself, namely, they were responses to the demands of the spirit in a post-traditional religious context.

Jung noted the pioneering desperation at the centre of theosophy, while also lamenting the state of its spiritual expressions and philosophical outlook. He admitted that to educated taste theosophy seemed crude, vulgar and 'an amateurish, indeed barbarous imitation of the East' (1928/31: 188). He acknowledged that to many Europeans who had cast off religion as superfluous superstition, theosophy seemed 'wholly irrelevant and fortuitous' and a 'regrettable aberration' (1928/31: 193). Jung felt that there was far too much emphasis on the literalistic, concrete nature of the spirit, so that spirituality was in danger of degenerating into 'spiritualism', or worse, a pseudo-science of astral bodies. Theosophy seemed to be misguided, poorly educated and slightly morbid in its otherworldliness and fantastic claims. It would not become a viable substitute for Western religion, although it perhaps contained within itself some possible clues and attitudes which pointed the way beyond the present impasse to a future religious renewal.

What we find distasteful we must nevertheless consider and even explore: that is the maxim upon which Jung's psychology and Freud's psychoanalysis are based. What the conscious mind rejects and scorns, the unconscious life finds infinitely attractive. 'The fascination of the psyche . . . is an attraction so strong that it does not shrink even from what it finds repellent' (1928/31: 191). In our time, the tried and true paths of religious enquiry no longer hold much attraction, and many are looking elsewhere for the exotic and the new:

> Along the great highways of the world everything seems desolate and outworn. Instinctively modern man leaves the trodden paths to explore the by-ways and lanes, just as the man of the Greco-Roman world cast off his defunct Olympian gods and turned to the mystery cults of Asia. Our instinct turns outward, and appropriates Eastern theosophy and magic; but it also turns inward, and leads us to

contemplate the dark background of the psyche. It does this with the same scepticism and the same ruthlessness which impelled the Buddha to sweep aside his two million gods that he might attain the original experience which alone is convincing.

(1928/31: 192)

The educated and sophisticated, along with the custodians of our official religious traditions, will hiss and snarl at such appropriations of exotic, Asiatic, indigenous and esoteric mysteries. The sophisticated will also, Jung says, 'prophesy an early and inglorious end to these movements'. But, he contends, such hostile voices

> overlook the fact that such movements derive their force from the fascination of the psyche, and that it will express itself in these forms until they are replaced by something better. They are transitional or embryonic stages from which new and riper forms will emerge.

(1928/31: 187)

This seems to provide a good rationale for taking the New Age seriously. It is not just a commercial fad or bourgeois escapism, though it might also be that. It is a spontaneous, archetypal expression of the unlived spiritual and psychological life of Western civilisation. Precisely because our official education and religion have not taken up this life, it finds its expression in avenues that are crude, vulgar or repellent. But such 'transitional or embryonic' things will not go away simply because they offend our taste. These things will only disappear when 'they are replaced by something better'.

Jung's chief interest in the New Age would be to guide this movement to greater maturity. He would look for the seeds of truth and try to weed the garden in which these seeds are planted so that they can prosper and grow. For instance, the obsession with the ego and its so-called 'spiritual' development might mask a deeper and more profound concern for the development of the soul and its interior life. In this situation, the task would not be to condemn the narcissism, but to deepen the narcissistic impulse so that the reality of the soul could be contacted. The narcissist thinks he is infatuated with the ego, but he is really in search of the soul, which is still obscured and out of reach, fused with the ego in an undiffer-entiated blur. The task is to lead the interest onward to its hidden object, rather than to protest, like an outraged moralist, that the entire enterprise is vain and wasted. Jung would seek to make the soul more apparent and the ego less controlling.

Jung's identity in professional and public domains

Although Jung's connection with the New Age was previously the subject of rumour and popular conjecture, his alleged influence on this movement is now being formally proposed and articulated. In *New Age Spirituality*, Duncan Ferguson (1993) argues that Jung has played a major role in the development of popular spirituality, and more recently in *The New Age Movement*, the sociologist Paul Heelas claims that Jung is one of 'three key figures', the others being Blavatsky and Gurdjieff, who are responsible for the existence of the movement (1996: 46). In similar vein, the New Age esoteric writer Nevill Drury maintains that 'Jung's impact on New Age thinking has been enormous, greater, perhaps, than many people realise' (1989: 25; also 1999: 10). A classic in New Age literature, *The Aquarian Conspiracy* by Marilyn Ferguson (1981), cites Jung as a major spiritual founder of the movement. Most sensationally of all, Richard Noll alleges that Jung is the intentional founder of the New Age, with Jung himself as its self-created Messiah (1994: 297). Everywhere the claim is being made that the New Age movement is a product of Jungian interest, and spiritually oriented therapists from a diverse range of fields claim to be Jungian, or refer to Jung as their spiritual ancestor, scientific authority, inspiration or source.

Importantly, none of the people who make such large claims about Jung's influence on the New Age are trained in Jungian psychology, but are sociologists of religion, historians of culture, New Age writers, public press journalists and social commentators who are responding to the popular perception that Jung is the father of this movement. As mentioned, professional Jungians are reluctant to identify the New Age as an offspring of Jungian enterprise. Indeed, the denial of Jung's influence on this movement was one of my original motives for taking up this project. In my earlier writings on this topic, I argued against the influence of Jung on the movement, since it seemed to me that the differences between Jung and the New Age were more apparent than the similarities (Tacey 1998a). I am still markedly conscious of the differences, and seek to delineate them in these chapters, but I am less inclined today to deny that Jung has had a considerable impact on popular spirituality, even if that tradition distorts or misinterprets him.

Jungian scholars and writers such as myself feel uneasy about making these admissions, since we do not wish to be reminded that the source of our scholarship and psychological insight is the same source that feeds popular forms of enchantment that are deemed to be spurious or vulgar. If Jung is acknowledged as a New Age guru then this has a negative effect on his reputation, and by implication on our own reputations, an effect that no professional Jungian analyst or writer would welcome. But Jungians are well versed in the art of encouraging other people, especially their patients, to look at their shadow side. It is high time that we demonstrated a similar willingness to encounter the unsavoury and potentially demeaning aspects of our own professional concerns.

There has been surprisingly little written by Jungians about the New Age movement, with the exceptions of Andrew Samuels (1993) and John Haule (1999). This, no doubt, is partly because most Jungians are clinicians who do not focus on social or public issues, but who are embroiled in the daily practice of individual psychotherapy. Many Jungians see the New Age as non-Jungian or even anti-Jungian and they refuse kinship with a movement that they instinctively dislike. But it could be that Jungians are too quick to dissociate themselves from this movement. It could be that Jungians are embarrassed about the New Age in a way that suggests resistance and a degree of helplessness in the face of a hugely popular movement.

Much professional Jungian culture operates within tightly circum-scribed and managed limits: clinical institutes, training analysts, trainees, in-house journals, conferences, and the hermetic containment of one-to-one analytical therapy. Around these professional cores are amateur organisations and networks: public Jung clubs and societies with member-ships, introductory seminars for beginners, libraries, tape collections, newsletters, Internet chat sites, and seminars on the web. There is an inward, centripetal force operating within professional and amateur Jung cultures alike, which would like to 'hold it all together', control the field, map out the divisions, locations, internal splits and disputes. This inward focus is inevitable in any organisational structure or network, but the end result is that the larger picture often gets lost, and the effect that Jung is having on the wider public domain is ignored or regarded as too difficult to discuss.

But there is a sense in which organisational culture regards things operating outside its own boundaries as chaotic, disorganised and beyond its control. If the effect that Jung is having on the public domain is only regarded through the jaundiced context of a 'leak' in the hermetically sealed vessel, then clearly such public influence is likely to be regarded suspiciously, negatively and critically. Professional Jungian culture all too easily turns a blind eye to what is patently happening to 'Jung' in the outside world, and this produces an ideal environment in which another phenomenon takes place: the semi-deliberate distortion and falsification of Jungian ideas for the mass market and popular consumption.

To complicate the situation even further, alongside the popular appropriation of Jung by the New Age movement, we have numerous Jungians who have defected to the other side, all too willing to convert Jung and his 'sayings' into precisely the disembodied, transcendental guru that the New Age wants him to be. In recent years, some Jungian writers and popularisers have rocketed to commercial success by breaking ranks with the professional culture and serving the popular need for spiritual guidance and prophetic utterances. These defectors are readily identified by the unrealistic poses they strike and the hyperbolic promises they make to their readers. I will have more to say about feral Jungians later, but for now I just want to note that not all Jungians are able to remain true to their professional training. The analysts and non-analysts who wish to make fast dollars have a detrimental effect on the field, since critics are all too willing to assume that these bastardised versions of Jung are representative of the classical Jungian position. Instead of correcting the New Age or offering it moral guidance and direction, this feral Jungianism panders to the worst in the New Age and supports its infantilism and narcissism. So whether we like to admit it or not, we Jungians are already up to our necks in New Age culture, either by way of popular appropriations of Jung's ideas, or by bastardised accounts of Jungian individuation theory by defectors and opportunists.

Jung's cultivation of the prophetic role

Jung, who was born in 1875 and died in 1961, was a complex figure who lived a long and extraordinarily creative life. He seemed almost to move in different directions at the same time. He entertained a professional career and demonstrated a centripetal, inward energy which was concerned with the separate but related disciplines of psychiatry and psychology. He was focused on the developing culture of Freudian psychoanalysis, and eventually this gave way to his founding of the school of analytical psychology. These professional concerns involved him in numerous conference networks and international associations, in the publication and editing of professional papers and books, in the organisation of seminars, meetings and colloquia, and eventually in the establishment in 1948 of his own training institute.

At the same time, a centrifugal, outward force was always operating in his life, his work and his thoughts. This centrifugal force appeared to develop slowly at first, but it gathered momentum, reaching a climax later in his life. This force involved intellectual and prophetic outreach, essays, books and writings for the general public, high-profile public interviews and media and television discussions. Jung could see that his scientific research and intellectual endeavour could not merely be confined within the circles of professionals, but that it should be shared with others and that it was imperative that this be done. Jung eventually developed a sense of intellectual responsibility toward the whole of society, responding as a prophetic commentator and interpreter of its major upheavals and wars, its political events, and its traumatic social transformations.

Arguably, this centrifugal force completely eclipsed the inward focus at the end of his life, so that finally Jung was more concerned with 'society' than he was with his own professional culture. Already, in the 1930s and 1940s, Jung was publishing hugely popular works with deliberately provocative and eye-catching titles, such as *Modern Man in Search of a Soul* (1933) and *Essays on Contemporary Events* (1946). Later, in *The Undiscovered Self* (1957), *Flying Saucers: A Modern Myth* (1958), and *Man and His Symbols* (published posthumously in 1964), Jung sought to dispense spiritual wisdom to the masses, and he was aware of his leadership role in this regard. John Freeman, co-ordinating editor of *Man and His Symbols*, describes this book as 'Jung's legacy to the broad reading public' (1964: 15). He encouraged readers to believe that there was a wealth of spiritual life within them, and that in secular culture this wealth remained 'undiscovered' and hence untapped by both individual and society. These thoughts alone, uttered by a respected authority, would be powerful enough to activate a mass popular movement.

Jung spent a great deal of his time and energy uttering prophetic remarks about the future, and he frequently contemplated the fate or destiny of entire nations, including Switzerland, Germany, France and, importantly, America, which supplied him with patients, followers, patrons, money and influence. Jung developed popular theories about the 'stages of life', about psychological adaptation to the world (subsequently mainstreamed as the Myers-Briggs Type Indicator), about the spiritual individuation of the human person, about the development of civilisation and even about the self-development or evolution of God (1952a).

Whereas Freud taught us to look to dreams and fantasies to solve the problems of neurosis and retarded childhood development, Jung instructed us to attend to dreams and visions to find the keys to our spiritual lives and to further our religious development (1912/52). He announced the presence of archetypes in the modern psyche, which were the imprints of the Gods and the keys to unlocking the inner life. He argued that the most important activity in psychotherapy was its 'approach to the numinous' (cited in Samuels 1996: 486). He wrote compellingly on the spiritual hunger of secular modernity, and he discussed the social and political dangers that befall us when raw spiritual energies emerge suddenly and destructively in modern times (1936a). He provides a religio-mythic explanation for the rise of political fascism based on the outbreak of misdirected archetypal vitality (1945). He clearly believed that the secular humanism of the West represented a potentially fatal error in the course of civilisation, and that the religious impulse would arise again, and would need to be formally recognised and re-incorporated by our culture.

Jungians would have to admit perhaps begrudgingly that the master did indeed cultivate the image of prophet and wise man actively and systematically. His influence on the wider world and the extended community cannot be seen as some kind of historical accident or failure of professional containment. Jung is a mentor of the New Age whether we like it or not. The New Age may misinterpret him, distort his psychospiritual message, and sometimes even reverse his intended or implied meaning, but the fact that they have 'claimed' Jung is not entirely illegitimate. Jung was reaching out to 'modern man in search of a soul', and those in search of soul and revitalisation of spirit have justly received his advances. He wanted to give nourishment and spiritual food to the needy, and the needy have responded, with open mouths, and at times, unfortunately, with empty heads. But no matter what chemistry develops when Jung's convictions go public and move beyond the professional therapeutic domain, Jung himself cannot be held fully responsible for the popular distortion or misinterpretation of his work.

The inevitable distortion of spiritual wisdom

The results of the public response to Jung's widely disseminated wisdom are ambivalent, to say the least. Jung could have predicted, and in fact he did predict, that his ideas and convictions would be misused by a large number of people who take hold of his ideas and try them on for size. For instance, he wrote in 'The Relations Between the Ego and the Unconscious':

> As I have said elsewhere, every analysand starts by unconsciously misusing his newly won knowledge in the interests of his abnormal, neurotic attitude.
>
> (1928: 223)

Jung was referring in this context to the tendency of the human ego to puff-up or inflate when it comes into contact with the forces of the unconscious. In the same essay, he wrote that an identification with the collective psyche often leads to the production of cosmic or astrological symbolism (as we find in the New Age), and that the suggestiveness of this archaic symbolism is such that all self-criticism and reality-testing is suspended. If the inflation is tacitly accepted, this can 'exalt [it] into a system' (1928: 260). In a passage which seems to present a summary of certain New Age types, Jung writes that when inflation has been accepted,

> One would be the fortunate possessor of *the* great truth which was only waiting to be discovered, of the eschatological knowledge which spells the healing of the nations. This attitude is not necessarily megalomania in direct form, but in the milder and more familiar form of prophetic inspiration and desire for martyrdom. For weak-minded persons, who as often as not possess more than their fair share of ambition, vanity, and misplaced naivete, the danger of yielding to this temptation is very great.
>
> (1928: 260)

What Jung saw in his clinic, that is, the temptation to identify with the archetypes and so become an overnight guru or seer, has now become a widespread public problem. Jung could supervise these problems in his patients, but who supervises these problems in the public domain? Jung describes the conditions that make the prolongation of inflation possible:

> Probably no one who was conscious of the absurdity of this identification would have the courage to make a principle of it. But the danger is that very many people lack the necessary humour, or else it fails them at this particular juncture; they are seized by a sort of pathos, everything seems pregnant with meaning, and all effective self-criticism is checked.
>
> (1928: 262)

Today, we appear to be relatively helpless in the face of this psychic problem, especially because we are so far removed from authentic spiritual experience that we can no longer discern between inflated madness and cosmic consciousness. Jung repeatedly stresses that the Promethean desire to make ourselves more than human ends up tragically making us less than human, because we have broken free from the temporal and spatial boundaries that compel us to ethical behaviour.

An alternative to self-deification and prophecy is the path of the acolyte or follower, which of course accounts for huge numbers in the New Age. Jung writes:

> besides the possibility of becoming a prophet, there is another alluring joy, subtler and apparently more legitimate: the joy of becoming a prophet's disciple. . . . The disciple is unworthy; modestly he sits at the Master's feet and guards against having ideas of his own. He can enjoy the archaism and infantilism of his unconscious fantasies without loss to himself, for all responsibility is laid at the Master's door.
>
> (1928: 263)

This is an enormously popular choice in the New Age movement today. The New Age man finds himself a guru, dead or alive, near or afar, at home or in India, California or Japan. The archaic wisdom of the collective psyche can be entirely projected upon the mana-figure, with whom the New Ager develops a strongly transferential dependence. Secretly, of course, he is completely identified with the guru, but his own self-effacing style and practised modesty covers up his arrogance, and the act of attending, promoting or defending the guru is used to shore up his own humanity. Before the guru he feels himself to be nothing, in fact 'mental laziness becomes a virtue' (para. 263), since to have thoughts or ideas contrary to the guru is to endanger this primordial situation.

Any thought of outgrowing this infantile dependence is treated as a sin, and the emotional intensity of this spiritual bond makes any criticism of the guru or of the follower's dependence on him virtually impossible. The avid New Age disciple naturally seeks out the company of other followers, 'not out of love, but for the very understandable purpose of effortlessly confirming his own convictions by engendering an air of collective agreement' (para. 263). Together, they can reinforce, reify and concretise the spiritual fantasy. Outsiders who make negative comments, or who point to ways in which the disciple's life has stopped growing, are treated with contempt and scorn. Insiders who begin to develop anger or resentment toward the infantilism of this bond are said to be 'unstressing', or else undergoing 'tests of faith' instigated by the guru. In other words, this primal situation is circular and self-perpetuating. It often takes a disaster or some scandal or controversy to break up the spiritually incestuous love-nest.

Jung recognises that the guru may actually be spouting elements of true wisdom, but that is not the point. The point is that the disciple is caught in an infantile situation, the free will of the ego is blocked, and archetypal contents have been morbidly attached to the mana-figure. In this state of psychic identification, 'the independence of the individuality suffers injury' (para. 265). The infantile quality can be found in the intensity and archaism of the spiritual bond, in the rigidity with which the ideas of the guru are expounded and reiterated, in the self-righteousness of the cult, in the paranoid fear of criticism, and in the morbid expectation that 'others' are working to undermine this state. The ideas of other philosophers and philosophies are frequently denied or treated as dangerous rivals, and one remains narcissistically attached to one's 'own' guru. Jung admits that 'since by no means all individualities have the strength to be independent, the disciple-fantasy is perhaps the best they can accomplish' (para. 265).

The historical irony of these words is that many Jungians conduct precisely this kind of relationship with Jung himself. Far too many 'weak-minded persons' (para. 260) become attracted to Jung, turn him into a guru and then convert all of his experimental researches into dogmatic articles of faith. Jung clubs the world over are full of these people, who may eventually drift away from Jung to find a 'real' guru, that is, a spiritual leader from India or Japan. But while they are fans and followers of Jung they can do a lot of public damage, by displaying cult-like behaviours and attitudes in their relations to Jungian thought. When cultism develops around the name of Jung, scholars, academics and journalists can go beserk. Seeing cultic behaviour or reviewing bad Jungian literature, writers with a commonsense basis and a desire to protect the common good immediately feel impelled to blow the whistle and bust the cult. Commonsense writers will feel impelled to point out that Jungians are suffering from delusional beliefs, and these writers will become angry and hostile. Ironically, they end up saying exactly the same things about Jungians that Jung said about weak-minded persons.

Lately we have seen a darker, more sinister twist to this dilemma. Richard Noll, author of *The Jung Cult* (1994) and *The Aryan Christ: The Secret Life of Carl Jung* (1997), observes, as I do, the presence of cult-like behaviours in low-grade Jungian followers and writers. But in a completely aggressive and unfounded gesture, Noll then begins to discern cult-like elements in the professional Jungian culture and ultimately in Jung himself. He reduces respectable Jungians to members of a contemporary cult, with Jung at the top as a kind of New Age guru. Noll manages this feat by what appears to be a deliberate and intentional misreading of the Jungian enterprise. Where Jung speaks about Gods and archetypes, and intends to be interpreted metaphorically by an educated audience,

Noll reads such statements literally, as superstitious assertions about spirit beings. Noll, at the Institute for History of Science at Harvard University, reads Jung's statements as an ignorant person might read the occult ravings of a deluded magician. By this method, Noll makes himself famous and Jung infamous. Noll reads Jung as a would-be Messiah who is bent on displacing Christ as the intermediary between man and God:

> Are we witnessing the birth of another religious movement that will one day develop into ritualized services and even cathedrals a la Emanuel Swedenborg? With the Jungian movement and its merger with the New Age spirituality of the late twentieth century, are we witnessing the incipient stages of a faith based on the apotheosis of Jung as a God-man?
>
> (Noll 1994: 297)

I will return to the invention of Jung as a New Age guru in later chapters, but for now I simply want to signal the possibility of dangerous misinterpretation and misreading at all levels. We misinterpret the contents of the unconscious as personally inflating forces, then we project these forces onto charismatic leaders. We perforce play-act the prophet, the martyr, or the modest disciple, because we are unable to objectify the cosmic forces and separate from them. And those who bear a vendetta against Jung, or who are envious of his visionary faculty, are willing to misinterpret his language to cause an international sensation. Misinterpretation, mistakes, and distortions abound in this field, and the field itself seems to be defined by the errors and blunders that are made either consciously or unconsciously.

The tragic incapacity of the normal ego

The root cause of most errors, it would seem, is an inability to distinguish between the ego and the soul. The ego needs to separate itself from the soul, but all too often the ego is fused with the soul in an unholy identification. The soul speaks to us in symbol and metaphor, but when the ego is fused with the soul it does not bother to learn this other language, but instead interprets the symbols in its own profane, realistic language. True spiritual teaching is always parabolic, analogical or symbolic, but the profane ego seizes upon this wisdom in its limited way, dragging it down to its level and destroying the poetry and transcendent value of what it finds intriguing. The greedy ego devours spiritual truth, and as a result it destroys its own sacred nourishment. This is how the normal ego responds to archetypal reality, how the New Age responds to ancient religions, the charlatan to his vision, and Richard Noll to the ideas of Jung. Our culture is in crisis, our psychological lives are contaminated and our hermeneutic interpretation is debased because we cannot objectify the soul and understand its separate reality. The price of our rampant materialism is that we turn gold into lead by refusing to acknowledge the reality of the soul.

Perhaps this is what makes professional Jungian culture right to insist on its closely monitored and checked dissemination of Jung's ideas and theories, because a fully creative exposure to these ideas is predicated on the possibility that the individual has the capacity to transcend the normal ego and its distorted or one-sided vision of reality. Psychological analysis creates the holding space in which people who feel called to change and transformation are able to venture beyond the ego in an atmosphere of safety and support, thus providing the conditions for the fostering of a new self that will listen attentively to the wisdom of the spirit.

The critical issue is that if Jung's invitation to contact the archetypes is appropriated by the normal ego, psychological disaster strikes. A typical pattern found in today's New Age culture might work this way. First, we have a relatively normal person who begins to feel that something is missing in his life, and who becomes tired and bored with the values and attitudes of conventional society. Energy withdraws from the day-world, and he seems to be depressed or fatigued, but the forces below the threshold of consciousness are stirred to new life. He commences some reading in spiritual matters, attends some inspirational workshops and begins to conduct self-exploration. Dreams and fantasies are monitored and recorded, and intuitions are listened to and developed. Feelings and emotions, formerly repressed or disregarded, are deliberately cultivated and deepened. In this condition of openness and exploration, Jung's invitation to enter the inner world and consider its contents with an eye to the sacred and the archetypal is found to be most attractive. A 'Jung phase' begins, and often at the same time, the seeker is exploring half a dozen other fields: shamanism, Indian yoga, Zen meditation, channelling, astrology, and I Ching.

This person has become a New Ager, but is he also a Jungian? He is certainly flirting with Jung, but I would say it would take some time before he recognises the depth and complexity of Jung's vision. Meanwhile, the forces unleashed in the unconscious, intensified by the withdrawal of libido and the dabbling in esoteric traditions, results in a flooding of the ego personality by archaic ideas and unusual convictions. The seeker has lost his normal boundaries, his social orientation and his connection with reality. He feels destined for big things and motivated by big ideas. Suddenly, the possibilities of his life appear to be endless, but always just a little out of reach, and away from his grasp. 'Thanks, Dr Jung', this person says, 'for waking me up from my shallowness, and for showing me this larger world.' But while celebrating his new-found spiritual life, some of his friends and family begin to suspect that he might be unhinged and unstable. 'What is all this talk about Jung?' his father enquires, and because of the association of Jung with such unrelated and grandiose illusions, Jung often acquires a bad name in normative or socially adjusted circles. If the name 'Jung' is only mentioned in the context of borderline psychotic experiences, and unhinged or other-worldly spiritual experiences, it is little wonder that some associate Jung with antisocial madness.

The unconscious of the seeker has been aroused, and the sleeping archetypes have been stirred to new life, but the problem now is where are these awakened forces to go? The New Ager, who thinks he can 'trip the light fantastic' (as was said in the 1960s about psychedelic experience), often fails to realise that he must take up a conscious and morally responsible attitude to the archetypes and their archaic powers. They do not exist for his delight or enjoyment, but demand a moral and creative response, and they need to be successfully integrated into his day-world experience. He is playing with dynamite, and these powerful forces can explode in his face, destroying the integrity of his personality and the unity of the psyche. At this point our seeker walks a tightrope between normality and insanity, but it is always possible that a third way is discovered: namely, the way of individuation, in which a new integration between consciousness and the unconscious occurs. The point is that the normal ego, almost by definition, will be unable to contain or transform the disruptive archetypal forces, and it will always be overwhelmed by them.

Building a new self, overcoming intoxication

What is required is the development of a different self, and this development requires discipline, work, effort, detachment, reflection and self-criticism. If the New Ager is enjoying the wonderland of the unconscious like a tourist in an exotic destination, he cannot develop the right attitude. If the primary aim is pleasure and intoxication, the contact with the unconscious remains negative, because the relentless pursuit of pleasure binds the person to the ego, and this egotistical state produces more inflation, grandiosity, anxiety and fears of being overwhelmed. In another sense, what is required at this critical moment is *initiation*. The seeker requires initiation into a new self, induction into a new sense of human identity. We need to build a larger vessel, because the ego is like a little saucepan buffeted by gigantic waves and high seas.

The New Ager protests: 'But I don't need initiation! I have already been initiated into the unconscious and plunged into the realm of the Gods. I am already transformed.' This is the inflated ego talking about its intoxicated state, and it is unable to see or appreciate the real danger it is in, or the problems that beset it. The Jungian response, as I understand it, would be to suggest that he has only achieved a partial or half-way initiation, which is almost worse than none at all. The plunge into the intoxicating sea of the collective unconscious is just the beginning, and it is relatively easy, involving a lowering of the threshold of consciousness. He has indeed been initiated into the unconscious, but not into his own selfhood, which is the necessary next step and the vitally important transformation or turn-around, which the Greeks called *metanoia*. Above all, the next step involves paradox and containment: the ability to live two lives at once, to recover the normal day-world ego and its sense of proportion, while still being able to experience the cosmic and archetypal dimension. When this paradoxical transformation begins, we can then say that he has embarked on the Jungian path of individuation, that he has graduated from the vulgar stage of infantile spirituality.

Again, the New Ager may protest against developing a more mature and integrated spiritual attitude. 'What is the point of individuation? The ego is worthless, beside the majesty and awesome power of the archetypes!' The typical New Ager has completely misread Jung in accordance with his own limitations and complexes, and the nature of this misreading is the subject of following chapters. The New Ager may become defensive-aggressive toward Jungian cultural attitudes at this point. Is Jungian culture merely trying to turn him back toward the normality and conventionality that he despises? Is analytical psychology just a sophisticated name for normalisation? These are the sorts of debates and conflicts of opinion that the Jungian analyst or therapist is likely to have with the New Age seeker.

The great irony of the New Ager is that all the while he intellectually undervalues and debunks the ego, he remains wholly caught up in its claims and cravings. He typically espouses an egoless state, and quotes approvingly from esoteric texts that condemn the ego and advocate nirvana, but because of his infantilism and irresponsibility, the ego is always dominant, always claiming the spiritual high for itself. In my own experience, New Age condemnation of the ego is rife, but the ego is not extinguished by mere talk or ideology, because the ego is archetypal and won't easily go away. If we try to destroy it, it will come back again, and seize more than its normal share of psychic reality. Unbeknown to the New Ager, the ego has divine sanction, and although it pales in significance beside the collective unconscious, gradually its significance is made apparent.

The ego acts, as Jung has said, as a prefiguration of the higher Self. The ego is swept aside by the unconscious, but it must recover because a vessel, or vehicle, is required to contain the sacred forces and to bring them into relationship with each other. In theological terms, the ego is the servant of incarnation, and it enables the divine to become known and manifest. At first, the ego is displaced by the unconscious, but the unconscious must, in turn, be displaced by the Self, the 'third' thing which transcends and replaces the conflict between the two. The Jungian vision involves a good deal of paradox, and paradox is not what New Age culture can sustain or understand. But unless the ego is strengthened and restored to significance, the new centre of personality, which Jung calls the Self, cannot come into being. The best service the New Ager can do for the Self is to withdraw from the excitement and danger of the unconscious, and work on more simple and mundane matters such as social adjustment, personal endurance and mental concentration. The motto at this stage in the spiritual experience is surely 'less is more', for it is not until the excitement of the collective unconscious is called off that the work of building the Self can begin. The primal attraction to the chaotic cauldron of the archetypes has to be resisted so that one can be inducted into the mystery of one's own selfhood.

The need for spaces in which transformation might occur

Jungian therapeutic culture might insist that the right kinds of changes and transformations of personality would most likely not take place in the wider public domain, or only in the person who is unusually gifted, and has the capacity to critique his own development. The professional advice might be that the vehicle of analysis is needed to facilitate a person's journey from normal ego-centredness to a new kind of wholeness. This is why many Jungian analysts look gloomily upon New Age culture, and why they doubt the effectiveness of Jung's wisdom in the public domain. I have known some analysts who have said that popular spirituality always ends up in narcissism, inflation and personal tragedy, because there is no vessel or *temenos* to effect any real transformation. I have much sympathy with this view and can see the therapeutic sense of it. But this view clearly leaves itself wide open to charges of elitism, exclusivity and money-making on the part of the Jungian industry. The whole world cannot go into Jungian analysis, and not everyone has the time, money or opportunity to enter long-term psychotherapy.

If the transformation from ego to Self is indeed willed by fate and belongs to human psychology, then perhaps we had better have more faith in the natural operations of the individuation process. The psycho-therapeutic purpose of the world religions, it would seem, is to effect precisely this kind of transformation. For people fortunate enough to be gifted by religious faith, or able to sustain a religious attitude in the modern era, religion may still be able to provide the context or holding space in which such changes occur. But the religions have been dramat-ically weakened and undermined by modernity and science, and in a Western society governed by individualism and a do-it-yourself approach to everything, the majority of educated people with spiritual impulses are likely to try do-it-yourself spirituality. In this case, we end up in our present situation, with much talk about ego-transcendence, but precious little evidence that people are able to bring such transcendence to healthy and life-affirming realisation. The pressing question we have to contend with is this: Are people able to induct themselves successfully into a new state? Are we able to conduct and manage our own initiations into wholeness and integration?

My own sense is that we need all kinds of help, especially with ritualising and symbolising the transformation of the new centre of personality. We need drama, art, music, ritual, religion and psychotherapy to support us in times of spiritual crisis and transition. The spiritual instinct to individuation is present, but it is so weakened by the claims of the ego, and by a social-political world saturated with ego-values and devoid of symbolic or spiritual awareness, that this instinct needs to be artificially strengthened and supported. Psychotherapy must become more widely and economically available, and our religions need to renew themselves to perform the vital role that they must play in the midst of human society and suffering.

The need to strengthen our sense of the Other

It seems important to ask whether our popular 'secular' spirituality, or our 'spiritual' psychology, is always bound to fail, to lead us into inflation and hubris, because it does not possess an adequate or good enough sense of the *otherness* of the sacred. By locating the sacred within the self, and by having a weakened perception of the holy as an objective agency, have we condemned ourselves and our culture to inferior or destructive forms of spiritual experience? In dethroning the idea of God, and in popularising the sanctity of the inner self, have we opened the floodgates to a gnostic revival that will continually involve us in psychic confusion and blurred mental vision?

In the Grail legend, the question that is always put to Parsifal is, 'Whom does the Grail serve?' It is vitally important to know that the object of spiritual desire, the Grail cup or chalice, serves a higher good and a greater authority. If the Grail is won by the greedy ego, so that its values and powers serve the ego and its development, then the whole point of the spiritual journey is lost. There is no doubt in the Vedic or Indian mind that the Atman serves the higher divinity of God, or Brahman, and not the personal self. But what about in our secular times, when our search for spirituality is operating in a purely secular context? How can we learn to know and relate to a greater authority, if the greater authority is not visualised, conceptualised or named? To the believing Christian, the higher authority is Christ or the Holy Spirit, and both are in turn viewed as agents of God the Father. But the adventurer in the New Age is disenchanted with religion and can no longer believe in the tenets or premises of its metaphysics. As such, the New Ager does not have a strong or clear enough sense of the sacred Other. Will the fashionable concept of the inner self, or the true self, enable the deep transformation to occur?

Paul Heelas, a sceptical sociologist of modern religious movements, puts the dilemmas facing modern spirituality this way:

> If indeed there *is* an inner spiritual realm, it might be supposed that the dawning of the New Age is in good hands. It [the spiritual realm] provides that guidance, that authoritative ethicality, necessary for life run without traditions; it provides that creativity, energy, power, love, responsibility (and so on) required for utopian times.
>
> However, as most New Agers unhappily acknowledge, the Self is only too subject to vicissitudes. That is to say, it is widely supposed that the ego, with its psychology of attachment, is continually striving to assert and reassert itself. And when it does, the Self ceases to function. New Agers are thus engaged in a perpetual struggle, combating the 'pull' of the ego by practising disciplines to make contact with the Self itself.

Depending on the state of play of the struggle, the Self – assuming it exists – is in control; or conversely, the ego is in command. Successful activity in everyday life thus depends on how the Self–ego contest is resolved at any particular moment. In sum, the New Age is not – in its own terms – securely and permanently *grounded*. There is the continual likelihood of the ego reasserting itself and disrupting the utopian life – at least until the time dawns, if this is conceivable, when egos are no longer constructed.

(Heelas 1996: 206)

This semi-humorous, ironic approach to contemporary spirituality is well positioned to grasp the contradictions and difficulties associated with our experience. As Heelas says, ours is a very precarious, unreliable and *ungrounded* spirituality. Reading his reflections, we remember the biblical narrative about the dangers of building our house upon shifting sand, which in this case would be the ungrounded reality of secular spirituality. Without the stable rock or ground provided by a historically based religious faith, much of this activity reveals itself as vain and futile. Here we begin to glimpse the wisdom of the church's traditional stand on these matters. The church believes that spirituality without religion is problematical, and that neither man nor God will be furthered by it. Religion provides a sense of direction, tells us what to look for, insists always on an attitude of humility, and formulates for us a strongly defined sense of the sacred Other. Without these things, our spirituality can be rudderless and vain, just as church teachings have long warned.

Popular confusions about ego and Self

Although Jung may have had a clear understanding in his own mind about the differences between ego and Self, it could be argued that he has not communicated this difference to the wider world, and therefore he is to some extent implicated in the mess we are in. In a Western civilisation already drenched in the 'self' and wallowing in egocentricity and self-referentiality, why would Jung call the highest sacred object or goal the 'self'? As we know, he did not even capitalise this term. It was only some (not all) of his followers who adopted the convention of capitalising it, to emphasise the distinction between it and the common 'self' or ego. Jung wrote:

When we speak of man we mean the indefinable whole of him, an ineffable totality, which can only be formulated symbolically. I have chosen the term 'self' to designate the totality of man, the sum total of his conscious and unconscious contents. I have chosen this term in accordance with Eastern philosophy, which for centuries has occupied itself with the problems that arise when even the gods cease to incarnate.

(1938/40: 140)

I have always found this passage puzzling. I don't think Jung chose the term 'self' to conform to the dictates and terminology of the Upanishads. Why would he? He had no debt or obligation to the Upanishads or Eastern philosophy. In fact he often speaks about the dangers of bringing Eastern ideas and terms to the West (1936b: 868).

The problem and danger of the term 'self' is that it is simply too common, too ordinary. It invites precisely the kind of metaphysical inflation that Jung strives to combat. If the indwelling human psyche and the God-image are ultimately one and the same thing, this is a gnostic or esoteric truth to be uttered very quietly and secretly in intense meditations, and not something to announce to the world at large. There is an ancient Jewish maxim that says 'God and man are in a sense twins' (cited by Neumann 1949a: 395), but no rabbi with a public ministry would ever popularise such a dangerous idea. Humanity is not ready for this dangerous revelation: indeed the world's major religions have always wisely avoided the gnostic tendency to equate the human with the divine, and have always insisted on strict lines of demarcation. In the sacraments we pray, 'Lead us not into temptation', but Jung's psychology leads us directly into temptation, the temptation to think of ourselves as Godlike, which is why so many Jewish and Christian theologians object to it.

It is a vastly different situation in the East, or at least, in the traditional East. When the yoga adept calls the Self the 'Atman', and then claims that Atman equals Brahman, that is, the Self = God, he does not conclude that man is God. There is already in Indian culture a sense of dimensionality in the soul, an awareness that the soul contains many worlds, and that inside these turning worlds there resides the silent, still world that we call God. T.S. Eliot captures this awareness memorably and beautifully in *Four Quartets* (1942), but Eliot was also drawing from the Upanishads and Vedic literature in that great poem. But the Westerner is largely ignorant of interior reality, partly because the churches have kept us in spiritual kindergarten by imagining God always 'out there', as an old man with a beard, in the sky. Nothing in our historical, educational or religious background prepares us for the great mystery of the coming age, which is the birth of God in the human soul. We desperately require a sacred psychology, a logos of soul, to help us navigate our way through the present confusion, but does Jung's psychology clarify the confusion or merely add to it?

Knowing well the dangers of inflation, it is surprising that Jung did not call his highest term something that could not be confused with the normal self. If he could not refer to Christ or Buddha, why not Atman or Perusha? If these seemed too exotic and difficult, why not simply call it the Second Self? There is great support for this term in Australian Aboriginal religion. During the rite that initiates boys into manhood, the grandfather steps forward and, showing the youth the sacred stone or churinga, says:

> Here is your body, here is your second self.
>
> (cited by Neumann 1949b: 289)

The 'second' self adds the necessary sense of mystery and otherness, and avoids all confusions. But if we only call it the 'self', the question arises: whose self? The New Ager replies, 'Well, mine, of course.' This term backfires and produces the opposite of what Jung intended.

I don't think Jung chose the term 'self' 'in accordance with Eastern philosophy', but rather in accordance with secular and scientific taste. He chose the term, I would contend, because it was the least religious-sounding term he could find. He chose it during a period in his career when he believed he was creating a secular science for the soul and its development. Jung was struggling heroically at the time to construct an alternative language and terminology to religion. He believed that blatantly religious terminology would alienate modern people from the domain of the unconscious, and create mystification and confusion. He was also, of course, concerned about his own reputation, and about the charges of mysticism and religiosity that were already being levelled at him by Ernest Jones and other hostile Freudians. The times were nonreligious or antireligious, and Jung wanted to keep with the times, and speak a language that would be effective.

Jung carried on for decades about the God-term and the God-problem, insisting that the psyche only reveals the presence of an 'image' of God, rather than God itself. But all of this reserve and quibbling was abandoned by the time he wrote his memoirs with Aniela Jaffe. In *Memories, Dreams, Reflections* (1961), he spoke openly about his religious convictions, and all former scientific reservation had fallen away. Some might say this was the product of old age, senility or loss of scientific integrity, but I would say it was the triumph of spiritual wisdom, no longer encumbered by the strictures of career and reputation. If Jung had employed openly religious terminology in mid-career, would he have been any worse off? Those who were gunning for him had already decided he was a religious nutter anyway, so I cannot see exactly what he had to lose. But it is what humanity might have won that concerns me here. If the 'self' had not been popularised, we might have stemmed the tide of narcissism – or perhaps not; perhaps it would not have made any difference. But the point is that this confusion did not help our innate tendency toward narcissistic grandiosity and inflation, giving spiritual narcissists everywhere the permission to quote Jung to justify their sanctification of the human ego.

My own view is that this places considerable responsibility in our own hands, in the present generation of thinkers and writers. Instead of singing the praises of Jung's theories of the self and its psychological formation, Jungians and especially post-Jungians ought to be deconstructing and reconstructing the theory in theological terms. We cannot fool around with sacred forces without an adequate theological understanding of what is taking place. At least, that is my own conviction, after working in this field for several decades. We are clearly facing a crisis of terminology: a self which is not a self, and a 'depth psychology' which is not considered a psychology by any university in the world. I think Jung is offering a science of life integration in the widest sense, but that there comes a point where we have to abandon science as conventionally understood if we want to become fully integrated. The final stages of life integration are clearly theological, and if psychology cannot openly supply that perspective we have to abandon or reinvent it.

Similarities

In concluding this chapter, I want to return to the similarities between Jung and the New Age. Both Jung and the New Age agree that spiritual meaning is no longer synonymous with, and can no longer be contained by, the religious establishments and institutions of Western culture. Jung and the New Age are interested in exploring non-Christian, pre-Christian and post-Christian sources of spiritual meaning. Both are interested in Gnosticism, alchemy and Eastern philosophical traditions. The New Age is particularly impressed by Jung's championing of the repressed spiritual values of our secular time, by his 'rediscovery' of the psyche, soul and spirit, and by his assurance that redemption and revelation, formerly obtained only within the context of strictly organised religions, can now be found within the lived experience of the individual.

Jung contributes substantially to the needs of the New Age by offering a psychological explanation for the enduring value and importance of the religious impulse outside conventional religious structures. We cannot pretend that Jung has been completely misunderstood by the New Age; one aspect of his work has been intuitively assimilated by those who are driven by deep-seated spiritual hunger. New Age people have been alienated by the established religious institutions for a variety of reasons, and they have become enthused by Jung's open invitation to participate in a spirituality without religion. Jung encourages people to seek spirituality within, to find God in the depths of personality and at the heart of the self. As Nevill Drury explains, this sent the New Age movement into paroxysms of spiritual excitement:

> Jung was making a momentous point that in many ways underscores the entire ethos of the New Spirituality today: namely, that divinity is not external to humanity but lies within, that it is an aspect of our humanness which we all share and can have access to.
>
> (Drury 1999: 6)

The idea of finding the sacred within the self is the constant preoccupation of Jung's life and work, and this has had an intoxicating effect upon the masses, encouraging them to seek the inward path to transcendence and liberation. The fact that the churches have been unable to offer such an inward or spiritual connection to religious mysteries has left them lifeless and listless. The lack of a connecting bridge between religious ideas 'out there' and the existential and feeling life 'in here' has had a devitalising effect on religion, and the tide of public interest has turned away from it. Interest will not flow back in its direction until clergy and theologians establish a link between religion and the soul, between spirit and psyche, or between God and the common ground of experience. The New Age exists partly because the churches have been unable to build this bridge.

The New Age is also excited by Jung's understanding that the best is yet to come, that God is evolving just as humanity is evolving, and that revelation is not only 'back there' in the ancient past or locked away in sacred scriptures, but also in our present experience, in nature and matter, and in divine immanence. In traditional religions, the emphasis is on an Absolute Truth that has already been revealed. The only challenge for the faithful and for ordinary believers is for them to 'grow into' that revealed truth, to know it more fully and completely. Jung, however, insists that there are very real and pressing spiritual challenges and adventures that belong to the present moment (the *kairos*, or 'right moment', as he announces), and this inspires people with a sense of meaningful and engaged spiritual adventure. Jung insists that because God is alive and the spirit is afoot, there are many exciting and challenging tasks that lie ahead, as it were waiting for us to respond to their call. This excites the New Age and fills it with a presentiment of present and future significance, finding in Jung's pronouncements the marks of true prophecy and inspirational insight.

But Jung delivers the New Age a mixed message which has been the cause of considerable confusion. While he encourages us to seek the 'undiscovered' spirituality within, he cautions us that such a discovery must not be pursued unaided, or without psychological or spiritual direction. Jung believes that people should stick to the historical pathways of organised religion wherever possible, unless they feel personally called to a direct spiritual encounter with the sacred. He often warns that it is a terrible thing to fall into the hands of the living God, and that we should expect to be shocked and disoriented by this encounter. Jung does not believe that this pathway of individual encounter with the sacred is for everyone, nor should it be taken casually or lightly. One must be qualified for it and ready for its onslaught, a cautionary warning that the New Age either completely ignores or regards as quaintly old-fashioned and a bit schoolmasterly. But if such an encounter is not meant for everyone, this makes it even more appealing to the elitism and individualism inherent in the New Age movement, a movement with a background in the soaring optimism of humanistic psychology (Carl Rogers, Maslow) and the human potential movement.

The true value of the New Age is not in how well or badly it applies Jungian theory to everyday experience, but in how well it demonstrates before our eyes the contents of the unconscious and the things that have been excluded or repressed by the Old Age. Its real value is in how it challenges Western religion to arrive at new and culturally relevant interpretations of the human spirit. The New Age is a 'cry of the heart' from the masses, a cry to make spirituality relevant to our times and emotionally related to individual human experience. It is a movement which reverses many of the attitudes, trends and views that are found in traditional Western religion, especially those concerning the body, sexuality, nature and desire. It is a movement which follows and extends an archetypal process which is based on the feminine principle, is compensatory to the patriarchal West and has historical links with romanticism, gnosticism, paganism, naturalism, nudism, theosophy and occultism.

Influence or coincidence?

If the New Age appears Jungian, it is not necessarily because it has always used Jung, but because it draws its life from a particularly strong archetypal current that we might associate with Jung because he clearly mapped this psychospiritual territory. In this sense, the question of Jung's 'influence' could be a kind of optical illusion, created by the coincidence between what Jung researched and what the New Age now experiences. Jung looked deeply into the Western psyche and he saw much earlier, in the opening decades of the twentieth century, the same psychospiritual forces that the New Age would have to contend with a half-century or more later. Andrew Samuels has developed a similar theory with regard to the supposedly 'Jungian' developments that have taken place within the post-Freudian schools of psychoanalysis:

> If we scan the post-Freudian development with as unbiased an eye as possible, we notice something rather odd about it, something of the greatest importance. . . . Many of the central issues and features of contemporary psychoanalysis are reminiscent of positions taken by Jung in earlier years. This is not to say that Jung himself is responsible for all the interesting things to be found in contemporary psychoanalysis . . . But, as Paul Roazen pointed out, 'Few responsible figures in psychoanalysis would be disturbed today if an analyst were to present views identical to Jung's in 1913.'
>
> (Samuels 1997: 4)

The link may not be causal or a matter of transporting ideas from one place to another. The link could be acausal and coincidental. Because Jung saw deeply into the collective psyche, he was actually looking into the future, given that what is deeply buried and hidden becomes revealed and exposed at a later point in history, possibly even a hundred or more years later. The argument about 'influence' can become a red herring, and we can thereby ignore the important issue, which is not that Jung is 'great' because he has so much influence over society, but he is great because he saw so much about who and what we are, and we end up living and acting what he saw. His works are too difficult to become widely influential, and as we have seen, bastardised versions of his ideas have more luck in gaining widespread currency.

Jung's research is based on those archetypal contents that contradict, oppose or compensate the traditional Christian canon and its espoused ethic of perfection, in particular the mother archetype, the feminine, nature, the earth, the shadow and evil. Jung was not interested in idealising or worshipping these archetypal contents, but in critically exploring them with a view to bringing them into relationship with the governing values of our culture. His method was to expand consciousness to include what had been rejected, not to become identified with the rejected contents. We must resist being seduced, and try to hold the tension between the opposites we encounter. Any social movement which identifies with one set of archetypal contents is by definition not going to be 'Jungian', because being Jungian is based on the ethics of integration and the continued struggle for a difficult wholeness.

Chapter 2

Oceanic spirituality and false wholeness

> If there is a sin against life, it consists perhaps not so much in despairing
> of life as in hoping for another life and eluding the implacable grandeur
> of this life.
>
> Albert Camus (cited in Miller 1995: 15)

Popular nihilistic mysticism

A favourite New Age metaphor is to experience the ego as a drop of water
poised above the ocean. In this configuration, spiritual work, or rather
spiritual relaxation, consists in allowing the drop to gently and effortlessly
fall into the ocean below. This path is about overcoming fear or anxiety
on the part of the ego, so that dissolution into nonbeing is seen as ultimate
ecstasy rather than as the obliteration of identity. But obliteration and
destruction is certainly one aspect of this process, albeit an aspect that the
New Age tends to overlook. It appears to be starstruck by the possibility
of nonexistence, and many of its techniques and ideals work toward this
end. For instance, a New Age handbook on spirituality describes the
concept of nirvana this way:

> In Hinduism and yoga, nirvana is union with the supreme Godhead
> – Brahman. In this state the ego is transcended and the self merges
> with Brahman, thus extinguishing one's individual nature. The
> mystic who attains this level of consciousness has no further need
> for rebirth.
>
> (Drury 1999: 188)

Such New Age 'translations' of Hindu philosophy are very common in
today's spiritual marketplace, but I am led to believe by Sanskrit scholars

and those better informed than myself that the New Age interpretation of Hinduism, like the New Age interpretation of Jung, is fundamentally wrong. It appears that Hinduism's advocacy of a transformation of consciousness, and of a displacement of the ego-based position, is constantly confused with the obliteration of all human consciousness. I have always been puzzled and dismayed by the New Age distaste for life, creation, rebirth and human manifestation. I love life greatly, and it has never occurred to me to believe that 'no further need for rebirth' could be seen as some kind of spiritual reward for being a good meditator. Moreover, to portray 'extinguishing one's individual nature' in such positive terms seems to be rather odd. Hinduism becomes the exotic and foreign carrier of a Western neurosis: a desire for self-extinction and death. Don't we have a longing for life and individual being that would protest against such extinguishment? Isn't there an instinct for life that would rebel against this love-affair with death and non-existence?

In the late 1970s, I experienced the misfortune of being the victim of a forest fire in the wooded hills around Adelaide in South Australia. In that fire, I lost my house and all personal belongings, including the results of three years' research toward my doctoral thesis, which was housed in an office that was destroyed by the fire. Soon after, I was greeted by a group of 'Age of Aquarius' friends who had heard the news. 'Isn't it wonderful', they began to chant, 'that you have been liberated of so much baggage and can now feel closer to nirvana?' 'This is a divine opportunity, bringing you much further to enlightenment.' I had to confess to these so-called friends that I simply felt closer to a nervous breakdown, and would they kindly leave me be and go away? At that time, I felt the need for 'ordinary' people who would commiserate with me and understand the human meaning of loss and devastation. I found some of my cosmic friends to be not only unfeeling, but downright inhuman and remotely 'spiritual' in the most negative sense.

Evidently, the instinct for life and individual existence has been eclipsed in such people, and there has been a suspension of normal human feeling toward suffering and crisis. The human loss is brushed away as meaningless, because they see before them the approaching glory of nirvana and nonbeing, which excites them with a different set of feelings about authenticity and divine radiance. Reflecting on this, I suddenly realised why so many religious cults end up in mass suicide, self-destruction, fires and conflagration. For such groups, life is merely a shallow and pale reflection of a greater reality which completely eclipses the importance and meaning of this life. The world of manifestation is somehow inauthentic and fake, and the exaltation of liberation only arises in such people when they can imagine the world on fire and consumed by flames.

The passion that some fundamentalist Christians have for the Last Days and the fires of the Apocalypse is of the same order as this. In those in whom the presence of the numinosum has 'broken through' into consciousness, there is often this terrifying idealisation of death, destruction and annihilation, usually by water or fire. The pain and terror of such destruction is suspended, and instead such people seem to feel warmed and heartened by the presence of the numinosum. This passion is well expressed by a fictional character in Patrick White's novel, *The Aunt's Story*:

> 'We have destroyed so much, but we have not destroyed enough. We must destroy everything, everything, even ourselves. Then at last when there is nothing, perhaps we shall live.'
>
> (White 1948: 168)

Such sentiments and attitudes are frequently put before us as spiritual and mystical, but I think their overriding feature is surely their extremely pathological character. In archetypal terms, I often find that a primal archetypal figure has broken through in the psyche of such people, causing them to radically undermine and devalue conscious life, and to experience a passionate desire for nonbeing.

In his important essay 'Mystical Man' (1949a), Erich Neumann presents a formidable defence for the mystical life, arguing that the poor reputation from which mysticism often suffers is a direct result of our failure to distinguish between different levels or kinds of mystic experience. At its lowest level, mysticism is simply a glorified attempt to destroy life, and this kind of otherworldly mystic 'is so frequently and unjustifiably regarded as the type of mystical man in general' (Neumann 1949a: 400). In this kind of mysticism, life is not valued because it is equated with suffering and conflict, and an infantile part of us longs to escape from conflict and to crawl back into the uncreated source or matrix, which Neumann calls the 'uroboros'. This kind of mystic has a fixation upon the mother archetype, and is prepared to sacrifice the world, the ego and all form in an attempt to sink back into the ecstasy of the matrix. This kind of mysticism is also called 'uroboric incest' (1949a: 389), because the ego yearns to enter into the cosmic womb and to lose itself in its ecstatic embrace. Neumann writes,

The uroboros mystic yearns to return to, to be gathered into, the maternal womb. His desire is to do away with the creative principle, which begets form, conflict, and suffering, and to achieve beatific nonexistence in the divine womb of nothingness.

(1949a: 399)

In low-level or nihilistic mysticism, the accent is on ecstasy and bliss, avoidance of pain, escape from the real, and beatific visions of another reality. This sounds very familiar to me, and it is as if Neumann's essay of 1949 were some kind of prophetic forecast of the popularisation of dangerous or anti-world mysticism several decades later. Neumann actually puts a vital question in this essay which requires an urgent answer today:

The question remains open as to what should be done to prevent the ideal of this state of perfection from poisoning humanity. For again and again the arduous heroic path of the ego into consciousness and suffering is endangered by the magic of the temptation to seek, or not to depart from, the state of perfection represented by an egoless unconsciousness.

(1949a: 379)

In archetypal terms, we have to do with a fatal erotic attraction, where the ego longs to 'marry' the archetypal mother in death. To educate us beyond this fatal attraction, the ego has to be shown how to serve the sacred reality in this life, and not to hanker after another life to consummate the erotic union. This opaque, dull, or inert world has to be made translucent, has to become the legitimate home of the sacred reality, so that in our longing for the sacred we do not always betray this world and flee to another world in ecstatic death or egoic dissolution. Jung's major work, *Symbols of Transformation* (1912/52), was hugely concerned with this problem, and with the way in which an otherworldly divine image can 'poison humanity' and bring about psychic destruction in individuals. In *Symbols*, Jung describes a case study in which an incestuous longing for fusion with the matrix subverts a human life, brings on fragmentation of mind, and engenders the illusion of creativity and power in the face of evident self-destruction. In my book *Patrick White: Fiction and the Unconscious* (1988), I show how this same destructive pattern is apparent in the life and work of a contemporary novelist.

Overlap between religion and pathology

Religious passion has certainly become a haven for psychopathology
and mental illness, but it has always been thus. Freud's unsympathetic
analysis of religion may be seen as excessive or unkind, but it nevertheless
contains a great amount of vital information about the overlap between
religious feeling and psychopathological disorder. What exacerbates the
situation today is that society has become virtually illiterate before the
realm of the spiritual, and idiots and fools can utter all manner of things
in the name of 'spirituality' or 'religion', and few are prepared to contest
their claims because we do not know any better. The unconsciousness of
the religious impulse in our time has aided and abetted the pathologisation
of this impulse, so that we can barely tell any more whether someone is
advocating spiritual health and life, or mental disease and sickness.

My own sense is that the New Age movement is largely about the
passion we feel for the Great Mother, but that evangelical and fundamentalist Christian groups are involved in a different kind of passion
relating to Our Father in heaven. The New Age is orgiastic, relaxing,
'natural', bodily, physical, and in pursuit of what Freud calls the 'oceanic
feeling'. But for all its apparent physicality and materiality, the New Age
is strangely otherworldly. Mythology and psychology show that the
spirituality of the Great Mother is often transcendentalist, involving a
high soaring of the spirit above and beyond the world (Hillman 1973).
On the other hand, the Christian cults are often transcendentalist in
a different way: non-bodily, puritanical, apocalyptic and pietistic. The
Great Mother cults experience their ecstasy through 'oceanic spirituality'
and immersion in a sea of bliss, while the Father cults pursue ecstasy
through work, toil and charismatic union with the law-giver, pantocrator
or Comforter who sends 'tongues' of fire. The feature common to both
cults is that the ego is enthralled by a numinous figure who stands on the
other side of consciousness, seemingly drawing the ego toward it as if
by a mysterious magnetic force. If this is a 'tug-of-war' between life and
death, the ego is not exerting any effort on its own side, and it gleefully
allows itself to be drawn out of life into the cosmic realm. This is an anti-
incarnational spirituality which does not understand the importance
of being anchored in this reality, or in providing a counterweight to the
otherworldly lure of the numinosum.

Negative religions of this kind are extremely dangerous to society,
since life is cheaply regarded, and disasters and crises that befall humanity
are likely to be overvalued as attempts at enlightenment (for the New Age)
or apocalypse and revelation (for Christian cults). But a loving, creative

and incarnational God cannot enjoy these religions either, since they are moving in the opposite direction to the evolutionary current of life and manifestation. If, as the mystic William Blake proclaims, 'Eternity is in love with the productions of time' (1793: 151), then eternity cannot benefit if the productions of time are constantly attempting to eradicate themselves and be drawn back into eternity. If the very point of creation and manifestation is to allow something eternal to know itself in time and space, and to take on form and acquire body, then this eternal longing is obviously frustrated by the nihilistic desires of humans who see no real point in the creation.

Ironically, such humans experience the numinosum as destructive and anti-creational, but only because, I believe, they have not allowed the numinous to speak for itself, but experience it through the distorting lens of a pathological complex. The task for people who are caught up in such psychic situations is not to flee from the numinous, but to know it more intimately and deeply, in which case the complex could be divested of its primitive and destructive features, allowing the archetypal figure to be revealed more fully. I do not believe that the archetype in itself is pathological; only the archetype which is encased in a complex, or which is encountered by a defective or weak ego, is pathological. We cannot blame the Mother or Father for destroying creation, but must ask ourselves why we invariably experience the archetypes in this way.

Contexts for the rise of the Mother archetype

The New Age is primarily a primitive religion of the Great Mother. The task of the future is not to get rid of it because it is dangerous, or to ban it because it is non-Christian, but to deepen and refine it so that we can know this archetypal figure more fully. Because of the strength and power of patriarchal religion, the Great Mother has been repressed and eclipsed for a long time in the Western psyche, only erupting in various exotic or fringe movements such as romanticism, occultism, primitivism, pantheism, or neopaganism. The decline of Christendom and the patriarchal social order has provided the ideal climate and opportunity in which the Great Mother archetype can return to society and make its presence felt again in consciousness and culture. But like any psychic content that returns to the surface after a long exile in the unconscious, its initial return can result in mental disturbance, disequilibrium, primitivity and inferior behaviour. If the New Age is primitive and uncouth, it is largely because this is the condition of the archetypal complex as it returns to society after prolonged banishment.

The Mother archetype has also been constellated on a grand scale because the Western ego has exhausted itself with its tireless addictions to 'development', 'progress' and 'advancement'. These addictions, which are largely the result of patriarchal drives and motivations, have left the Western ego exhausted and depleted, just as they have exhausted and depleted the body of the earth and its natural resources. As a direct result, a compensatory process has been activated in the Western psyche, in which our restless addictions are being countered by a desire to slow down the pace of change, to re-experience the wonder and splendour of the natural world, and the wonder of our own bodily, natural selves. The Mother archetype rules the world of nature and the body, and it is 'she' to whom we must return if we want to experience the natural cosmos again. Moreover, as the personification of the unconscious matrix or source, it is she to whom we return when we absent ourselves from the manic craziness of the world and retreat into the oceanic depths of peace and inactivity.

With the New Age, the spiritual impulse has regressed to an early, primitive situation which actually precedes Christianity and patriarchal religion by thousands of years. It resides in a deeply regressed posture, and it knows 'God' only as the World Mother, that is, as the fluid, amniotic ocean of life, in whom the individual swims around much like a fish or marine creature. It is little wonder that the dolphin and the whale have become key symbols of the New Age, because they express perfectly the condition of oceanic engagement and at-one-ment to which the New Age aspires. The only snag in this paradisal scenario is that we are not dolphins or whales, but rather complex human beings who have got ourselves and our culture into a mess. It is wonderful that we strive to save dolphins and whales from the dangers and violations of governments and predatory industries, but we also need to rescue ourselves from our romantic identification with the dolphin and the oceanic feeling.

New Age spirituality is mainly about returning to the mystical source-situation, and the methods used to facilitate this return are primarily techniques of relaxation: meditation, silence, reflection, retreats, introspection, massage, perfumed oils, ambient music, celestial teas and cosmic harmonies. The whole point of New Age spirituality is to move outside or beyond the busy ego and its complex world and to penetrate to a level of reality where there is peace, harmony, gentleness and renewal. In a modern world obsessed with achievement, scores, progress and striving, the New Age instinct is an understandable and reasonable compensatory reaction to our manic style. In 1949, Erich Neumann wrote:

The mystic's striving to rid himself of the world, his isolation, and his ego – to vanish in the area of creative nothingness and thus recapture the unified experience of self and totality, perfection and paradise – is the understandable countermovement to the movement of the ego into the solitude of consciousness.

(1949a: 388)

The legitimacy of the New Age is discovered just here: in its expression of a collective need for balance, inwardness, internality and silence. But even 'compensatory' reactions to human craziness are themselves liable to become crazy in turn, creating a new one-sidedness in the opposite direction. The New Age tends to create a cult experience around the need for quietude, retreat and return, so that while it offers a way out of life, it does not really offer a way back into it again. There must be a return to the world, after there has been a leave-taking from it. If we follow the ebbing of the cosmic tide back into the ocean of nonbeing, we lose the very tension and energy that makes life possible and that advances civilisation.

In the New Age movement, the archetype of the seductive, 'terrible' mother has been constellated, the mother who draws the exhausted ego into her womb, but who fails to release it back into life. Typically, however, the New Ager is caught up in a gross idealisation of the cosmic womb and of the Great Mother, which are perceived as kind, loving, gentle, healthy and restorative, so that the demonic or life-denying aspect of this same archetypal field is not – or cannot be – experienced in relation to these idealised objects. Instead, the demonic aspect is projected upon society and the 'world', which is felt to be evil, stifling, choking and destructive of human integrity and worth. When New Agers leave the tribal commune or vegetable farm and climb into their trucks and vans and head into the city, they experience the city as filthy, destroying, dehumanising and foul. It is in these highly charged and emotional reactions that the long-repressed aspect of their own infantile spirituality expresses itself; but of course, in projection upon a demonised fallen world.

The choking, stifling and crushing elements that are projected upon the city are the same elements that describe their unconscious relationship with the Great Mother and her primordial womb or matrix. The task of therapy is to direct psychological and not merely ideological or ecological attention to the emotions experienced in the city. However, there will be great resistance to the psychologising of these emotions, since any deeper awakening will challenge the cosy lifestyle that has developed in response to the idealisation of the Mother archetype. It is far easier to condemn the world for being fallen and corrupt than it is for the New Ager to understand that he or she has fallen under the spell of an ancient archetypal pattern which threatens his or her integrity. When the ego sinks into the oceanic sea of the cosmic womb, the pleasurable aspect is identified with the beloved object, but the maw that crushes life, the *vagina dentata* that devours life, and the aggressivity of the primal matrix are all experienced outside the blissful experience in projection upon the world and others.

Cosmic bliss, peak experience and the avoidance of suffering

The person who is attracted to oceanic spirituality faces two kinds of suffering, and he or she generally attempts to escape from them both. The first is the suffering experienced in the source situation, as the ego is drawn toward, and then dissolved by, the oceanic waters of the cosmic matrix. Call this, if you will, mystical suffering in the pursuit of self-annihilation. The second kind is the ordinary suffering experienced in life, the suffering that afflicts the ego as it encounters grief, loss, frustration, failure, anguish, isolation and, above all, the tensions that arise as it comes into collision with the demands of eternity and fate. Call this, if you will, incarnational suffering in the service of life and creation. Being in life involves us in a 'crucifixion' of sorts between the demands of the ego for freedom and its own pleasure, and the claims of invisible forces over which the ego has no control. In life, we have to hold the tension between these opposites and attempt some kind of resolution, usually by the ego's acceptance of a fate that it can do little to alter. We reduce the high stress and tension of any life when we willingly accept the path that fate has already established for us.

Jung believes that the ultimate symbol for this aspect of our lives is the Christian cross, which symbolises, among other things, the pain and anguish of being pulled in different directions and of being 'crucified' between the human and the divine. The cross is experienced by the modern mind as a mournful and bleak symbol, but the cross is itself paradoxical, representing not only the pain of crucifixion but also the exaltation, holiness and release of resurrection. According to Jung, the spiritual and therapeutic value of the cross today is that if we accept the contrary forces that pull us in opposite directions, if we learn to contain the suffering generated by the conflict between divine and human imperatives in our lives, we too can experience something of the joy and triumph of the resurrection. The path of such reconciliation is tough and difficult, but the creator does not delight in our suffering, rather, the creator suffers with us as we are drawn now this way, now that way, in the pursuit of personal wholeness. As Mahatma Gandhi wrote, 'Suffering is the one indispensable condition of our being, but the purer the suffering the greater the progress.'

The New Age responds to this traditional wisdom like a child. It is irked by suffering, and tries to find ways to avoid it. The New Age often says that it prefers the image of the Buddha sitting in ecstasy beneath the Banyan tree, rather than the image of Christ writhing in pain upon the cross. The New Age has the sense that if it journeys to the East, and pursues the oceanic ecstasy and bliss that appears to be on offer there, it can avoid the suffering and pain of the West. The New Age wonders why religion has to be such a morbid affair. Why must the Messiah be nailed in agony to the cross? Can't we have a better guiding image and a more progressive and humane religious symbol? New Agers find Christianity too pessimistic and mournful, and Western humanism is disliked as well, since it too has a tragic vision of life and bears witness to a human world which is inherently limited and flawed. In the West, neither humanistic nor religious culture pretends that it can get rid of suffering, but these cultures attempt to make our suffering endurable by awarding it higher meaning.

The New Age replaces the Western sense of tragedy with an intense optimism about individual and social transformation.

> A 'new' age is possible; human potential is limitless; its dynamics are beckoning and available. Emphasis on sin and evil, on redemption and conversion must yield to a world of 'original blessings' in a good creation.
>
> (Kelly 1993: 41)

Man need no longer crucify himself in the image of Christ; he can get off the cross, and celebrate his corporeal, fleshly existence and his capacity for entering into transformative dialogue with the divine. Central to New Age culture, then, is a consciousness which is unable to experience the value of pain or the meaning of suffering, partly because pain and suffering are split off from the highly regarded 'spiritual' experience. This consciousness produces, among other things, an obsessive preoccupation with the state of bliss, and an addiction to ease, satiety, rest, relaxation. It is this kind of preoccupation that makes it extremely difficult to face the inevitable suffering that life delivers.

The New Age man searches for highs, peak experiences, altered states of consciousness, and avoids lows, depressions and bleak pessimism. He looks for spirituality, for which read 'devices and techniques that will connect me with the divine', and he often avoids or rejects established religions, for which read 'those dogmatic structures that limit my individual freedom, inhibit spiritual expression, and diminish personal expectations of glory'. Spirituality promises highs, but religion threatens with its emphasis on moral restrictions, social conscience and ethical obligations. The New Age man wants the goal (unity with the divine) without the way (the discipline, ethics and self-effacement that make unity possible). He wants blissful union without the suffering of the cross, spiritual rebirth without having to endure spiritual death. He is 'hooked' on the sacred, addicted to spiritual techniques and practices, and his credo is: 'Follow your bliss' (Joseph Campbell and Bill Moyers 1988).

A Jungian response would be to doubt the authenticity of this so-called 'spirituality' if it is merely designed to provide instant gratification for the ego. Jung would be suspicious of the marked separation of spirituality from religion, if it is designed simply to separate highs from lows, or light from shadow. Jung would see any unbounded optimism as a defence against darkness, especially given the tragic character of the twentieth century and its long and arduous struggle with darkness, and he would support the Christian West in its emphasis on unavoidable suffering. According to Jung, suffering can never be escaped, but must be embraced and accepted as part of the human condition.

A major difference between Jung and the New Age concerns their discovery or location of the sacred. As already argued, despite the New Age rhetoric about the immanence of the divine and the worldliness of its vision, the New Age appears to be caught up in a transcendentalist interpretation of the spirit. The New Age tends to find its spiritual experiences away from life and beyond the ground of ordinary experience. It is attracted to the bizarre and the exotic, to the extramundane and the shamanistic. A spiritual experience is a flight away from the real, and hence the importance of the word 'high' to describe this popular spirituality. The New Age is not redemptive or transformative, and in this sense Christianity is a far more radical social philosophy insofar as it attempts to engage and redeem the elements of this world. Could it be that the New Age has inherited the otherworldliness of historical gnosticism, with its impatience with the real and its metaphysical focus on a distant cosmos?

By contrast, Jung discovers spirituality in and through our human pathologies, not by transcending them. Jung maintains that for modern humanity 'the Gods have become diseases' (1929a: 54), and we meet our rejected and repressed sacredness at the centre of diseases, at the core of psychoneuroses and in the midst of mental anguish. If modern man does not consciously sacrifice to the Gods, he finds himself unconsciously sacrificed to the many pathologies and diseases that assail him, forcing a kind of literal or destructive displacement of the ego in favour of archetypal realities. Any collective movement that finds psychopathology morbid, dark or unworthy of interest is actually missing the spiritual opportunity of the time and does not deserve the name of 'spirituality'. The New Age, from this Jungian position, works tirelessly to avoid any encounter with the true sacred, preferring instead to follow some abstract, and entirely conventional, ego-ideal about what the sacred is like.

In religious practice, it is the soul that finds release and liberation, for that is the immortal part of the person. Paradoxically, the salvation of the soul is at the same time a mortification of the ego, hence the formulation: 'whosoever will lose his life for my sake shall find it' (Matthew 16.25). In the past, the necessary mortification of the ego has been confused with the mortification of the body, sexuality and the feminine, and this arose largely from the split in the Western psyche between spirit and matter. But today, with our greater psychological knowledge, we get closer to the Christian mystery by seeing that it is the personal self, the ego, which must be displaced so that salvation might take place. In the New Age, there is no real separation between the personal self and the transpersonal spirit, so the first stage of true religious awareness is not achieved; or rather, a religious process is conducted and at every point of this journey the spiritual life is contaminated with the desires and longings of the ego. As the spirit is released from its bondage and is lifted into heaven, the ego wants to travel along with it, and the ecstasy of the spirit's release is an ecstasy that the ego wants for itself.

In similar manner, the hungry New Age ego espies the grandeur and power of God, and it identifies with that power, viewing God as some untapped supernatural resource which can be utilised for the expansion of human potential. This is a wild and boundless Promethean fantasy, and the New Age actually believes in its heart of hearts that man can become God. With its early roots in the humanistic psychology movement, it weds the optimism of Maslow and Rogers with the esoteric claims of Blavatsky and Gurdjieff. In most of the popular literature, the New Age boasts about breaking conventional boundaries, realising hidden potential and aspiring to divine heights.

The impossible fusion of ego and spirit

The New Age man blasts his way into the spiritual realm, expecting to find bliss, but because he is so narcissistically wedded to the ego his experiences often meet with disappointment. The ego cannot be sanctified by the divine, but can only be sacrificed to the divine. Because this fact is not realised, the sacrifice often occurs unconsciously and involuntarily. Intellectually, the New Age man espouses a dreamy, heavenly philosophy, but in actual fact he is full of complaints and bitterness, because nothing appears to go right, other people seem bent on undermining or ruining him and even his spiritual teacher or practice is criticised for being inadequate. The 'loss of self' that should be occurring consciously falls into the unconscious, and, like anything unconscious, is projected outward upon others and the world.

However, not only the loss of ego takes place unconsciously, but the necessary development and building up of the ego occurs unconsciously as well. This is a different, but related, side to the tragic and undifferentiated fusion of ego and spirit. The ego needs to separate from the spirit in order to discover its own identity and life. The ego must actively embrace its own separateness and even risk alienation from the spirit to come to itself. As Jung made clear, ego development is archetypally sanctioned, and any attempt to stifle this development must result in disaster. When asked about their spiritual practice, or why their lifestyle is so different from ordinary people, New Agers will often declare that they have 'stomped on', 'trodden on', or 'dropped' the ordinary ego. What they mean by this is that the usual things associated with human development have been abandoned in favour of a lifestyle that is more pointedly related to the desires of the spirit. However, the ego has not been dropped, and by definition cannot be dropped; it has merely been fused with the life of the spirit. This is the psychological background for the notorious problem of rampant egotism, emotionality, splits and competitiveness that plague New Age groups, cults, sects, ashrams, clubs, societies and communes. Although all these groups strive to transcend ego in favour of spirit, they are often destroyed by a secret, dark and malignant egotism, which eats away at the high ideals and eventually causes the whole edifice to collapse, often with devastating consequences to society and to all concerned.

The basic drives of the ego, especially the power drive and its push for identity and esteem, cannot be got rid of by an intellectual attitude which espouses focus on higher things. Although the conscious emphasis is on openness to the divine, merging with a higher will, and negative capability, the power drive of the ego makes itself felt in the fixity and dogmatism with which these 'expansive' goals are pursued. The devotees declare that they are nothing before the divine, or worthless before the charismatic teacher, but in the background there is fierce jockeying for privilege and special place, for power and influence within the group. Nor can the sexual drive be willed away by an incense-smelling devotion to ethereal and heavenly concerns. What is neglected or rejected comes back to visit us, and it usually comes back with considerable vengeance, so that the local New Age ashram can end up as a den of iniquity, busted by the police and featured on page three of the local newspaper. Although espousing the pathways of Eastern bliss and enlightenment, the tragic West finds its revenge in engulfing such naive groups in negativity and the return of the repressed.

Jung would agree with the New Age that the Christian West has become overly wedded to a downbeat and constitutional pessimism, a pessimism that scares many away from Christian practice. The transformative possibilities of self-development and individuation give rise to a certain degree of optimism, and a positive spirit that lifts us out of despair and misery. He would also agree that there is a greater need for self-knowledge in Western religion, and that we find too much 'blind faith' in Christianity, with too many people adopting beliefs and doctrines without testing these precepts against experience. We need spiritual exercises, contemplations, devices, wisdoms: the call from the pulpit to 'believe' is not enough. Jung condones much of the New Age spiritual apparatus; its emphasis on diversity and pluralism, on pre-Christian and post-Christian wisdoms, on meditation, introspection and direct personal experience. However, unless the right attitude has been adopted, the apparatus and self-help technologies are worse than useless; they are positively dangerous. The New Age man would be better off closing his box of tricks, shutting down the suburban ashram and going back to church to learn lessons of humility and modesty. There can be no genuine spiritual transformation unless the ego and the spirit are separated and firmly differentiated.

The ego and the spirit have both to be lived, expressed, celebrated and enjoyed. We must live two lives simultaneously, and especially for all Westerners, as Jung warned, the life of the ego cannot be surreptitiously forgotten beneath the claims and passions of altered states of consciousness. Western man's ego has been differentiated over many centuries, and no weekend seminar or meditation course will get rid of it. The ego, our personal self, our mortality, our separateness from God, is the instrument of our suffering, but if this instrument is exploded in order to transcend suffering, we end up in more pain than ever before. Humbly, our suffering and incompleteness have to be accepted, and only then is transcendence possible.

Incarnation, meaning and suffering

At the heart of the New Age is a nihilistic theology that claims that the point of life is to return to God. A true theology would insist that the point of life is to live life to the full, so that God and the eternal can be incarnated and 'made present' in the life of the suffering individual. The idea of incarnation, found not only in Christianity but in all affirmative religions, insists that the sacred wants to enter into life and to become manifest in time and space. The sacred wants to enter our lives and to be transformed by this experience, just as we long to enter into the sacred and be transformed by our encounter with the eternal. The world and creation involves a two-way movement between the sacred and the profane, the creator and the created. Christianity has made a dramatic and bold statement about the incarnation of God in the person of Jesus, but all religions emphasise this immanental direction of the sacred, for instance in the Jewish idea of the Shekinah, and represent this direction as integral to the fulfilment of the divine intention, and as part of destiny itself.

The human element must not merely sink ecstatically into the cosmos, but it must 'hold out' in the face of this unbearable longing, allowing itself to become the vehicle or instrument for the incarnational self-development of the divine. In Jung's terms, God wishes to 'individuate' itself in and through our lives, and this is a psychodynamic way of speaking about the theology of incarnation. We have a responsibility to allow ourselves to be creatively employed in the work of incarnation. Our task is not to be born so that we may melt softly into the divine pleroma; rather, we must maintain our position in this world and hence allow something greater to be born in and through our lives. The unavoidable element here is tension and suffering, and the ability to withstand suffering so that this process might be realised. We must suffer within ourselves the coming together of the divine and the human, the mortal and immortal, the infinite and temporal. To capitulate to the lure of the sacred is to abort the incarnational process. We must maintain our hold upon social realities, human facts and political responsibilities, so that the integrity of time and space is assured. The devotion to social reality and political justice is, in this sense, a devotion to the sacred, because by these efforts we ensure that the created world can become a fit and worthy vessel of the infinite love and mercy of the divine. By making the world a worthy place, we allow the divine radiance to become ever more transparent in the opaque places of the earth, transforming these places with its effulgent glow.

Sometimes, the New Ager who gives up on life and who follows the downhill course of ecstasy into the ocean, reaches the point of merger, the nadir, only to find that God wants him or her to remain in life and to become responsible to time, place and community. When the sacred is authentically encountered, and not just glimpsed through the distorting lens of the mother complex, we discover, often in a critical moment, that we must turn around and go back into life, because the God of love and compassion loves the world and does not want to destroy it. In my own experience, the typically New Age phenomenon of fuzzy, world-denying spirituality is often dramatically terminated as soon as the divine pneuma is consciously encountered. The true spirit seeks life, not death; it seeks community, not isolation. The spirit seeks social engagement and human relationship, not retreat from life or immersion in the ocean of bliss. The true spirit seeks work rather than the cult of relaxation, and that is why work, effort, toil, have been sanctified and endorsed by religious traditions. In work, toil and endurance, the human and divine intersect with each other in ways that are purposeful, creative and transformative for both parties.

The theology of incarnation leads in turn to a metapsychology of the human ego, insofar as the ego carries the incarnation forward and is the locus of suffering in the human person. The human ego is not just a useless appendage, but is a divinely sanctioned entity. The human element is made in the image of the divine, to perform the work of the divine. In psychological terms, the ego is not merely a barrier or hindrance to the archetypal field, but a vehicle of manifestation for that field. For Jung, the ego is a prefiguration of the archetype of the Self; it is our partial, human, incomplete experience of that greater Self which will always remain elusive and beyond our full realisation. The ego must not be dissolved, despite the exhortations of James Hillman and his archetypal psychology, because the ego is itself an archetype and needs to be respected as such. It is therefore ironic that 'archetypal' psychology displays such a systematic vendetta against the ego, a recognition that allows us to conjecture that 'archetypal psychology' is in fact the New Age version of Jungian theory, or the Jungian school that most nearly approximates to the oceanic, anti-incarnational philosophy of New Age experience. There are real philosophical and cosmological differences between a psychology of life integration and a cult of the unconscious. These reflections now lead us to a consideration of the problem and language of wholeness.

Wholeness as dynamic interplay between opposites

> No one knows better the true meaning of distinction than they who
> have entered into unity.
>
> Tauler

Jung speaks of 'wholeness' as the new psychological and spiritual ideal, and one which will occupy us in the future as we work our way out of the spiritual wasteland of modernity toward a new religious high culture. He frequently contrasts the psychospiritual ethic of wholeness with Christianity's historical emphasis upon 'perfection', an ethic which has sprung from a dualistic awareness and which has kept numerous splits and divisions alive in the soul, notably that between *pneuma* and *physis*, or spirit and nature. The New Age adores this Jungian criticism of Christian ethics, and it swoons at the thought that this age-old ethics is to be debunked and replaced by a new moral and spiritual standard. The New Age has fully appropriated Jung's discourse about 'wholeness', and it uses this term in its literature, its advertising materials, its downtown bookstores and its centres of awareness. The New Age famously borrows the Chinese symbol of the Tao, or the Yin–Yang symbol, also used extensively by Jung, to demonstrate a condition in which life is balanced and in harmony with itself. The Yin–Yang is for the New Age a symbol for the 'new' cosmology of wholeness.

For the New Age, the world is self-evidently 'one', all things are equal, and the 'ten thousand things' of a complex reality are simply different aspects or facets of the one true reality. The Western mind that perceives splits and divisions is merely projecting its own neurotic dividedness upon the unitary reality of the uni-verse. According to the New Age, and here its attitude chimes in with certain prevailing attitudes in constructivism and postmodernity, splits, dualities, distinctions are merely fictive creations of an imperious, patriarchal, judging mind. The task of advanced consciousness is to see through these divisions, dissolving them and returning the world to its original oneness. The primary goal of New Age meditation and spiritual practice is to break down the barriers that so preoccupy the rational intellect (the busy, monkey mind), and to break through to the primal unity or wholeness. 'All things are one' is a standard expression, and many people within this movement agree that to achieve this realisation is to advance Western consciousness beyond its present condition.

At first glance, the Jungian attitude would appear to be in full accord with the New Age and its rhetoric of wholeness. In its desire to replace

Western dualism with a new holism, the New Age is almost axiomatically assumed to be following a Jungian direction. But the New Age completely misses the dynamic condition of Jung's concept of wholeness. The New Age concept of wholeness is quietistic and peaceful, linked with its preoccupation with relaxation and massage. For the New Age, wholeness is that pleasurable feeling achieved when we drop the stresses of daily life and reduce our anxieties by drifting into a tensionless state. This popular concept of wholeness has an affinity with the 'oceanic feeling', in that our difficulties, tensions and stresses are discharged into the unconscious, as into an ocean of peacefulness. In this deeply relaxed state, which is one of the goals of New Age activity, we feel 'at one' with the universe and spiritually whole. But this is a far cry from Jung's concept of wholeness. For Jung, wholeness is achieved, not in some relaxed state of mystical reverie, but in the daily battlefield of competing psychological forces.

Wholeness for Jung is not just a Tantric orgasm, or listening to Bach while being suspended by a saline solution in a Californian flotation tank. It is an endless wrestling with the parts of ourselves that do not want to be reconciled, an endless encounter with the unsavoury, the fragmented, the lost and repressed. Jung's wholeness is sinuous, muscular, and is arrived at through the constant interplay of dynamic energies. In *Psychology and Alchemy*, Jung writes:

> Without the experience of the opposites there is no experience of wholeness, and hence no inner approach to the sacred figures.
>
> (1944: 24)

When these opposites are dramatically at odds with each other, the psyche is fragmented and torn, and very little can be achieved. But when they are able to be brought into relationship with each other, then the possibility of 'wholeness' suggests itself. According to Jung, symbols of wholeness, in particular images of the mandala (1934/1950), often appear in moments of desperate conflict and fragmentation, as the psyche's spontaneous attempt to restore a sense of order and suggest alternatives to meaningless disorder. These symbols of wholeness often have a healing and restorative effect on the conscious life, and if we meditate on them the psyche's natural predisposition toward order can be reactivated (1950).

Jung's 'wholeness' is achieved through a conscious encounter with the competing forces of life, not by abandoning those forces or by escaping the tension of opposites by diving into an ocean of peacefulness. His concept of wholeness is heroic and active, and we only achieve it by first 'having it out with' the various psychological forces that are making competing demands on the self. It is a wholeness that presumes long and sustained bouts of psychological conflict, during which we have got to know 'both sides' of a conflict and can arrive at a meaningful resolution. Jung's wholeness therefore results from the valiant attempt of the individual to maintain the tension between archetypal opposites that might otherwise rip the individual apart. The whole point is not to get the opposites to coalesce and subside into a undifferentiated soup, but to allow them to work toward a state of complementarity and interplay, where each 'side' of the conflict maintains its own character while also engaging in dialogue with the 'other' side. This does not result in static inertia, but on the contrary, it allows us to develop an effective fund of psychospiritual energy (1916b). The image that comes to mind is the interplay between negative and positive polarities in the current that creates electricity, and electricity in this example is an image of the dynamic energy that is obtained when the archetypal forces are in relationship with each other.

The primal archetypes have an inherent tendency to split along weak 'faultlines', and although these faultlines are at first hidden, thus preserving an original appearance of 'unity', a splitting often occurs as the archetypes are drawn into consciousness. When such dissociation occurs, the opposite ends of the archetypal spectrum are turned against each other. Battles break out between, for instance, spirituality and sexuality, intellect and heart, good and evil, light and darkness, old and new, or heaven and hell. The development of consciousness is thus attended by suffering and pain, and this can only be resolved, according to Jung, by the gradual emergence of a 'both/and' perspective in which both sides of the archetypal split are accepted and incorporated into a new 'whole'. It is this 'both/and' perspective that distinguishes Jung's philosophy from the 'either/or' perspective of conventional morality, where generally the 'light' side is preferred and privileged above the 'dark'.

But Jung argues that conventional religious morality has misread its own religious symbols. The way of Christ is not, he argues, a way that leads to the privileging of the light above the dark, but a radical way that leads to the integrative or both/and perspective. This is why Jung often argues that Christ is a symbol of the Self, namely, the archetype that leads to psychological integration and whose dynamic energies lead to 'wholeness' (1951). For Jung, the symbol of Christ upon the Cross is a major world-symbol for the inevitable suffering that results from the human experience of being pulled in opposite directions, or from enduring the pain of the tension between the archetypal opposites. Again the New Age distorts Jung's meaning by throwing out the Christian elements of his work. For the New Age, wholeness does not involve struggle and strife, but rather it is achieved by dropping the pain and suffering that prevents us from experiencing the sublime unity of the world. The New Age experiences its 'wholeness' prior to the advent of consciousness and prior to struggle and strife, whereas for Jung the only valuable wholeness is achieved in and through the meaningful sufferings of consciousness.

Wholeness today, for instance, would mean bringing the demands of Christianity and the demands of the newly uprising paganism into some kind of integration. It means being aware of our ancestral heritage, our parents and grandparents, even as we are sitting in a Buddhist meditation hall trying to forget the embarrassment of our modest Methodist or Swiss Reform origins. Wholeness means we can never divorce ourselves from our origins and our past, and we can never aim for full enlightenment or constant transcendence. Wholeness means coming down from New Age peak experience and looking at the valleys and the depressions of life. It means listening to the soul as well as to the soaring spirit. Viewed in this way, the popular use of the term 'wholeness' seems to have little in common with Jung's original meaning. For Jung, wholeness is not what we 'want', but what life forces upon us; therefore, it could hardly be expected to become 'popular'.

The new rhetoric about 'wholeness' barely disguises the fact that the New Age is privileging a new style of one-sidedness. The New Age is a reaction against the old one-sidedness of patriarchal, rationalistic, supremacist and intellectualist culture. It champions what has been repressed or ignored in the old cultural regime, including the world of mystery, the feminine, the natural, the intuitive. It extols Jung's advocacy of these repressed archetypal elements and substances, but it misses Jung's vital point. These lost or forgotten archetypal elements are not to be identified with or indulged, but are to be *critically* encountered. The object of this encounter is not to 'go over' to the opposite, but to reach into the unconscious to integrate its contents into consciousness.

Two kinds of wholeness

Jung and classical Jungians such as Erich Neumann and Edward Edinger distinguish between two kinds of unity or wholeness. Jung refers to a preconscious wholeness, the wholeness of the primal and amorphous universe, an undifferentiated soup-like unity that exists prior to consciousness. In this early unity, the pairs of opposites are fused, not because they have been brought together but because they have not yet been separated. Everything is 'one' because the 'many' have not yet been born. This wholeness is discovered in ancient mythologies that idealise an original paradise from which we have fallen or departed. It is also discovered in certain kinds of mysticism, in otherworldly cosmologies, and in the dreams and fantasies of deeply regressed patients who find difficulty in accepting the torn or conflicted nature of reality. Jung associates this original, preworldly wholeness with the archetype of the Great Mother, and those who seek the incestuous return to the mother are likely to idealise this condition. As mentioned, Neumann developed Jung's thesis of the 'great round' by designating this symbol an *uroboros*, or tail-biting serpent, and those who worship this source are referred to as uroboros mystics:

> Living in the image of this prenatal paradise, the uroboros mystic denounces the real world. This pleromatic prenatal phase of the uroboros exerts so great a fascination because it offers the joys of the paradise of the unborn. Psychologically it corresponds to a situation in which the tension between consciousness and unconscious is no longer, or rather not yet, present.
>
> (Neumann 1949a: 399)

In the uroboros model of unity, tensions are 'not yet' present because we have regressed to a vision of reality prior to the development of conscious existence. When the uroboros governs our experience of unity, we always point backwards in time, to our own childhood or to the childhood of early humanity, because the psychic gradient is backwards, toward the source.

Jung posited and championed a second kind of wholeness in which the pairs of opposites, split apart by the advent of a polarising conscious-ness, have come together again in relative unity. This wholeness, he felt, is the goal or *telos* of conscious realisation. Jung felt it was crucial to differentiate between these two kinds of wholeness, because to view the first kind of wholeness as an 'ideal' leads to the pursuit of infantilism and escapism. If the first wholeness can be paralleled with Eden or Paradise, the second can be compared with William Blake's New Jerusalem. If the first wholeness is the Alpha, the second is the Omega. According to Blake, the pursuit of the First Paradise is a false spiritual striving which leads only to an encounter with whirlpools and demonic forces at the Gates of Eden:

> Downward 'tis sunk beneath . . . the feet,
> A raging whirlpool, draws the dizzy enquirer to his grave.
>
> (Blake 1794: 242)

The New Ager is certainly a 'dizzy enquirer' who gets more than he bargained for when he goes in pursuit of the primal source. The true spiritual path, for Blake as for Jung, must accept our exile from Eden and must take on the burden of consciousness that our exile forces upon us. We can no more recover the First Paradise than we can our original innocence. But we can and must work toward a Second Paradise, in which the opposites torn apart in the Fall are brought into relative harmony again, and through a second innocence we can participate mystically in the wonder of this recovered wholeness, as if through the eyes of a child.

Importantly, Jesus did not say that we must 'remain' as little children to enter the kingdom, but that 'unless you change and *become* like little children, you will never enter the kingdom of heaven' (Matthew 18.3). The New Age movement attempts to idealise the first innocence and to strive backwards in search of it, but there is a true, authentic path toward harmony which is life-affirming and creative. Some theologians refer to the first unity as 'gnostic', in which the forms of the world are terminated in primal dissolution or cataclysm, and this unity is contrasted with an 'incarnational' unity in which God and world enter into relationship. The second kind of unity does not seek the obliteration of the real in an ideal, inchoate void, but seeks the establishment of a new unity in which the forms and qualities of the world are protected, preserved and valued. This exalted unity is symbolised for Jung by the mandala, the 'magic circle' of Eastern philosophy.

Jung would immediately recognise that the popular image of 'wholeness' is nothing other than the reappearance of the age-old image of Edenic Paradise, a primal harmony that has haunted humanity for countless millennia, and that has arisen again to haunt and plague our own time. Mario Jacoby has made an important contribution to this area in his book The *Longing for Paradise* (1980), where he attempts a psychological investigation into the phenomenon of nostalgia. When exhausted consciousness retreats into the ocean of nonbeing, it is the pleromatic harmony of the uroboros that stands as the insignia for this regression. This image is all the more dangerous because it is lavished with spiritual terms and metaphors, thus obscuring the psychopathology that usually attends this ancient image. Blake cursed this original harmony as 'false' because it underestimates the creation, and is prepared to forfeit the whole world for a glimpse of an otherworldly ecstasy or bliss. The New Age advocates a return to the World Mother, and its craving for unity is the infant's craving for oneness with the mother.

When the infantile image of wholeness operates, consciousness is actually 'blamed' for the splitting apart of the pairs of archetypal opposites. Nature and the cosmos are viewed as perfectly whole, with all forces and elements securely in their place. Because infantile wholeness has no way to understand the divided nature of the universe, all divided-ness is projected upon the ego and the intellect, which are viewed as destructive forces which bring division and conflict into the Garden of Eden. Hence, the pleromatic mysticism of the New Age idealises nature and demonises man. Nature is embraced and adored for its completeness, while humanity is seen as the source of all pollution and contamination, both literally, in terms of the environment, and psychospiritually, in terms of originating the pairs of opposites, conflict, competition and strife. Although Heraclitus said that strife is of the essence of the cosmos, New Agers see strife only in terms of man. In its extreme form, this can lead to hugging trees and hating humans.

The New Age does not see itself as the inheritor of Western history, and is not interested in completing that history, but merely in deleting or transcending it. It does not want to bring together the archetypal opposites that have caused conflict in the West, but it wants to be rid of those forces and achieve a state of quietude through meditation and relaxation. Through Eastern meditation techniques, we can now transcend the fury and strife of the Western world and bring society into a new golden age of peace and harmony. The New Age tends to dismiss the conflicts of the West as largely unreal and self-created. Culture and its conflicts are looked upon as vain, silly, frivolous and unnecessary, since nature has already supplied us with a magnificent image of harmony, and thus with everything we need.

The New Age does not recognise that the opposites, dualities and conflicts with which the West has dealt for centuries are part of the archetypal structure of the universe, and therefore our strife and conflict has archetypal backing and is not merely self-generated. God and eternity are involved in our struggle, and the opposites with which we wrestle are part of the divine nature of God. If the human psyche resembles a battlefield at times, it is only because we have been co-opted by the sacred to perform and further its work of reconciliation and integration. The forms and figures that we deal with, such as Christ and Satan, or God and his Adversary the Devil, are the forms of the cosmos itself, not just 'figments' of human imagination. This was Jung's great insight in his *Answer to Job* (1952), a work which argues passionately for the divine sanctioning of the human struggle with opposites. The New Age God, on the other hand, does not know storm and fury, strife and conflict, but only harmony and rest. These are entirely different experiences of God, and different kinds of theologies.

In some of his writings, Jung refers to the false unity as the *pleroma*, which is imagined as a kind of cosmic acid-sea in which the instrument of consciousness is dissolved. In his 'Seven Sermons to the Dead', Jung writes that 'It is quite fruitless to think about the pleroma, for this would mean self-dissolution.' The pleroma is conceived as indistinct and undifferentiated, and is viewed as the destroyer of individuation:

> We fall into indistinctiveness, which is the other quality of the pleroma. We fall into the pleroma itself and cease to be creatures. We are given over to dissolution in the nothingness. . . . Hence the natural striving of the creature goeth towards distinctiveness, fighteth against primeval, perilous sameness. This is called the *principium individuationis*. This principle is the essence of the creature. From this you can see why indistinctiveness and non-distinction are a great danger for the creature.
>
> (Jung 1916a: 380)

Jung's language here is stilted and artificial, yet he was writing a mystical 'sermon' and consciously adopted this style. It is ironic that some Christians accuse Jung of the sin of 'gnosticism', by which they mean a love-affair with the uncreate matrix or disincarnate source, because here Jung clearly argues in favour of *incarnation* and *embodiment*, which he identifies as the driving force within individuation and life.

I do not believe that all New Age spirituality is necessarily a gnostic love-affair with the pleroma, but at least some of it can be classified in this category. Whenever the New Age devalues consciousness and the ego, whenever it scorns the tragic fate of Christ, whenever it berates culture and undermines human striving for a greater wholeness, then we discern the seductive fascination of the pleroma at work, and its 'call' to infinite bliss. This call can easily be interpreted as a call to suicide and self-destruction, since the self, the body, the person, is viewed as a meaningless speck of knotted tension that would gain immediate release if it were returned to the pleroma. This may account for some of the darker activity in New Age youth spirituality and postmodern popular music culture, with its often morbid fascination for nirvana, death, enlightenment and suicide.

However, Neumann points out that the constellation of the uroboros symbol does not necessarily lead to certain destruction, and that this mysticism will not always be detrimental to the individual or to society. The uroboros, Neumann asserts, can be viewed as an infantile vision of wholeness, or as an *anticipation* of the mandala (1949b: 11). When the archetype of wholeness emerges in our fragmented world, it will not necessarily manifest in its highest form first of all, but it will bear the stamp of archaism and primordiality. Hence the New Age fascination with nihilistic mysticism, while not to be encouraged, may perhaps be seen as a kind of low-grade anticipation of a higher mysticism that may be expressed at a later stage in our individual or cultural development. It could be a doorway through which we have to pass, as our civilisation recovers its spiritual orientation and begins to reawaken to its religious life.

Chapter 3

Jung as Lucifer

Inventing a New Age guru

> There are so many great ideas that do no more than a bellows: they
> inflate and make emptier.
>
> Nietzsche (1885: 89)

This chapter attempts to explore the psychological landscape in which
the making of a New Age guru takes place. It is not so much concerned
with specific instances in which Jung has been converted into a guru, as
it is with the philosophical and theoretical problems attached to such
myth-making in our time. I am astonished and frequently appalled at the
wildly negative images associated with Jung, especially in high cultural,
literary and theological circles, where he is viewed as a kind of devil. I
am convinced that what we need today is a depth psychology of reputation
and public image, since the things that make up any reputation or public
image seem to be largely irrational, and often have little or nothing to do
with what a famous person actually said or wrote. The sticking-points that
define a public reputation have often to do with prevailing social currents
of the time, and with powerful psychological forces that almost forcibly
draw public figures into their service, making such figures 'stand' for
certain definite things. Jung stood out in the twentieth century as a public
figure willing to risk large statements and pose big questions, and as such
he drew numerous projections toward himself and can almost be made to
'stand' for a whole range of contradictory intellectual and philosophical
positions.

In his impassioned 'Reply to Martin Buber' (1952b), Jung indicated
that he had already, in his lifetime, been characterised in numerous
conflicting lights. Count Keyserling, he claims, had characterised him
as 'unspiritual', while the theologian Buber saw him as profoundly

'spiritual', albeit in the context of 'early Christian Gnosticism, which has always been looked at askance by theologians'. Jung goes on:

> Funnily enough this opinion of Buber's coincides with another utterance from an authoritative theological source which accuses me of agnosticism – the exact opposite of Gnosticism. I have in my time been regarded not only as a Gnostic and its opposite, but also as a theist and an atheist, a mystic and a materialist.
>
> (1952b: 1499–1502)

Jung speaks of the 'concert of contending opinions' about him, and dismisses all of these tags and labels, claiming that they tell us more about others than about himself. Jung's preferred self-description as a 'psychiatrist' is hardly satisfactory, and his reply to Buber merely reminds us that the question about who or what Jung is is far from being settled.

What I want to explore here is my hunch that Jung has become a carrier of the image of Lucifer, the fallen angel who symbolises the deadly sin of pride or hubris. Jung, Lucifer and Nietzsche appear to me to be all tangled up together, and separating the strands may prove useful.

The unconscious religious life

Jung insisted that when the 'Gods' disappear from view, as in secular modernity, they fall into the unconscious and become factors of disturbance. 'The Gods have become diseases', he declared (1929a: 54). If we are not conscious of the Gods, they are likely to act on us from below, contaminating our humanity with archetypal contents. Secretly, they 'puff up' the ego and fill it with dreams of God-likeness. Although the contemporary ego typically denies the existence of God and refuses to believe in a divine ground of reality, it is unconsciously identified with the divine reality it denies. In truth, we cannot cut ourselves off from the sacred because we are constructed in its image, and we continue to draw our lives, consciously or otherwise, from its source. But the New Age, which draws on the unconscious religious life of secular modernity, is hugely burdened by an inferior religiousness. Because so much of this religious life is below the threshold of consciousness, it has become a haven for psychopathology and mental illness.

The New Age spirituality movement views its own activities and attitudes as authentic and valuable. Indeed, it considers itself in an heroic light, in that it lifts the bans on the spiritual and thus sets the spirit free.

But it sets free demons as well as spirits, complexes as well as Gods, and psychopathology as well as health. It sets all this free because it lifts the lid of Pandora's Box, and allows a promiscuity of spirits and demons to spring forth from the unconscious. The New Age is pathetically unaware of the moral ambiguity and complexity of the deep unconscious. Precisely because it is so 'new', it has no historical sense and no spiritual discernment. It is like a helpless infant playing with forces over which it has no control and about which it has little understanding. It is largely blind to the perils of the soul, partly because it suffers from a naively optimistic view of the realm of the spirit. It fails to understand that, in the unconscious, Gods can turn into demons, and Lucifer and Satan are psychic forces to contend with, not just empty fictions from the past.

The New Age tries to perform the function of a modern religion, but it is not a religion. Rather, it simply provides a receptivity or openness toward the spiritual realm, creating a 'climate of validity' in which the nonvisible forces can be contacted and encountered. True religion involves us in a careful consideration of the forces of the deeper reality. Religion can tell the difference between a God and a demon, a spirit and a complex, because it understands this deeper reality in the same way that science, for instance, understands the material world. Religion has a developed language and understanding of the sacred, and it encourages discernment and caution at every turn of the spiritual path. It certainly does not run under the simple slogan, 'If it feels good, do it', because what feels good is sometimes demonic or evil. True religion understands that we cannot have spiritual highs without moral obligations, we cannot have ecstasy without attendant suffering, nor can we unite with the cosmos without ethical obligations to this world and to its creator.

According to Jung, religion serves a paradoxical role in the psychic economy. Religion performs the double function of relating us to the divine, yet also of protecting us from annihilation in the divine. Religion teaches relationship without fusion or identification, and when the ego is tempted to identify itself with the divine, religion warns that such grandiosity is sinful and evil. The Christian worshipper says in prayer: 'Lead us not into temptation, but deliver us from evil'. Religion keeps the person sane by insisting on the necessary humility and separateness before God. At the crucial moment of the Catholic Mass, the faithful are asked to repeat: 'Lord, I am not worthy to receive you, but only say the word and I shall be healed.'

Religio means a 'binding back' to the sacred, but when a balanced relationship with the sacred is no longer possible, or has been denied us by modernity and science, what can the wretched ego do? When the burden of its separateness has become intolerable, and it cannot rest upon a secure relational connection with God, there is always the temptation to abdicate its position entirely and to merge dangerously and psychotically with the divine figure. Its longing for comfort and security will then activate the infantile desire for fusion and the desire to be contained in the sacred embrace. This leads to an impossible explosion of its normal boundaries, and even if the body remains intact, the mind can nevertheless be exploded and destroyed by this fusion. Although seeking comfort and support, the ego then experiences a sudden loss of reality, an absence of boundaries, a false identification with the creator, and a demonic increase in power. In searching for heaven, the ego without a conscious relationship or *religio* experiences only hell. In the absence of functional or effective religion, a kind of psychotic or mad mystical frenzy can take over, as is reflected in the New Age credo of spiritual advocate Shirley MacLaine, who cries:

'I am God, I am God, I am God.'

(1990: 13)

Satan as an unconscious archetypal complex

My contention is that much New Age spirituality is effectively 'Satanic' in the classical sense. Conservative priests will tend to agree with me, but probably for the wrong reasons. Satan is nothing more or less than the human tendency to identify ourselves with God. Satan is the mythological expression of psychotic spirituality. In particular, the story of Lucifer has profound relevance for us today. The name 'Lucifer' means in Latin 'light-bearer', and Milton makes extensive use of this symbolic meaning in his *Paradise Lost*. Lucifer was originally one of God's angels, and he was much loved by God. While remaining in the company of heaven, and while actively and productively serving God, Lucifer personifies for us the creative and even divine aspect of the human being, and hence the idea of bearing 'light' in this context. This divinity of the human person is only realised in the process and awareness of instrumentality, that is, in the stance of remaining 'secondary' to God, and in service of a greater reality. But as soon as we claim for ourselves 'primary' status, our divine aspect is immediately lost, and we become wretched and fallen. The divine light turns to darkness, and the energy at our source turns against us.

Lucifer grew tired of his secondary role, and decided that he could no longer serve God or the good. Instead, he would serve himself and defiantly rebel against God's wishes. For this act of supreme disobedience, God expelled Lucifer from heaven and cast him into hell, or sheol. In psychospiritual terms, 'heaven' in this context would represent the condition of harmony and unity that can be experienced when the ego accepts its instrumental and creative role, while 'hell' would symbolise the condition of alienation from the true and the good. In 'hell', all the psychic energies become destructive rather than creative, burning the ego up in unquenchable ambitions and unrealisable longings. The impossibility of our achieving eternal or immortal status 'consumes' us in a fire of unearthly desire, and the will of creation works against us rather than for us. The divine light no longer illuminates but only burns to a cinder. This story has been highly moralised by Western religious tradition, and notoriously misused as a justification for racism and prejudice against dark-skinned peoples. But the story refers not to literal conditions of blackness or whiteness, but to the placement and attitude of human consciousness. Nor is it an allegorical tale about the consequences of being 'good' or 'bad' in the narrow moralistic sense. The story has to be lifted out of its puritanical meaning, and restored to its larger existential and psychospiritual meaning.

In Isaiah, the existential dimension is clearly evident. The human being, mythologised as Lucifer, has the choice of two states or conditions. He either can serve the higher good and be mindful of his secondary role, or can become 'inflated', break his human boundaries, attempt a false ascension, and be condemned to eternal misery in the sulphurous pits of hell:

> How are you fallen from heaven, day star, son of the dawn!
> How you are cut down to the ground, conqueror of the nations!
> You said in your heart,
>   'I will ascend to heaven
>   I will raise my throne above the stars of God. . . .
>   I will make myself like the Most High.'
> But you are brought down to Sheol
>   to the depths of the Pit.
>
> (Isaiah 14.12–15)

In longing to climb so high, in desiring to usurp God's power and to become like God, the Satanic figure and the power-hungry ego he symbolises is laid low, reduced and brought down. The Satanic process is one in which we are inflated, only to be made emptier.

The eternal problem of the ego is that it constantly attempts to over-reach itself. It seems to distrust its own instrumentality, or it cannot draw enough esteem from its ancillary role. Perhaps it cannot see the true dignity in being a channel for the sacred, and it seeks to realise its dignity in ways that are more apparent to its own perception. It is as if the ego is continually prone to making a category error, which is perhaps what Western theology refers to as its 'original sin'. It gets bored with its ancillary role, and it reads 'service' as 'servile', or it sees 'secondary' as 'second-rate', and it longs to usurp the position and power of the Most High.

In *The Origin of Satan*, Elaine Pagels writes that

> What fascinates us about Satan is the way he expresses qualities that go beyond what we ordinarily recognize as human. Satan evokes more than the greed, envy, lust, and anger we identify with our own worst impulses, and more than what we call brutality, which imputes to human beings a resemblance to animals ('brutes').
>
> (1996: xvii)

Pagels strives to release Satan from the dreadful cartoon-like figure of traditional folklore. He is not just a caricature with horns and a pitch-fork, who represents our 'base desires', our anger or wrath, our lust or depravity. He is more than what moral allegory will allow. He is not just an allegory of what we already know about ourselves, but a living symbol of what we don't yet understand about ourselves. He represents life lived away from wholeness and the divine radiance. He is discovered not only in what is 'worst' about humanity, but also in what is 'best', insofar as our best is sometimes governed by narrow egotism and narcissism, rather than by devotion to the greater good. The most sophisticated of human activities can be Satanic, if they do not lead us to light, but only to alienation from the light.

> Thousands of years of tradition have characterized Satan instead as a spirit. Now he stands in open rebellion against God, and in his frustrated rage he mirrors aspects of our own confrontations with otherness. Many people have claimed to see him embodied at certain times in individuals and groups that seem possessed by an intense spiritual passion, one that engages even our better qualities, like strength, intelligence, and devotion, but turns them toward destruction and takes pleasure in inflicting harm. Evil, then, at its worst, seems to involve the supernatural; what we recognize, with a shudder,

as the diabolic inverse of Martin Buber's characterization of God as 'wholly other'.

(1996: xvii)

Satan is not a lifeless, dreary allegory of a schoolboy's 'bad' qualities, but a living symbol of what happens to us when the big picture is lost, when we no longer guide our lives according to a greater vision, but only see life in terms of 'what we can get out of it'. Satan is what happens when we approach the unconscious from an egotistical viewpoint, when we use the unconscious for entirely personal and trivial reasons, rather than adopting an attitude of service and selflessness toward it. *Satan* comes from the root *stn*, meaning 'one who opposes, obstructs, or acts as adversary'. In similar manner, the Greek term *diabolos*, often translated into English as 'devil', literally means 'one who throws something across one's path'.

Jungian individuation in the image of Lucifer

It is my belief that Jung can become a carrier of the image of Satan or Lucifer for us today. In this sense 'Jung' is a popular distortion or mytho-logical construct, and largely the opposite of what he is in reality. Jung spent an enormous amount of intellectual time and energy warning readers and patients against the dangers of psychological or spiritual inflation, and urging us to maintain our human limitations and proportions as we encounter the archetypal field of the collective unconscious. But insofar as the unconscious today is charged with high-level energies and complexes that take over consciousness as soon as they are encountered, Jung becomes willy-nilly associated with these complexes and identified with the inferior religiousness to which they give rise. Jung is popularly seen in the New Age movement as the important scholar-philosopher who gives us permission to enter into the unconscious and become fused with its contents. This, as I have said, flies in the face of reality and defies common sense, but it is a popular view that is widely abroad and therefore has to be taken into account. It is not simply that people are misreading Jung or are failing to attend to what he 'really' said. It is that complexes or disturbances have been aroused in the collective psyche, and these complexes actually coordinate and control our perception of Jung's work.

In the next chapter, I will give several examples of the systematic dis-tortion of Jung's meaning, especially by New Age Jungians who convert the theory of individuation into a theory of inflation and grandiosity. Much popular Jungianism is actually Jung-in-reverse, a kind of feral Jungianism that misreads Jungian psychology in accordance with the demands of inferior religiousness. But in this chapter I am more interested in the theory of this process, and in the psychodynamics that conspire to turn Jung into a prophet of New Age inflation.

Where has Satan got to in our time? Both secular modernity and the New Age movement are convinced that Satan does not exist. Secular modernity says that Satan is a mere invention of medieval imagination, a construct of superstition that enlightened people can safely do without. It claims that Satan, like God, is a human invention that we can jettison in the higher knowledge that such figures never existed in the past and never will exist in the future. The New Age movement, on the other hand, wants God back again, but not Satan. The New Age is convinced that the universe is governed by light and love, and that whatever happens to us happens for the 'good' of ourselves and of all beings. The New Age is ruled by an extremely naive and one-sided consciousness that is oblivious to evil and the presence of darkness. This, of course, is a mental atmosphere in which evil and darkness can thrive. The New Age forgets history, junks the past and fails to believe either in Lucifer, Satan or the power of evil, since its philosophy only allows it to believe in a world of good things. Blind to Satan or Lucifer, it fails to see how these ancient realities have incarnated as the very basis of its thinking and worldview. Satan's ultimate triumph is to convince the New Age that he does not exist and is therefore nothing to worry about.

Jung becomes constructed in popular imagination as a figure who invites us to enter the inner world to become fused with the archetypes and Gods who live there. The energy-charge of the collective unconscious is so great in a secular, non-religious culture that we are immediately seduced by the powerful world of the archetypes. Jung's image as a scientist and empiricist, as a man of restraint and caution, as a psychiatrist who warns against mental disease, is immediately devoured by another image of Jung as New Age guru, shaman, spirit-guide, or psychopomp, who shows the way into the unconscious so that we might bury our brokenness in the mighty powers that reside there. We do not enter that world to seek a true relationship, but to lose ourselves in the majesty and wonder of the eternal. We are not interested in incarnating the divine reality in time and space, by holding our position in time and space so that something great can emerge in and through our own lives. Rather, we seek to obliterate our smallness in the largeness of the divine embrace, an attitude which reverses the incarnation and which *opposes, obstructs, or acts as adversary* to the creative process.

God and Satan present themselves to us as a pair of mythological opposites, and we cannot have the good one and pretend that the bad one does not exist. In reality, we have to become conscious of both pathways and options, before we can choose our own path with responsibility and discernment. God is that sublime and irresistible force in the universe and in all of its component parts which moves towards wholeness, evolution, sanctity and the common good. We can resist that force for a time, or blind ourselves to its magnitude and light, but ultimately it breaks through the manifest world of creation and draws things onward to a greater state. God coordinates the course and direction of creation, and God subordinates the part to the whole, making the part aware of its instrumentality, its incompletion, its utter dependence on a greater life and upon the whole for its own existence. God ultimately asks the part to sacrifice itself for the good of the whole, which is paradigmatic of the death and resurrection of the dying Messiah or God-man.

Jung's work basically offers a psychological understanding of this same process. He provides us with a psychology of the sacred, with a new and modern rationale for adopting a fundamentally religious attitude toward our life and to the world at large. The religious attitude is above all sacramental and sacrificial. It understands the importance of sacrifice, and the need to subordinate the mortal and limited life to the guidance and direction of the larger life. Jung's work calls us to the path of wholeness, sanctity and the common good, but this pathway readily gets contaminated by darkness and overwhelmed by instinctual forces that subvert the entire process. Where the 'way to God' is opened up, there Satan automatically appears with his wily ways and his deceptive works. In this context, Satan represents that other life which always seeks to disrupt the unity of creation and to create havoc rather than moral order. Satan seeks to promote the part against the whole, and contrary to the will of the whole. He informs the part that it can rebel against the whole, and need not be subordinate to it.

Confusing higher consciousness with arrogance and hubris

In the same way that the New Age often represents identification with the collective unconscious as nirvana and enlightenment, so too has Satan always represented identification with the divine reality as a 'higher' form of consciousness. In the Genesis story of the Fall, the wily serpent tempts Eve with the prospect of achieving a higher form of existence and a new, elevated awareness. The serpent proposes: 'Did God really say,

"You must not eat from any tree in the garden"?' Eve repeats what God had told her, and the serpent replies:

> 'You will not surely die. For God knows that when you eat of it your eyes will be opened, and you will be like God, knowing good and evil.'
>
> So when the woman saw that the tree was good for food, and that it was a delight to the eyes, and that the tree was to be desired to make one wise, she took of its fruit and ate; and she also gave some to her husband, and he ate.
>
> (Genesis 3.1, 4–6)

There are significant features here that have a bearing on our present theme. The first is that Satan puts doubt and confusion in the mind of the original humans. We know what is right and what supports and upholds the whole, but we are tempted to challenge the laws of creation and to move counter to the instructions of the creator. The second point is that Satan portrays rebellion against the wholeness of creation as a *clever* act which will lead to a higher state of existence. Eve is urged to rebel for the sake of self-interest, so that her and Adam's eyes will be opened, and they will know good and evil. The third point is that self-interest leads ultimately to inflation and hubris – 'You will be like God' – so that the serpent is actually drawing forth the latent human desire for prestige, greatness, immortality and primacy.

When God walks through the garden and demands a response of Eve, she says 'The serpent deceived me, and I ate.' The Satanic forces in our lives work essentially through deception, through clouding our perceptions, muddying our thoughts and blurring our boundaries. The true laws of our being are situated deep within the psyche or soul, but these laws are readily transgressed when we are encouraged to break our boundaries and become bigger than we are. Self-interest, flattery, narcissism and grandiosity are the ever-present temptations which seduce us into betraying the whole and inflating the part. A crucial element here is the word 'delight'; the fruit from the forbidden tree 'was a delight to the eyes . . . and was to be desired to make one wise'. Initially, the temptations of narcissism appear to be delightful. The false prophecy that invites us to leave our human boundaries and to become like God seems at first a delightful prospect. We are not content with our human limitations, and our subordinance to a higher authority seems to be a burden and a bore.

And so, even today, we reach for this false prophecy with delighted hunger in our eyes. We reach for our grandiosity, only to find, of course, that as soon as it is grasped we are infinitely more wretched than before, more hollow, and stricken by guilt. We are made aware that we have betrayed the laws of creation, which are the same laws that govern our own inner being, laws to which we have access through conscience and contemplation. The fall from grace did not just happen 'back then', but happens all the time. We discover the counter-will constantly in our experience, and especially we encounter it when matters of the spirit and soul are raised. When the possibility of developing a spiritual life is put before us, we often greet this possibility with a delighted response, seeing in it an opportunity to become larger and more important than we are. We do not want to relate to God as a secondary or servile subject, but we want to become the primary object, to become like God and to achieve wisdom and immortality through this process of explosive transcendence, where we explode the boundaries that separate creature from creator.

But to return to the construction of Jung in the popular domain, we have to do with an imagined New Age guru whose voice is remarkably like that of Lucifer, Satan or the Devil. The 'Jung' of New Age production appears to be saying: 'Take and eat this fruit of the tree of self-knowledge, and your eyes shall be opened, and you shall become like God, knowing good and evil.' A voice is attributed to Jung which is not unlike the age-old voice that wrecks humanity and its relationship with truth, largely by filling humanity with the temptation to overreach its limits. One can almost hear the serpent's rattle through the figure of a dummy, blown-up, phony Jung, who promises bewildered moderns that if we do as he says we shall have enormous riches and everlasting life. It virtually does not matter what Jung actually said, because once this myth takes over we are deceived into believing that this is what he did say. People no longer feel the need to read Jung, because they think they know what he said.

I believe that Jung is actually saying this: 'Take and eat of the fruit of the tree of self-knowledge, and your eyes shall be opened, and you shall develop a *relationship* with the divine.' The crucial difference is that Jung calls for relationship, and Satan calls for identification, for humanity to 'be like God'. In the relationship that Jung imagines, humanity is to remain as humanity, not to go over to the other side. It is a relationship in which the human remains human, and in which God remains Wholly Other, even as each party comes to know and to understand each other. Jung is actually saying: 'If your eyes are truly opened, and not just clouded over with cosmic deception, you will recognise that you remain human and mortal in this encounter, and God remains essentially other than human.' Jung's important twist to this primal scenario is that we must attempt to develop a conscious relationship with God, but not make the mistake of imagining that we are God. If we believe that we are God, then everything will be lost and the spiritual journey aborted.

It has to be admitted that Jung does have a devilish twinkle in his eye, and therefore some things in common with the traditional depiction of Satan. He does seek, like the Devil, to terminate the innocent sleep of humanity. He does seek, like the Devil, to break up and destroy our primal unity with the world. He does seek change and transformation, and invite us to become other than we already are. He does seek to open our eyes and to encourage a new kind of consciousness. He recognises our restlessness, our striving, our hunger to become something more. If these desires are 'devilish' and contrary to God's will, then they are also 'Jungian'. But the Jungian position represents, I believe, a middle term between the Devil and God. We are invited to wake up and become conscious so that humanity and God can know each other more intimately, and know each other as separate, though also related, beings.

Jung is a religious prophet who seems to conventional religion to be desiring evil, but who in the final analysis is seeking a higher good. If Martin Buber and numerous other theologians construct Jung as an alien or outsider, it is because they quite rightly see the devilish twinkle in Jung's eye, and become critical. The disaffection, the opposition, the antagonism to Jung in theological and religious circles derives, I believe, from the unearthly and threatening glow of Satan which attends his work. It is this same unearthly glow, of course, that makes him so wildly popular in the unholy New Age.

It *seems* to the theologians that Jung is seeking to make God too intimate, too known, too close to the human self, and not 'wholly other' enough. It seems to the theologians that Jung is a heretic, that he is psychologising God, and making theology a mere branch of the human sciences. But for want of this intimacy, this closeness, God is being lost and ignored in our time. Jung understands that if religion is to survive it must become an inward experience, and not merely an article of faith or a matter of blind belief. Jung is seeking to revive the religious impulse by making it intimate and profoundly human. Many psychologists and therapists understand precisely what Jung is doing, and what a great blessing it is for the future of religion. But many theologians 'smell' the presence of Satan, the dark one who asks us to ignore our boundaries and to become like God. Theologians do not have a strong enough sense of the God within, or of the objective realm which underpins our subjectivity. If they understood the objective realm within, the mystical interiority, and our capacity to be in relationship with that interiority, they would not immediately assume that to know God intimately is to commit the sin of hubris.

Ironically, what the theologians fear is on full display in the New Age. There, in the wider public sphere, people talk of having spiritual journeys and of their affection for Jung. The mystical interior life is 'claimed' by the New Ager as his or her own inner life, there is a fundamental identification between personal subjectivity and divinity, and then the theologian turns aside in horror and disgust, and rests his case against Jung.

Superman as Lucifer: is Jung confused with Nietzsche?

It often seems to me that Jung is confused in the popular imagination with Nietzsche. It is not that Nietzsche himself is so very popular (many students cannot even spell his name), but his basic story or predicament is well known, and acts as a container for the Lucifer complex in our time. Friedrich Nietzsche announced the so-called 'death of God' and then declared the birth of the Superman. To this extent, Satan and his deceiving works can make good use of this narrative. But unfortunately Nietzsche went mad from syphilis and psychosis soon after his famous declaration, and the popular mind needs a more healthy or attractive figure upon which it can project its hubristic complex. The Lucifer complex, like any product in the marketplace, needs to promote itself, to appear valuable and worth supporting.

Jung is more appealing than Nietzsche since he was not a raving lunatic, or at least not as far as we know. Perhaps it is the fear of the charge of lunacy that prevents the Jung family from releasing the famous Red Book, with its visions of fantastic creatures and mystical figures, to scholars and biographers. But to most of us today, Jung was not mad like Nietzsche, but only a little crazy. He was crazy enough to make him endearingly eccentric and attractive to popular sentiment. As in the famous postcards, Jung is viewed as a quaintly old-fashioned Swiss-German eccentric who made engravings of the mythic figures in blocks of stone beside the Lake of Zurich. This has irresistible appeal to popular imagination, as does the fact that this same mystical man was rejected by the Viennese founder of psychoanalysis, whose authoritarian rationality prevented him from furthering his association with Jung.

Nietzsche was a sort of nineteenth-century philosophical entrepreneur and power-broker, who clearly saw the death of God as a spiritual *opportunity* for humanity. Nature abhors a vacuum, and Nietzsche believed that man, and specifically himself, could move into the emptiness left by the death of God, and so become enormously powerful. He wrote:

> If we do not make a great renunciation and a lasting victory over ourselves out of the death of God, then we must bear the loss.
>
> (cited in Frey-Rohn 1984: 87)

In numerous contexts and writings, both within *Thus Spoke Zarathustra* and elsewhere, Nietzsche implores us to go for broke, to take the spiritual opportunities that present themselves to us today:

> Our way is upward, from the species across to the super-species.
>
> (1885: 100)

> God is dead! . . . I teach you the Superman [Ubermensch]. Man is something that should be overcome. What have you done to overcome him?
>
> (1885: 41)

> The Superman is the meaning of the earth. Let your will say: The Superman *shall be* the meaning of the earth.
>
> (1885: 23)

The fanatical nature of all this, the insistent tone, the desperate longing to overreach ourselves, should alert the reader to the awareness that this could be unsound. Is Zarathustra a spiritual liberator, as Nietzsche intends, or is Zarathustra a false prophet, cult leader and possessed maniac? His fanatical discourse sounds more like a dictatorial Hitler than an enlightened Buddha, Lao Tsu or Christ, but for young or alienated readers in search of spiritual power, this is inspiring stuff. Moreover, because of our notorious separation from our instinctual nature, we seem to lack the nose for detecting truth from falsity, and when someone holds out the possibility for us to overreach ourselves, we do not think of evil, Satan or the serpent, but we only think of the dream of success.

Nietzsche adopted the view that God had not deserted man, but rather that man had killed God by virtue of his intellectual enlightenment and secular progress. Nietzsche recognised the enormous cost involved in the civilisation process, which was our eventual alienation from the highest source and origin of human meaning. As Nietzsche's madman proclaims in the marketplace:

> 'Where has God gone?' he cried. 'I shall tell you. We have killed him
> – you and I. We are all his murderers. But how have we done this?
> How were we able to drink up the sea? Who gave us the sponge to
> wipe away the entire horizon? . . . Are we not straying as through an
> infinite nothing? God is dead. God remains dead. And we have killed
> him. That which was holiest and mightiest of all that the world has
> yet possessed has bled to death under our knives – who will wipe this
> blood off us?'
>
> (cited in Frey-Rohn 1984: 71)

Nietzsche was aware that the demise of the metaphysical world had been
evident for some time, since the forces of humanism, rationality and
positivism had threatened to replace transcendence with materiality,
eternity with history and God with man. We have killed God with our
own rationality, with our failure to respect mystery, with our infantile
longing for certainty, demonstrable fact and the 'evidence' of the senses.
We have not been able to tolerate the rupture to our lives that knowledge
of the sacred entails, and thus we have opted for a false and banal security
which has destroyed mystery and revelation.

The destruction and killing of God was such an overwhelming reality
for Nietzsche that he could only see one adequate response to this
enormity: we should make ourselves Gods to fill the vacuum:

> Must not we ourselves become gods simply to seem worthy of [this
> deed]? There has never been a greater deed – and whoever shall be
> born after us, for the sake of this deed he shall be part of a higher
> history than all history hitherto.
>
> (cited in Frey-Rohn 1984: 71)

In one sense, Nietzsche was an instrument for the *Zeitgeist* or spirit of the
time. He was telling the civilised world about the terrible cost of its
civilisation. He was telling us about the state of the world in mythic and
religious terms, although the world was not necessarily ready or willing
to hear. The visionary philosopher or writer sees the events taking place
in the soul before these are clear to the majority of people. The visionary
thinker responds to a mythic event in the collective psyche, and only much
later can others see what he had witnessed. Hence Nietzsche was forced
to endure enormous suffering, personal isolation and misunderstanding,
since he was far ahead of his time. Nietzsche's madman is met with
incomprehension and amazement as he utters his prophecy of the death
of God. In a despairing gesture which must reflect Nietzsche's own

personal agony at being misunderstood, the madman throws his lantern
on the ground, and cries:

> I have come too early . . . My time is not yet. This tremendous event
> is still on its way, still wandering; it has not yet reached the ears
> of men.
>
> (cited in Frey-Rohn 1984: 71)

Jung spent much of his life trying to unravel the complexities and
difficulties of the Nietzschean dilemma (Jung 1988). Jung seemed
to believe that the 'modern' man was almost by definition confronted
with Nietzschean problems: the death of God, the absence of meaning,
existential despair and the temptation to install man in the position once
held by God. But Jung clearly believed that the modern man must learn
to deal with this predicament in different and creative ways. Nietzsche's
way would lead to inevitable madness, because the archetypal energies
that were formerly invested in the divine figure would flood back into
the human psyche, leading to an inundation of consciousness and a
disintegration of mind. For Jung, the human person is mortal, limited and
bound by time and space. For man suddenly to assume the role and mantle
of God would result in a psychospiritual catastrophe far greater, and with
more devastating consequences, than the depressive psychosis which
followed the death of God and meaning.

In drawing into himself the energies of God, man would suddenly
light up like a demon of the underworld, and he would not be 'greater'
than human or larger than life, but essentially less than human and
lower than animals. When an archetypal figure falls from 'heaven' and
contaminates the human realm, the result is not the divinisation of man
but the dehumanisation of humanity, because the archetypal forces can
only act negatively when they burst in upon the human arena. Jung wrote
of the 'demonisation' of the spirit as a consequence of its assimilation by
consciousness:

> Man conquers spirit . . . without realizing what he is doing. . . . The
> integration of the spirit means nothing less than its demonization,
> since the superhuman spiritual agencies that were formerly tied up
> in nature are introjected into human nature, thus endowing it with a
> power which extends the bounds of the personality *ad infinitum*, in
> the most perilous way.
>
> (Jung 1946/48: 454)

Throughout Jung's work we find endless warnings and statements about the dangerous character of the modern predicament. The once-divine forces, as he says, have 'fallen' to earth, and this causes our ordinary human world to become filled with darkly malign energies:

> Since the stars have fallen from heaven and our highest symbols have paled, a secret life holds sway in the unconscious. That is why we have a psychology today, and why we speak of the unconscious. All this would be quite superfluous in an age or culture that possessed symbols. Symbols are spirit from above, and under those conditions the spirit is above too. . . . Our unconscious, on the other hand, hides living water, spirit that has become nature, and that is why it is disturbed.
>
> (Jung 1935/54: 50)

Nietzsche spoke in similar metaphors, but in ecstatic rather than cautionary tones: 'Truly, it is a new good and evil! Truly, a new roaring in the depths and the voice of a new fountain!' (1885: 101). Jung said he was deeply chilled by Nietzsche's exalted support for the 'new roaring in the depths', and his striving for complete transcendence of the human condition. Jung was disturbed by the entire mythopoetic thrust of *Thus Spoke Zarathustra*, and by the not so subtle passages where we find that the laugh of the mountain-dwelling Zarathustra was 'no human laugh'. The maniacal tendency is never far from view: 'I love him who wants to create beyond himself, and thus perishes' (1885: 91).

Nietzsche, isolated from the social community and intensely intellectual, was an ideal candidate for the inflation of the spirit. The pneumatic energies of spirit, no longer contained in deity or icon, were heading toward him at enormous speed, and Nietzsche felt the inflation and the uplift that resulted from this invasion as sheer ecstasy, as inspiration, and as a calling to a kind of post-human condition. In this process, his consciousness and his mind exploded, his health deteriorated and he went mad. Spirit which falls to earth becomes an earth-spirit, entangled with instinctual and pagan forces. It is therefore significant that Nietzsche saw himself as Dionysus Zagreus, the ancient God of wine, of ecstasy and of chthonic earth-mysteries. Possession by this God felt pleasurable, wild and momentous, but he was destroyed by the very thing which brought this inhuman joy. At the end of his tortured life, Nietzsche signed his letters, 'Dionysus Zagreus', showing the world how this archaic God had replaced and annulled the man, how tragically his ego had become absorbed into a demonic archetypal complex.

Undergraduate recollection: Jung, Nietzsche, Yeats and the Beast

In a bid to uncover the popular myth of Jung, I reach back in my own memory and personal past to the first time I heard Jung's name. It was during an undergraduate tutorial at Flinders University in South Australia in 1972, and the session was on Yeats's poem 'The Second Coming' (1920: 124). Various students in the literature class were trying their hand at interpreting this enigmatic poem. Several of them were discussing Nietzsche and his famous declaration of 'the death of God'. In this context, the name of Jung arose several times, and at first I thought this man must be an ancient Chinese sage, or so it sounded to my untrained ears.

One bright student said that the philosopher Nietzsche had replaced God with man, or with the so-called Superman. Nietzsche's term 'Ubermensch' is translated as 'Superman', but some translators prefer the English word 'overman'. This student also said that Jung had replaced God with the self, and that this effectively equated with Nietzsche's substitution. Jung believed, he continued, that the space previously occupied by God was now to be occupied by our own consciousness, and that we would all be divinised by this new event. He argued that Jung and Nietzsche were philosophical twins; both saw, like the poet Yeats, that the old God had died, and both saw an elevated or transformed humanity as the new God.

This excited me very much, but I had yet to read Jung, so I could hardly contradict this highly intellectual student's interpretation of his work. As a young, ambitious student who was battling with my own sense of impotence and bewilderment in the face of the wide world opening up before me, I was keen to overcome this bewilderment with a new-found sense of spiritual power. Ever since I had renounced my own religious faith at about the age of fourteen, I had felt assailed by a sense of emptiness and absence, and I wanted this to be filled with something exciting and new. Old-style religion could no longer provide the longed-for nourishment, but perhaps direct contact with the spirit could. What had drawn me to the writings of Nietzsche as a teenager was the exhilaration and release he seemed to offer; we could let go our tawdry and flawed humanity and aspire to heaven on the wings of the spirit.

By the age of eighteen I had developed a small circle of acquaintances who all read Nietzsche and who listened to Jimi Hendrix sing of ecstatic mystical release. We also listened to Jim Morrison and the Doors scream of 'breaking through to the other side'. In the 1960s, many youths seemed possessed of Nietzschean longings to transcend the merely human and to reach for a higher reality. I can remember one serious teenager saying, 'Let's sit down and talk about the art of self-overcoming.' It was clear to me at the time that the adults around us had no idea how serious we were about the business of transcendence. But my generation had assumed that religion was dead and that something else was needed, desperately and urgently. It struck me that much teenage behaviour is about the longing for transcendence, and that even drugs, sex and various other addictions can be understood as symptomatic attempts to transcend the mundane and its tyrannical and empty hold over our lives.

The student who spoke about Jung was involved in drugs, sex, poetry, astrology, cinema and the 'Age of Aquarius'. The 'New Age' was not yet invented by business and industry; in those days we only had the 'Aquarian Conspiracy'. He not only watched films but he also made them, and he was majoring in drama. He was a bit 'hippy', but not fully so, for he seemed too intellectual to be a hippy. He was tall, somewhat charismatic, and, with a deep and resonant voice, he often quoted Jung in all sorts of contexts. This student had long curly hair, a serious, pale and often frowning face, and he usually wore a dark red velvet gown with a hooded cape. In part, he reminded me of the character Damian in the Herman Hesse novel of that name. Years later, I would understand this brilliant young man to be what Jung called a *puer aeternus*, an 'eternal youth' with a kind of unbroken link with the creative unconscious, and an abiding passion to return to a state of mystical oneness with the source or matrix.

He modelled for me the *puer aeternus* element in myself, and I was later somewhat surprised to discover while reading von Franz that *pueri aeterni* in history and myth often wore heavy gowns and hooded capes. Marie-Louise von Franz wrote in *The Problem of the Puer Aeternus* (1970) that the taste for secretive behaviour and concealing clothing came from the fact that the puer was not yet 'born' into the world, and he clung to secret spaces as to the bosom of the world mother. James Hillman (1973) later denounced von Franz's reading of the *puer*, claiming that the *puer* had nothing to do with the mother, and attacking von Franz for imposing the mother complex onto this mythic figure. In her correspondence with me in 1978, von Franz, in turn, denounced Hillman, declaring that he was denying certain facts about the *puer aeternus* because he had a personal identification with the archetype. Von Franz assured me that Jung would not have followed Hillman's position, since for Jung 'the *puer aeternus* only lives on and through the Mother' (1912/52: 258). I sided with von Franz in this dispute, and recognised that the *puer* was indeed a son of the mother, and that his mysticism was a secret attempt to return to her.

This, then, was my first introduction to Jung, and it had a lasting impact. I must confess that at first reading, I could not quite determine what Jung was actually saying. Jung seemed to assume Nietzsche's 'death of God' as a cultural and metaphysical catastrophe, but what Jung was proposing to take the place of God was not clear to me. From the very outset, I found his concept of the *self* to be ambiguous, if not downright confusing. If God was to be replaced by the 'self', then this seemed to be a Luciferian solution to the death of God, not unlike Nietzsche's mad conception of the Superman. Of course, as discussed in an earlier chapter, Jungians who 'know' Jung are aware that by 'self' he did not mean 'self' in the normal, colloquial sense of the term. But obviously, as soon as his theories and writings leave the professional Jungian circles and enter the public realm, there is bound to be enormous trouble in understanding and interpreting his elusive meaning. Was the hooded student so wrong to see Jung and Nietzsche as philosophical twins? Was the student wildly wrong in his assertion that Jung wanted to replace God with self? Indeed, in the lack of clarity in his formulations, and in the invitation to misinterpretation at the heart of Jung's terminology and conceptions, there may be more than a little trace of Lucifer in the Jungian opus.

The real problem, as Renos Papadopoulos was later to argue, was that Jung experienced considerable difficulty in articulating and explaining his concept of the 'Other' (Papadopoulos 1992). The concept of the 'self' was not sufficiently 'other' to act as an adequate carrier of the sacred. Although the old God was dead, Jung found it difficult to convince his readers that anything of similar greatness was to replace this concept. In the early 1970s, I lived for years with the impression that Jung and Nietzsche were twins, and that both sought to abolish the human and reinstate the divine as a 'higher' form of humanity. I read Jung's warnings about inflation, but the hubristic complex within, and my own background in Nietzschean philosophy, was actually doing the reading and the interpreting for me. When Jung came to cautionary warnings about 'godlikeness' and such, I think I skipped over these bits without much recognition, as the hooded student seemed to have done. But I also remember at one stage feeling that Jung wanted us to accept our new-found divinisation with humility. The fact that Jung called the presence of God inside us the *self* only made matters worse for me, since, like most others new to this game, I only had known the term 'self' as a synonym for ego. Unlike Jung, I had not developed a different awareness of this term through Buddhism and Eastern sources. It seemed hardly credible to me that the word 'self' could be used to describe an objective, almost independent 'Other' that completely transcended the personal ego on all sides.

My hooded friend explained that Jung had turned Nietzsche's philosophical speculations into a psychological system, and even into a method of therapy. We are all sick, he said, because we have witnessed the death of God and are suffering from a depressive psychosis and alienation from the world and each other. By showing man that he need not mourn the death of God, because this same reality will come to birth again within ourselves, man is cured of his depressive malaise and is given hope of an unexpected kind. This is the popular, though utterly mistaken, formula: a formula which converts Jung into a false prophet and which poisons much of his work with the venom of the serpent. Reading Jung as an illustration of Nietzsche turns depth psychology into poison, and virtually makes a philosophical system out of hubris. Nietzsche's Zarathustra announces, without any hint of irony: 'It is power, this new virtue; it is a ruling idea, and around it a subtle soul: a golden sun, and around it the serpent of knowledge' (1885: 101).

My last comment on this undergraduate recollection is to refer to the unconscious irony of that university discussion. We were, after all, examining Yeats's poem 'The Second Coming'. This poem is about the death of God and the end of the cultural order that God brought to our lives. But after the death of God, according to Yeats, we do not move forward to a new sublimity in which man is elevated to the status of God. Rather, the breach in the cultural order allows the Beast or the Anti-Christ to enter the human realm. For Nietzsche, the death of God gives rise to a better world; one in which 'the earth shall become a house of healing' (1885: 103). But for Yeats, the collapse of God leads not to earthly utopia but to fear and trembling:

> Things fall apart; the centre cannot hold;
> Mere anarchy is loosed upon the world,
> The blood-dimmed tide is loosed, and everywhere
> The ceremony of innocence is drowned.
>
> (1920: 124)

Decades after Nietzsche's announcement of the death of God, the world plunged into the blood-bath of two world wars, and savagery and barbarism were experienced on a scale unknown even in the ancient pagan world. Yeats does not see a rosy future in which man 'celebrates his journey to his highest hope and a new morning' (Nietzsche 1885: 104).

For Yeats, what follows the death of God is not the birth of Superman, or Ubermensch, but the unleashing of the Beast.

> The Second Coming! Hardly are those words out
> When a vast image out of Spiritus Mundi
> Troubles my sight: somewhere in sands of the desert
> A shape with lion body and the head of a man,
> A gaze blank and pitiless as the sun,
> Is moving its slow thighs . . .

This 'rough beast', writes Yeats, 'slouches toward Bethlehem to be born' (1920: 124). When the Christian era collapses, the next big mythic event, the next figure to be born in Bethlehem, is not the Second Christ, but the rebirth of chthonic nature and instinct.

If our tutorial had stuck to the imagery of the poem, instead of wandering away from it in ramblings about empowerment of the personal self, we would have noted that the death of God is an ominous, dark event which is not cause for celebration but for absolute caution. The death of God releases not human growth and optimism, but rather the rough beast from the dungeons of the collective unconscious. We were misinterpreting and ignoring the poem, overvaluing Nietzsche, misreading Jung, and all in service of personal aggrandisement and the Luciferian complex. We were defending against the awful truth of the poem by flight into New Age speculations about transcendence and human potential.

Inventing the guru of a new religion

There is a saying that if God did not exist, we would have to invent him. As Freud discovered, we often invent God in the image of our own unconscious complexes. However, I depart from Freud if he assumes that 'God' is nothing more than the sum total of our collective neuroses. The thing we call 'God' is clearly an amalgam of genuine spiritual insights, scriptural revelations, pathological formations and cultural constructions.

'Jung' is a similar kind of amalgam, a composite of popular delusions and mistakes, together with some genuine elements that are constantly being threatened by delusions. From time to time, the image has to be purged and cleansed of accretions and evil. However, once it has attached itself to an image, evil has a notorious capacity to stick and not be moved, or to return as soon as it is removed. I am particularly interested in our exploitation of 'Jung' as the oracular presence who delivers the age-old hubristic fantasy, or what I have termed our Lucifer complex, namely, the persistent idea that we are Gods, despite our evident humanity and mortality. We ignore what Jung actually said in favour of an alternative moral philosophy which derives from our complexes and which is dictated to us by an unconscious process.

In *The Aquarian Conspiracy*, Marilyn Ferguson (1981) published the results of a survey in which she asked New Age people in the United States to nominate the international spiritual figures who had influenced them most. Overwhelmingly, the respondents indicated that Teilhard de Chardin and C.G. Jung were the key, formative figures in their spiritual development and awakening. But how much Jung had these people read? My own experience leads me to conclude that they have hardly read any Jung at all, beyond a few pages of *Man and His Symbols*, and perhaps a couple of chapters of *Memories, Dreams, Reflections*. Jung's serious and difficult work is hardly ever encountered, and most people have in their minds the image of the old, pipe-smoking sage who lives beside the Zurich lake, uttering prophecies of the future and chiselling out figures of myth from large blocks of stone.

For a great many people, I would contend, 'Jung' is an empty signifier into which they project their own psychological content. But because this content is collective, not just personal, it gains a life of its own and begins to assume enormous importance. The popular image of Jung eclipses the reality of the man and his work, or we could say that a public myth is superimposed upon, and gradually replaces, the human and textual realities. We have to go through the difficult process of becoming conscious of our collective fantasies, especially because the popular 'Jung' is to some extent spiritually toxic and dangerous.

In the popular mind, Freud is a sex guru just as Jung is a spiritual guru. Both are viewed as anti-establishment or revolutionary figures who seek to overthrow the existing cultural order. Freud is constructed as the naughty and sexy radical who seeks to debunk the moral order, and Jung is seen as the radical 'son of a preacher' who wishes to overthrow the religious establishment, in defiance of the law of the father. In the same way that Freud allegedly capitulated to the sex instinct, so 'Jung' capitulates or caves in to radical, gnostic or weird expressions of spirituality. Jung is seen as the advocate of free and unrestrained indulgence in the cosmic or spiritual dimension of existence. He gives us 'permission' to be spiritual, just as Freud gives us permission to be sexual. But the spiritual permissiveness of Jung, like the sexual permissiveness of Freud, is far removed from reality. Although Jung constantly warned people not to identify with the sacred forces in the psyche, his moral authority is often invoked to sanction a (con)fusion of our human identity with the identity of the Gods. 'Spirituality' is sometimes popularly conceived as an excuse for us to slough off our painful humanity and to don the brilliant and wise personae of the Gods. It is such misconceptions that give Jung a bad reputation and that reduce his psychology of the sacred to a debased parody of itself.

In the popular imagination, Jung is a New Age guru who sits in judgement on the old age, condemning it to irrelevance and impotence. He is anti-Christian, and one of his early prophetic experiences which Marilyn Ferguson's New Agers recall, is his vision of a giant turd falling upon a Swiss cathedral, which is recorded in *Memories, Dreams, Reflections*. This vision, the New Age believes, indicates that Jung has personally witnessed the end of Western religion, and he has been instructed by God to get rid of the traditional church, and to found a new religion under the sign of Aquarius. This New Age has no use for historical religion, with its negative view of the self and its emphasis on the transcendence of God. The New Age announces the death of the old, and the birth of a new gnostic awareness in which the self is divinised and God is encountered at the inner level, as the core of our own selfhood. The wisdom of the gnostics, which the traditional church has always opposed, has finally achieved its apotheosis in the New Age, and this gnostic movement is set to rise to new heights, just as the traditional church is rapidly heading into decline and ultimate oblivion.

Jung is perceived as the natural leader of a new international gnostic religion, a perception that Jung did much to foster, given his self-identification with the alchemists, and his frequent statements that he was bringing the wisdom of the esoteric traditions into the modern world. But in actual fact, Jung's vision has more in common with W.B. Yeats than with the optimism of the New Age. After the death of God, for Jung, comes our confrontation with our own wretchedness, our nakedness, our disorientation and chaos. 'Things fall apart', and we fall apart with them, which is why we need psychotherapy, to glue together the fragments of self that threaten to split apart after our God dies. Then, according to Jung, we are plunged even deeper into darkness and despair, as we encounter the personal shadow, and then, even more menacingly, the archetypal shadow, which is similar to Yeats's vision of the rough beast. The death of God does not precipitate a new religion of light, but rather leads to a darkening of the light, an eerie and foreboding phenomenon.

> There are times when the spirit is completely darkened because it needs to be reborn.
>
> (Jung 1934: 941)

In Jung, too, a darkened spirit slouches toward Bethlehem to be born. Jung did not welcome this any more than Yeats welcomed his vision of the rough beast, which had 'troubled' his sight. Yeats's vision was not a personal fantasy, but an eruption from the *spiritus mundi*, which in Jungian language would be the collective unconscious. Jung and Yeats had to face the reality of evil, because they both felt that the spirit of the time demanded it. It would be nice to wish for better things, but a confrontation with the forces of darkness seemed to belong to the destiny of modern humanity. Nietzsche denied the confrontation with evil, since he considered himself to be 'beyond good and evil' (1886). But this denial only made Nietzsche succumb all the more tragically to the dark forces.

Popular gurus as collective complexes

The New Age is interested in promoting Jung as a 'light bringer', as anti-establishment, anti-Christian, gnostic, alchemical, ecological, mystical and celebrative. The popular Jung is on the side of the individual, and promotes individualism above conformity. Jung and Joseph Campbell are fused together, so that Campbell's motto, 'Follow your bliss' (Campbell and Moyers 1988), is attached to Jung. Like the popular Freud, the popular Jung encourages pleasure, satisfaction and freedom of desire, but at the level of spiritual rather than sexual experience.

The idea of Jung as a spiritual guru, who gives moral sanction to all manner of spiritual ideas and activities, constitutes a kind of 'spiritual promiscuity' similar in some ways to the sexual promiscuity that the popular 'Freud' was felt to encourage years ago. Freudian scholars and historians were quick to discover that the popular Freud was considerably different from the scholar's Freud. They have also conceded that there are different 'Freuds', different voices, directions or themes in the great man's work. But the popular image of Freud as sex guru, as anti-establishment advocate of free and unrestrained eros, is a fabrication which is a far remove from 'what Freud really said'.

Freud had a complex view of eros, and he was by nature conservative and defensive of the moral order of society. However, the popular image of a permissive or rebellious Freud 'sticks', despite what scholars, biographers or academic researchers say or prove to the contrary. The reason it sticks is because it is willed by something powerful in the collective mind, and this powerful reality constructs its own image of Freud, in accordance with its psychodynamic and expressive needs. The same process takes place with the popular construction of Jung, but we are only just beginning to understand how this process works. The recognition of the unconscious complexes governing our public perceptions helps us to liberate these thinkers from the iron cages in which they are held and contained.

The tell-tale sign in the construction of a popular persona is the *one-sidedness* and *narrowness* of the public image. Split-off aspects of mind or complexes of the psyche are notorious for their obsessive or compulsive character. Complexes are never well-rounded or whole, but are always partial and fragmentary, and such partiality transfers itself to a public figure, making that figure 'famous' and ensuring him or her an afterlife in the public gallery of important figures, but also ensuring that he or she is condemned to partiality and one-sidedness. This kind of fame is problematic and all-consuming, insofar as the complexity of the public person is 'devoured' by the narrow psychic content that is attached to him or her. For evermore, the public figure is lost to a fabricated and tyrannical persona, which never does that figure justice. In short, the gurus of popular imagination are the personified forms of obsessive and one-sided complexes.

In recent times, one can see how the complexity of various human figures has been sacrificed to one-dimensional stereotypes: Marilyn Monroe to the stereotype of a Sex Goddess, Elvis Presley to a Sex King, Freud to a Sex Guru, Princess Diana to the Victim Bride, Prince Charles to a New Age Prince who talks to cabbages and flowers, and Jung to a New Age Guru who discovers giants and fairies where no-one else finds them. When the collective persona takes hold, these people are forthwith prisoners of these stereotypes, and victims of a universal one-sidedness. Scholars, writers and historians can show in their detailed accounts that these people are vastly different from the stereotypes that have been imposed upon them, and biographies often emphasise the ironic disproportion between reality and fantasy. But despite what evidence can show and what reasoned argument can present, nothing much changes in the popular imagination, which is virtually impervious to reason because it is based on irrational psychic factors.

In these examples, either 'sex' or 'spirituality' is the split-off component that is confused with the public figure. Freud and Jung are respectively fused with sex and spirit, and although this division roughly corresponds to reality, their highly complex and ambivalent responses to sexuality and spirituality are repressed, so they emerge as simplistic and crude advocates of narrow positions. The human mind has a distinct tendency to polarise and separate spirituality and sexuality, and the construction of Freud and Jung in this binary oppositional relationship accords fully with the neurotic splitting that frequently takes place in the psyche. The fact that these figures terminated their relationship in circumstances of dispute and controversy only serves to reinforce the breakdown of relationship between the sexual and spiritual parts of the public mind.

It is worth considering what problems attend to a split-off spirituality complex. In a sacred or non-profane culture, in which religion is central to everyday life, our longing for God is a positive impulse which grants us a legitimate connection with the divine. It is only when the instinct for connection with the transcendent is repressed and denied that it becomes a complex in the unconscious, drawing energy and attention to itself. When it functions as a complex, our spiritual impulse can undermine the health and direction of the ego, leading the ego away from life to an otherworldly reality. When an invented 'Jung' is enlisted as a guarantor of this complex, we justify otherworldly and antisocial behaviour by referring to this as our 'spiritual journey' or as our 'Jungian' experience.

Chapter 4

American New Age
Jungian inflation

Do not listen to what the prophets are prophesying; they fill you with
false hopes. . . . I am against those who prophesy false dreams. They
tell them and lead my people astray with their reckless lies.

(Jeremiah 23.16, 32)

The sacred in service of the ego

We have looked at the potentially toxic effect of the figure of Jung in the
popular imagination, and I would now like to consider the problem of
toxicity and contamination in the secondary Jungian literature. Once
again, it is not the correct use of Jung that causes these problems, but
the misuse of Jung's ideas that has the poisonous effect. One simply has
to turn the Jungian compass a few degrees either side of the position of
genuine balance to find that damage can be done by Jung's ideas. It seems
that the capacity for error and travesty arises from a fundamental problem:
Jung encourages contact with sacred forces, but because his psychology
operates as a 'secular' science, the atmosphere is not always appropriate
to respond to the sacred forces in the correct way. Sacred forces require
sacred responses, which means that when we encounter the divine, we
must respond with humility, otherwise the entire project loses its integrity
and everything goes awry. Jung insisted that one must adopt a 'religious
attitude' toward the contents of the unconscious, but this is difficult to
achieve, especially when he insisted at the same time that his work is a
secular, empirical science (1952b).

A religious attitude would promote disciplined thinking and moral
sanctions, and enforce an attitude of humility and service. Part of our
contemporary problem is that the term 'religion' carries so much baggage,
and has such negative publicity, that few wish to be associated with it.

For this reason, Jung coined the term 'religious attitude', in contrast to formal 'religion' as such, to refer to an attitude of reverence and respect for the sacred Other. But for many people, 'religious attitude' still has too much religiosity about it, and I suppose it is because of this that our society today elects to speak of 'spirituality', and to contrast this to 'religion'. What Jung called the 'religious attitude' we today call 'spirituality', but the term is still not an ideal one, because 'spirituality' has, like everything popular, become tinged with narcissism, personalism and individualism. People talk about 'my' spirituality, and 'my' spiritual development, and this kind of discourse has become yet another way in which the ego and its power complex has begun to extend its empire across the breadth and depth of the psyche. What we need – regardless of what term we use for it – is an attitude toward the contents of the psyche that promotes humility, awe and wonder before a reality which is greater than we are. This is clearly difficult, and perhaps impossible to achieve when a set of ideas go out into the public domain, and become subject to commercial manipulation, mass psychology and a consumer mentality.

When Jungian psychology is popularised, it automatically becomes a way of developing the ego and of realising human potential. Readers are often encouraged to identify with archetypes and thus to become inflated and important, at least in their own estimation. Indeed, it could be argued that the reason why so many Jungian books become hugely popular is because they present readers with a programme to become 'huge', to transcend ordinary human boundaries and to take on the likeness of the heroes, Gods and Goddesses. Jeremiah is a useful guide when dealing with the false prophecy of New Age conjurers: 'The prophets prophesy falsely, and my people love to have it so.'

Typically, the American Jungian populariser tells a story, a myth, a fairytale or a legend, and readers are invited to identify with the significant figures and to transcend their human ordinariness. The mess of an ordinary life is thus artificially 'resolved' by an identification with a larger-than-life character. The messy psychological and emotional problems of individual experience are gloriously transcended by our identification with spiritual or cosmic patterns. Little wonder this kind of process becomes popular, because we are offered an escape from the demands of the present by a flight into myth and archetype. In this way, 'archetypal' psychology (Hillman 1983) can become a defence against development (in the sense of individuation), and 'myth' becomes a way of avoiding contact with what is really going on in the psyche.

There are, of course, ways to present archetypal narratives and myths so that they do not have inflationary effects upon readers. Jung, Carl

Kerenyi, Neumann, von Franz and the classical European Jungian writings provide many instances of archetypal and mythic narrations that do not puff up readers, but simply offer narrative materials upon which they can feast their imaginations. But in recent years, Jungian popularisers – and almost in every case Americans – have refined the art of seduction and power, by presenting the stories as 'raw materials' upon which readers can develop the fortitude and resilience of the ego. In this popular literature, the emphasis is not upon developing imagination, but upon developing personal power, growth, efficiency, human potential and a vast range of other 'useful' products. This is the use of myth and archetype in the service of the ego.

It is hard to 'develop the imagination' if people do not have a sense of what the imagination is. This is clearly the crux of our problem, and why Jungian psychology is having this inflationary effect on people everywhere. The realm of story, myth, image, metaphor, symbol, poetry, narrative, is being covered over by the ego and colonised by its interests. People are far too eager to identify with whatever image or archetype is presented to them, and as a result we tend to say 'I am That' to every mythic figure or beast that passes our way. Spiritual bankruptcy is expressing itself today as imaginal illiteracy. If we had a fuller sense of the imaginal, we would allow the archetypes to remain in their own space, and not seek to colonise that space and impose our own personality upon it. Scripture warns us that where there is no vision, the people perish (e.g. Proverbs 29.18), and we can see this in our own time: we are perishing in our own egotism and narrowness of vision, extinguishing the imagination and the realm of spirit by constantly 'owning' or 'buying' whatever we see. It could be that rampant capitalism and consumerism in the world has invaded our souls as well, and that we are caught in a negative spell of our own weaving. Ironically, the richness and value of the psyche is immediately rendered worthless when the ego lays claim to it. Consumerism has taught us not to turn things into gold, but rather how to turn inner gold and treasure into lead.

The inflationary popular literature is part-Jungian, insofar as it derives from Jung and uses his words and language, and part anti-Jungian, insofar as it is conducted in a spirit that is antithetical to his ethics and orientation. The Jungian element consists in inviting the reader to encounter the archetypes and to enter the field of myth and fairytale. The non-Jungian element is what follows from this encounter, and the attitude in which it is conducted. Using Jungian language, terms, concepts and methods to pursue non-Jungian ends is a pernicious activity that must be identified and made conscious in contemporary popular culture. Jung would probably have much sympathy for old Yahweh, who complains to his prophet Jeremiah:

> Therefore I am against the prophets who steal from one another words supposedly from me. Yes, I am against the prophets who wag their own tongues and yet declare, 'The Lord declares'.
>
> (Jeremiah 23.30–31)

The problem of becoming popular

To some extent, these problems relate to the difficulty of becoming popular, and ask us to reflect on what it means to be 'popular'. Why do we want to be popular? How can we be popular? In my view, the Jungian field certainly needs to become popular, since it is one of the few areas of enquiry and discourse that is seriously investigating the problem of meaning in our society, and the importance of meaning for mental health, personal well-being, and social stability. We need to become popular, but how? Does being popular mean selling out? Must we make unreal promises to readers about spiritual rewards and personal wholeness? Must we wave carrots and chocolates and prizes before them, so that they will enter the inner world and begin to take it seriously? Is this approach misguided, patronising and condescending toward the general public who buy these Jungian books? Are there other ways to proceed, ways with more integrity and value? I will return to these questions later in the chapter, when I explore the cases of James Hillman and Thomas Moore.

To a high degree, the New Age spiritual movement supplies the 'kiss of death' to any cultural or religious form which attracts its curiosity or interest. The New Age makes popular the spiritual insights and wisdoms of Jung, Buddhism, Yoga, Jewish mysticism and Sufism, and perhaps it advances the causes of these traditions by exposing them to wider audiences and communities of interest. But because the popular representations of these traditions are so impoverished, one feels that more harm than good has been done. All too often, popularisation is synonymous with vulgarisation. As a teacher and public speaker, and therefore as one who is forced to 'popularise' a great deal, and to make complex material appear comprehensible to a range of students and listeners, it saddens me to think that the 'popular' is by nature flawed, cheap and denatured.

We must discover alternative ways of being popular, because if the genuine approach can only be found in learned or difficult writings we have failed as teachers and as communicators, and we have also failed our traditions by keeping them locked up inside specialist academies and professional in-house jargons. The greatest spiritual teachers do not preach only to the converted, but engage with an entire people, and by their ability to reach into the hearts and minds of many they exert a profoundly transformative influence on individuals and society. At the moment we live in a time where contact with the many is almost synonymous with shoddy or corrupted spiritual products, and where the 'pure' path is difficult to access outside closed traditions. This is not to say that only an elite few practise pure spirituality; on the contrary, this is clearly not the case. I am only attacking the way that spirituality is represented to the many, and am making a plea for a more responsible and conscious approach to the public dissemination of spiritual knowledge. We must reverse the current trend if society is to be spiritually revived, and if the fabric of community is to be restored.

A further problem arises: How does one make popular a science, art or therapy which is essentially a criticism of the human condition? To articulate the process of individuation is by definition to engage in a prophetic criticising of the structures, defences, habits and conventions of ordinary consciousness. To discuss the possibilities of individuation is to discuss possibilities that people are not living, or are not prepared to realise or understand. Such is the stubbornness of the ego and its conventional adaptations that the perspectives of wholeness, authenticity and the sacred have frequently to shatter the encasements of the ego in order to be admitted to the human frame of reference. Readers of popular books like to be flattered and admired. They like to be told they are doing well, that they have already accomplished much, rather than that they are only at the very beginning of the journey, and are merely in spiritual kindergarten. Unless writers are prepared to point to our falling short, to the gap between what is and what could be, they are not keeping faith with the larger vision of individuation, but are betraying, rather than fulfilling, Jung's prophetic vision of a more integrated humanity.

Seductive strategies

So my interest in the popular New Age production of Jungian thought is intimately connected with broader questions about the dissemination of knowledge and the integrity of communication. I am interested in how spiritual ideas are disseminated, and am keen to track down where, precisely, this dissemination goes wrong, and where and how popularisation turns vulgar. The New Age popular literature has established the models and patterns for this kind of distortion of spiritual truth, and popular American Jungianism has gone down the same path, as if intoxicated by the material rewards of this kind of industry. The nature of the game is to adapt sacred materials to profane goals, and to use spiritual narratives for boosting confidence, personal prestige and power.

Typically, this game involves opening the reader to the prospect or possibility of making contact with the sacred, and then telling the reader that such contact can make them rich, famous, attractive, efficient, sexually virile and more successful at their jobs and marriages. The signature of the New Age, and what makes it profoundly non-spiritual, is that it always looks for what the individual can 'get out of' the sacred, rather than for what the individual might be able to contribute to the sacred, or to the human community as an expression of the sacred in time and space. In the New Age, the sacred exists for our personal use, delectation and delight, and we are to set the sacred to work for us. The most recent 'Jungian' book in this tradition is a work entitled *Making the Gods Work For You* (Casey 1998). But there are countless others, including Robert Johnson's *Inner Work: Using Dreams and Active Imagination for Personal Growth* (1989b). There is no regulation of this popular market, and works that offer delusions and dangerous distortions of psychological theory can seemingly get away with murder, and all in the name of industry and capitalist enterprise.

In the non-Jungian field, Deepak Chopra represents the typical example of what I have just described. In his book, *The Seven Spiritual Laws of Success: A Practical Guide to the Fulfillment of Your Dreams*, Chopra offers as his first principle the belief that 'when we realize that our true self is one of pure potentiality, we align with the power that manifests everything in the universe' (1994: 7). The first gesture is toward relating us to the sacred, and our innate spiritual hunger is activated. Especially attracted are young readers who are shopping around for a sense of the sacred, yet who are alienated by the churches and traditional forms of religious devotion. The initial move to the reader seems innocent and genuine, but even here our suspicion might be aroused by the description of the human being as 'pure potentiality', which should alert us to the presence of another agenda which stands behind the overt claim that we need to be linked to the sacred. This other agenda is clearly about empowerment and mobilisation of the person, who is to use the sacred as a kind of free-to-the-public, readily available and accessible energy supply.

The sacred in this picture is nothing more than a power centre that can boost our profits, efficiency and performance if we know how to plug into it. There is never any concern for the sacred itself, and rarely any sign that reverence might be an appropriate attitude before the presence of the sacred. Chopra displays his true interests when he tells the reader that success 'is the ability to fulfill your desires with effortless ease' (1994: 2). At this point, the power drive has usurped the spiritual concern, and we hear whispers of the serpent telling Eve to eat the forbidden fruit. In this model, our spiritual interest is caught by the promise of spiritual connection, and then our power drive is activated by the promise of influence and wealth. The combination of immature spiritual interest with the power drive is what creates the context for profane instruction and New Age vulgarity. Such guidance is presented to audiences as 'inspirational' or 'positive' thinking.

This same process takes place in the New Age popularisation of Jung. For instance, here is just one example of how the idea of the 'Collective Unconscious' is interpreted and produced by a popular New Age writer. The text comes from *Crystal Awareness*, by Catherine Bowman.

> This is what the New Age is all about: it's a major change in consciousness found within each of us as we learn to bring forth and manifest powers that Humanity has always potentially had. Individuals struggle to develop talents and powers, and their efforts build a power bank in the Collective Unconscious, the soul of Humanity that suddenly makes these same talents and powers easier to access for the majority. You still have to learn the rules for developing and applying these powers, but it is more like a re-learning than a new learning, because with the New Age it is as if the basis for these had become genetic.
>
> (Bowman 1992: i)

This is the aggressive discourse of the personal will and individual empowerment. It is worth noting that, in the course of these three American sentences, the word 'power' occurs five times. Jung's Collective Unconscious is actually referred to here as a 'power bank'. We can connect with that bank and withdraw from its inexhaustible funds when we are feeling depleted or down. Moreover, the more we do this, and the more others do it, the 'easier' it all becomes. Our spiritual dream is coming true, and we can make it all happen simply by doing it more often. This is the language and sensibility of consumer capitalism disguising itself as a spiritual technology. The whole point of the unconscious, in this new and influential discourse, is that it exists to serve our own ends, not we to serve its needs. The traditional sense of the sacred, which gives rise to humility and worship, has been cashed in for a new attitude, which has to do with empowerment, 'ease of access' and ego therapy. The Gods exist only as powers to make us happy. We are certainly in spiritual kindergarten, playing with dangerous toys.

Making Jung work for you

The phenomenon of best-selling books that exploit Jung's insights for the purposes of advancing power, commercial success, emotional security and gender certainty has not yet been sufficiently documented. Andrew Samuels has begun to open up this difficult and controversial debate, both in *Jung and the Post-Jungians*, where he discusses the problem of unreal Jungian optimism and 'panglossian excess' (1985: 28), and in *The Political Psyche*, where he exposes the regressive social agenda of the Jung-influenced New Age men's movement (1993: 181–200). But the list of writers indulging in escapist or unreal representation of Jungian psychology is considerably large, and growing all the time now that writers have glimpsed the market potential of Jungian thinking.

I try to keep abreast of these works because I have an interest in the representation of Jung's thought, but I cannot pretend to be apprised of this entire popular literature, because much of it is difficult to access through university libraries, which generally do not acquire purely populist writings. But in this category I would place the works of such writers as Robert Bly, Robert Johnson, Robert Moore, Douglas Gillette, Clarissa Pinkola Estes, Guy Corneau, Carol Pearson, Jean Shinoda Bolen, Caroline Casey, and the later writings of James Hillman, among others (see References for individual works). When I am critical of these writers, it is sometimes said that I am envious of their success. This excuse can be used as a way of avoiding criticism, and the intellectual debate can be shut down by resorting to reductions of this kind.

Some of these New Age Jungian writers, such as Bly, author of the blockbuster *Iron John* (1990) and Casey, author of *Making the Gods Work For You* (1998), have not had any formal education in Jungian thought, and are basing their writings on a minute theoretical foundation. But others, like Robert Moore, Hillman, Estes, Corneau, Bolen and others are trained, professional Jungians. The recipe for fame and publicity is simple: if a writer can offer a program whereby people transcend their normal limitations by ascending to spiritual heights, success is guaranteed. The New Age literature drops the idea into people's heads that they are actually Gods, or that they can command the Gods to work on their behalf, or that they can perform heroic or God-like tasks. Just by reading the latest book, the humble reader can be marvellously transformed into a man who bends iron with his bare hands, or a gifted knight who discovers the grail or draws the sword from the stone. Any ordinary neurotic can suddenly transform into Hermes or Zeus, or a broken life can miraculously arise from its depression as Innana, Ishtar or Persephone.

When we are feeling uncertain about our identity, or vulnerable before a new difficulty or problem, we simply have to look up Bolen's *Gods in Everyman* (1989), or her *Goddesses in Everywoman* (1985), and automatically we swell to superhuman proportions. Suddenly we get high on the greatness that is locked inside us, and 'take on' the Gods as a replacement for our troubles and problems. This let's-go-shopping approach is typical of the New Age movement, and its ease, its lack of psychological effort, its consumerism, and its manic defence against depression, are reflective of the commercial marketplace in which this activity is situated. If the motto of our consumerist society is 'Toys 'R' Us', which is the name of an international enterprise, then the motto of consumerist spirituality could be 'The Gods 'R' Us'. The New Age replaces our human confusions and difficulties with the certainty of archetypal figures, with which we then identify to overcome our human frailty. The Gods work for you best when they act as alternatives to anti-depressants and expensive personal therapy.

We need to befriend the archetypes, but certainly not identify with them. The difference between befriending and identifying, which Jung makes in his writings, is deliberately blurred by the New Age profiteers. Jung argues that if we renounce the position of the ego, we can be taken over by collective forces which could destroy our individuality. At the end of the day, it is our humanity that must remain as a counterweight to the collectivity of the archetypes. Sailing away with the archetypes and imagining oneself to be Zeus, Aphrodite, Artemis or Iron John may provide some escapist relief for a time, especially if reinforced in a group setting by a New Age men's or women's movement, and administered by practitioners who claim to be Jungian authorities. But eventually the ego has to face its own frailty and unadorned vulnerability. When the bubble of irreality bursts, as it must, so that life can resume its course, we have to pick up our ordinary human personality again. This means that we have to affirm our brokenness, inadequacy and weakness, and not give in to the false strength that can be gained from the archetypes. In affirming our brokenness, we protect our integrity and keep ourselves human. The encounter with archetypes is and must remain a moral problem, one that is fraught with difficulty.

In my list of New Age inflationary Jungians, I would have to include the works of other notable 'stars' in the Jungian galaxy, including some of the more popular writings and television productions of Joseph Campbell. Campbell's famous motto, 'Follow your bliss', which is an adaptation of the 1960s slogan 'If it feels good, do it', has trivialised the archetypal field, and again has presented that field as an unlimited resource for personal narcissism and peak experience. *The Power of Myth* (Campbell and Moyers 1988) develops the familiar New Age theme of finding 'power' from myth, although Campbell indulges his own personal power to such an extent that he fails to acknowledge that most of his insights derive from Jung. James Hillman, who in late career also jumps on the New Age wagon, similarly attempts to popularise Jung's ideas while conveniently forgetting that they are Jung's ideas, not his own. One aspect of American psychopathology, it seems, is that this nation likes to appear as a 'source country', as a place where crucial ideas and theories happen 'first', and this desire to be original is so strong that writers are prepared to borrow from European forebears without the humble gestures that would make such borrowing forgivable.

The archetypes will look after us

The typical New Age Jungian book tells us to stop worrying and be happy. High levels of optimism and a childlike or naive belief in the goodness of archetypes is a typical characteristic of American popular Jungianism. Although the old moral and cultural order is collapsing around us, we can rest assured that things are in good hands, that 'the archetypes' are guiding us, and we simply have to learn how to seek their guidance. In a variation of the old religious idea that we must 'let go and let God', we have the new idea that we must 'let go and allow the archetypes to take over'. Everywhere we find this childlike belief that our fate is not in our hands, that benevolent archetypes are watching over us and leading us to a new wholeness. This is very seductive 'good news' to the men and women of today's world who feel torn, whose lives are broken, and who crave a new foundation for modern life. In the popular texts, the archetypes are always good, and always working to support us. As Andrew Samuels has said,

> Talking to some Jungians, it is often hard to see how anything bad could ever have happened, everything is given a purposive colouring and tragedy is denied. Everything is seen as being for the best or as part of some giant benevolent plan.

(1985: 28–9)

But in Jung's work, there is great emphasis on evil, and every archetype has a dark side. Indeed, according to Jung, the archetype often reveals its dark side first, before its more positive aspects are apparent. In Jung's theory, it is primarily the archetype of the Self that adopts a benevolent, supportive role toward the ego, assisting it in its plight and helping it through difficult times. The Self often helps the ego along its way, sometimes offering a prophetic dream, a clear insight, or a dream-animal which shows the way through the impasse. Marie-Louise von Franz (1973) shrewdly observed that at the Jung Institute in Zurich, students were often taking it for granted that the Self would come to the ego's rescue, and were actually becoming blasé about the healing and helping capacity of the psyche. She insisted that such an attitude, which we now find rampant in the New Age, can have a stultifying effect on the psyche, and can give the ego a completely false sense of security and well-being, as if taken up in the arms of a benevolent God.

Jung's optimism about the archetype of the Self appears to have contaminated all the other archetypes, so that people are hardly ever frightened or terrified by the figures of the deep, but see them as aspects of a giant benevolent plan. A kind of sugary optimism has been smeared over the entire archetypal field, distorting our vision of this world and interfering with our discernment of what we experience. The New Age has seized hold of Jung's optimism and blown it out of proportion. Something foolish has taken place, but as with everything in the New Age, it has glimpsed an aspect of psychological truth and has distorted its meaning.

It is clear that the modern ego is burdened by huge amounts of stress. Change is taking place in all fields of human experience, and the rationalism of consciousness has taught us to take this stress personally and to feel responsible for it. As a result, the ego is often unable to cope, and sometimes breaks down under the load it is carrying. In this event, a reduction of tension in the ego personality is a wise move, and we reduce tension best by imagining that support and relief is at hand, either in other people and in positive forces in society, or in forces within the self. Stress is reduced when we see that the ego is not the only player in the house of personality, but that there are many archetypes that operate within the totality of the psyche. However, an unrealistic capitulation to these other authorities is clearly dangerous and to be cautioned against.

Handing over our lives to archetypes and instincts is a renunciation of our individuality and an abdication of ethical responsibility. It is ironic to see some New Age Jungians offer us 'individuation', because what they propose is the reverse of individuation. It is a loss of the individual and unique character in favour of the comfort and support of archetypes. Walter Mitty-like, and in a systematic recapitulation of James Thurber, we lose our individual smallness and acquire the greatness of the King, Warrior, Magician, Lover and so on. But these archetypal personae are masks which hide or disguise our individuality. They do not represent opportunities for individuation in Jung's understanding of the term.

The Hillman phenomenon: sensitivity and refusing to fight dragons

Whatever happened to Jung's sense that struggle and strife is the hallmark of genuine individuation? Jung quoted Heraclitus, 'Strife is the father of all things', not Joseph Campbell, 'Follow your bliss'. Whatever happened to Jung's good sense that the collective archetypes are not to be trusted, because they are capable of devouring our individuality in an instant? For Jung, the archetypes are often imagined in their most basic and primal form as monsters, dragons or demons, and Jung argues that we sometimes face situations that demand an heroic response. There are times when a dragon must be slain, or a monster must be outwitted, so the treasure-hard-to-attain can be won for consciousness. The treasure is the boon, the gift of new life, often personified (for men and patriarchy) as the anima or soul-figure who is held captive by an oppressive mother-figure. The primal archetypes do not willingly renounce their treasure. They behave 'as if' they were dragons who seek to hoard and defend their wealth.

A typical New Age response is to marry the dragon and ignore the anima, a reversal of the classical heroic pattern, and clearly a sign that a collective or universal mother complex is at work, playing a huge role in the New Age construction of spirituality and psychological life. When the father is absent, when the God of our culture is dead, he is no longer present to act as guide or influence on our spiritual journey. In a culture that lives 'after God', the classical patterns are often reversed and a new set of values take over. Unfortunately (or otherwise), the ego needs the father to act as guarantor and benefactor of its journey, and this is true for the ego in either men or women. Although it has become fashionable to attack the father, knock patriarchy and denounce the 'violence' of dragon-slaying (all, let us say, for good historical and political reasons), this puts the ego in a double-bind, and prevents it from fulfilling its journey into consciousness. The values that emerge after God can become a 'political correctness' that has a detrimental effect on the psyche. It may mean that we are championing the feminine far too literally, or we are doing so in a way that ignores the continued claims of the father and the masculine. The negative element is not our championing of the feminine, but the extreme way in which it is often done.

The first major Jungian thinker to cast doubt on the classical heroic paradigm was the American James Hillman (Tacey 1998b). Before Hillman, major Jungians such as Erich Neumann (1949b) and Edward Edinger (1972) had reinforced, not critiqued, the masculinist elements of Jung's theory of consciousness. So Hillman was a phenomenon which in a sense 'had' to happen. In his essay 'On Psychological Femininity', Hillman reached the following conclusion, which was applauded by progressive thinkers at the time:

> We are cured when we are no longer only masculine in psyche, no matter whether we are male or female in biology. Analysis cannot constellate this cure until it, too, is no longer masculine in psychology. The end of analysis coincides with the acceptance of femininity.
>
> (Hillman 1972: 292)

I was fascinated when I first read this daring manifesto, but it was informed by a feminine poetics that was one-sided. Acceptance of the feminine is not synonymous with cure or healing of psyche, especially not for the person who is already drenched in, or overwhelmed by, the feminine. For such a person, healing or cure could come only by way of the acceptance of a larger wholeness, in which the masculine would play a vital role. Anyway, Hillman himself would later have to swallow these words, as his very public advocacy of the hyper-masculinist men's movement in the 1990s would loudly announce. The spirit of the time has great vitality and a sense of daring release, but those who follow it too closely are likely to become victims of the time and cramped by one-sidedness.

It was Hillman who advanced the sensitive or 'New Age Guy' approach to psychological exploration. He argued that the killing of dragons was antiquated, psychologically unhealthy, macho and ideologically unsound. In a defiant essay of 1973, in which he indicated his departure from the values of individuation, Hillman argued that if we slay the dragon we kill the unconscious:

> Killing the dragon in the hero myth means nothing less than killing the imagination, the very spirit that is the way and the goal.
>
> (1973: 169)

Here, as elsewhere, Hillman's rhetoric is persuasive, but he is nevertheless wrong-headed in psychodynamic terms. He argues that if we kill the dragon we do inherent damage to the inner world and to the ecology of the soul. This leaves us, he claims, high and dry in the sterility of consciousness, without the imagination to relate to or befriend. However, he is relying on the anti-heroic fashions of late modernity to carry the argument. It seems that dragons are presented to us by the unconscious to be grappled with, outwitted or defeated. Dragons symbolise the destructive forces of the archetypal world, forces that would destroy consciousness if they had half a chance. The ego must attempt to ward off this evil influence if it is to survive. No anti-heroic or anti-masculinist rhetoric can attempt to explain away our biological and spiritual responsibility to protect consciousness against the crushing forces of the unconscious. Hillman's love for the matrix and mother is so strong that any attempt to ward off her evil influence is unthinkable to the ego.

The mother's son only longs to be 'true' to the mother, a commitment which stifles his masculinity and has all kinds of repercussions and compensatory problems, such as instability, self-doubt and emotionalism. But by refusing to fight dragons, to separate from the primal unconscious, the son involuntarily falls victim to an inflation, since the boundaries between himself and the unconscious are not clear, and he becomes filled with the pneuma and psychic life of the unconscious. The dragon fight may be unpleasant, and may cause the ego to feel isolated and apart from its source, but it is the one guarantee that we have against the tyranny of inflation. Remaining wedded to the source has the automatic effect of causing the ego to expand its boundaries, to puff up with the dragon.

Far from the dragon fight causing us to lose our relation to the unconscious, Jung would insist that such a fight enables us to relate to the unconscious for the first time (1928: 261). Jung argues, and Neumann clarifies this theme at greater length (1949b), that so long as the unconscious is symbolised by a dragon, a monster or some other primal symbol, there is no 'relationship' at all with this realm. We are held captive by it, 'captivated' and caught under its sway. If we refuse to ward off the evil element, and if we refuse to respond to evil as a danger, there can be no humanising of the unconscious, and no relationship with it. The fact that the dragon often holds a princess in chains is the symbol that the more human and positive face of the unconscious needs to be released from its primal enchantment. Energy has to be exerted in favour of development, and although 'progress' is unfashionable, our fashions cannot be used as a way of avoiding what must be accomplished in the journey of individuation.

The ecological argument in this context is also without foundation. Dragons are not to be taken literally, as if they were African animals in a game reserve, so that by killing them we commit heinous crimes against nature. Dragons are presented to be slain, so that something new can be born from the configurations of the libido. The wily and cunning archetypes will make full use of our ecologically sound arguments if it means that they can cling to their archaic power and maintain control. I am sure Hillman's green ideology has the full support of the Dragon Mother and the Devouring Father, who are chuckling behind the scenes, eternally grateful to political correctness, which solidifies their power. Hillman denounces Jung as old-fashioned and heroic, but in this case it is the older view that is wiser, and the new view that is suspect. Just because ideas are 'post-Jungian' does not mean they are better than Jung. The whole point of Jung's hero/dragon model is that the ego has to exert strength to combat the retarding and stifling effects of archetypes, which the dragons symbolise for us, even today.

The New Age men's movement

The Sensitive New Age Guy or SNAG wanders into the unconscious and starts patting the dragon on the head: 'Nice, friendly dragon; you wouldn't want to hurt me, would you?' 'Nice dragon, would you kindly give up your treasure; would you fill my soul and my flagging self-esteem with your spiritual boon?' If these archaic figures strike back, and inflict damage or wounds, we are surprised at our woundedness, but why? We have forgotten the power they have over us, and forgotten our responsibility to defend ourselves.

It is little wonder that, two decades after defining this anti-heroic program, Hillman found his way into the North American New Age men's movement, as a co-leader of this movement with Robert Bly (Hillman, Bly and Meade 1994). In psychodynamic terms, this can be seen as an acting-out of his need to gain the masculine strength that formerly he wanted to give away, renounce or deny. The problem, however, with the New Age men's movement is that it does not apply its search for strength to the inner level, but only protests about 'men's rights' at the social, political and external level (Tacey 1997). Men can 'get tough' with each other and against feminism, but at the inner level they can still be pussy cats curled up in mother's lap. For too many men today, 'feminism' becomes the dragon that is to be slain, and strong women become the figures who must be heroically opposed (Faludi 1991). Hillman's complaints about his 'dismembering encounters with radical feminists'

(1992: xii) have been more frequent in recent years, and this is clearly an external projection of forces that assail him from within. If men refuse the dragon fight, they end up simply fighting with women, since the need to differentiate themselves from the feminine is an archetypal imperative.

Hillman's life and work reveals the dangers of an incomplete understanding of Jung. It is as if Hillman reads Jung with one eye open, and another eye shut. He would endorse, for instance, this line from Jung with great enthusiasm:

> It is precisely the strongest and best among men, the heroes, who give way to their regressive longing and purposely expose themselves to the danger of being devoured by the monster of the maternal abyss.
>
> (Jung 1928: 261)

But the next sentence reveals the side of Jung that Hillman could not appreciate, and would subsequently reject in his theorising:

> But if a man is a hero, he is a hero because, in the final reckoning, he did not let the monster devour him, but subdued it, not once but many times.
>
> (Jung 1928: 261)

The men who join Hillman and Bly's North American mythopoetic men's movement imagine that 'being a hero' means banging drums, howling at the moon, complaining about their mothers, or denouncing radical feminists. But Jung imagined a far more subtle method for becoming a hero: the art or discipline of resisting one's own infantile desires to crawl back into the belly of the mother, or the unconscious. The hero is the one who resists the seductive attractions of the unconscious, and who, even while journeying in the psyche, understands his debt to consciousness and society. Like Odysseus, he dialogues with seduction but does not surrender to it.

Refusing to see the negative

The New Agers who surrender to archetypes are generally not paying close enough attention to their own dreams and psychic imagery. The dreams of such harmless Jungians would probably reveal the true story: that they are losing their grip on life and abandoning individuality to collective forces. Being swamped by the collective can be represented in dreams in a thousand different images of devouring, terror and disintegration. A man in the New Age men's movement might dream of being devoured by a tyrannical giant, partly because he has fallen into an unconscious idealisation of the archetypal father. But when he awakens, he will attribute the bad dream simply to the cheese he ate the night before. There is almost no capacity for understanding the terror or dread of archetypes. A woman in 'women's spirituality' might dream of herself as Little Red Riding Hood, and may be eaten up by a wolf who is dressed as her beloved grandmother. But because her idealisation of the Earth Mother and the Goddess is so strong, she will not be in a position to see the evil omen in the idealised archetype. Instead, she will probably attribute the fault to her own weak ego, to her lack of courage, or refusal to drop her conventional consciousness and run with the wolves.

The idealisation of archetypes that we find in the New Age blinds us to the shadow side of these archetypes. We think it is a miraculous thing to run with wolves, but the wolves have appetites, teeth and jaws that can rip us apart in seconds. The Great Mother is idealised in the New Age, and especially by its eco-philosophers and eco-psychologists, but the Mother too is 'red in tooth and claw', and in ancient times she sponsored the seasonal sacrificial slaughter of her phallic consort and son-lover. Christianity arose as a direct challenge to the bloodthirsty world of the Great Mother, and now, centuries later, we have forgotten what Christianity is all about, and we have forgotten the brutality, danger and tyranny of the Great Mother's world. For us, it has the rosy glow of magic, romance and natural living, but this is an illusion which history may have to shatter for us once again.

The notion of letting go and letting God must be balanced by a sense of discernment between the archetypal figures, and a realistic sense of moral responsibility toward what happens in the psyche. As Jung conceived it, the individuation process is processual, dynamic and a two-way street. Sometimes the ego has to give way to the archetypes, and at other times the psyche waits for the ego to show the lead. We must not be led to believe that the psyche is a fully autonomous unit, and that what happens inside it has nothing to do with us. The ego cannot afford to relax totally and to give way every time to the archetypal currents. The ego must act in partnership with the psychic community, and not passively forgo its leadership role in favour of the authority of archetypes. Jung argued that to capitulate to archetypes was individuation in reverse. He said that to hand over moral responsibility to the archetypes was a psychological disaster and a moral fraud (1928). The ego must maintain its ground, and continue the battle of life, even as it discovers other powers and centres of authority that have to be reckoned with.

Hostility toward the ego as a New Age strategy

Thirty years ago, James Hillman's archetypal psychology did not look anything like an expression of New Age ideology. He seemed to represent the antithesis of the New Age, in that he championed a psychology that was progressive, highly intellectual and avant-garde. He appeared to be anti-fundamentalist, anti-patriarchal, processualist and deconstructionist. Yet beneath the intellectual complexity, there were several assumptions and guiding ideas that were close to what we now refer to as New Age sensibility. In particular, Hillman's work carried the central insignia of the New Age: a devotion to the Great Mother and a refusal to do anything to injure, wound or harm her pristine domain. This devotion took place for the most part secretly and under cover, since he often displayed verbal hostility toward the Mother, presumably as a symptomatic attempt at detachment. As a result of devotion to the matrix, there was a refusal to develop the 'masculine' ego or to encourage any 'development' that would challenge the power of the maternal unconscious. In Hillman we discover a strong verbal rhetoric opposed to the ego, and a celebration of the archetypes and myths, in whose guiding wisdom and loving care we must entrust our lives (1979). But not all myths were celebrated: any myth that seemed to champion the logos, spirit or father, such as Christ, Yahweh, Herakles or Zeus, was denounced.

New Age spirituality worships the cosmic source and condemns the ego, and yet it unconsciously indulges it. This relentless verbal attack on the ego, yet indulgence of whatever is pleasurable and ego-syntonic, is what makes this movement neurotic and contradictory (Heelas 1996: 206). It condemns the ego because it seems to stand in the way of cosmic fusion with the primordiality that it celebrates. The ego is experienced as upstart, unlawful and without validity, and is systematically opposed; the dissolution or relativisation of ego is called 'spirituality'. But because there is no development of an alternative authority in the psyche – no sense of a Christ, Buddha, Atman, or Self – the psychic energy activated by this 'spirituality' has nowhere to go, and so floods back into the ego, inflating it beyond all proportion. Precisely because the ego refuses to believe in its own boundaries, it becomes inundated by the source.

These same patterns and contradictions can be found in Hillman. He provides glowing reports about the wonders of the unconscious and the majesty of archetypes, and as he attends to these mysteries he is always undercutting the ego and debunking its moral status. As the *New York Times Magazine* reported, Hillman is 'intent on dismantling ego, hero and self':

He has devoted decades to dethroning our culture's faith in the ego, to deflating our worship of heroic action and to deprecating our certainty in the concept of the self.

(Yoffe 1995: 46)

Like his anti-heroic response to dragons, these attitudes are presented as up-to-date and fashionable, but they ignore the fact that the ego and its heroic activity are archetypal and given by the psyche. They cannot be got rid of as merely human postures and encumbrances, because the ego is, as Jung argues, an early prefiguration of the Self. The ego has to be taken seriously and not simply swept away as irrelevant. As in the New Age, Hillman claims to be transcending the ego, but because there is no sense of any alternative authority in the psyche, no Self, Christ or Buddha, the actual effect of his archetypal activity is to puff up the ego he is theoretically opposing.

Hillman's adoration of polytheism, plurality and the many forms of daimonia acts as a retarding factor against the building of a higher authority in the psyche. For him, the unconscious is conceived as a rushing river of ever-changing images and possibilities, and the psychic energy released by what Hillman calls 'soul-making' has nothing to attach itself to. We have an archetypal need to build an alternative authority, and to devote our attentions to this authority with religious zeal and interest. There is a need to discern, discover, attend, love and finally to worship a sacred Other, but when the unconscious is experienced as a rushing river of endless possibilities and configurations, there is nothing for us to build on.

The formation of a higher authority in the soul is a monotheistic impulse, and this is the historical importance of monotheism in Western cultural development. There is a 'monotheistic' impulse in the psyche that Hillman's work represses, in favour of entertainment, excitement and the running river of possibilities. This militates against authentic soul-making and instead builds excitement, addiction and fascination. Hillman's Americanisation of Jung is found just here: the unconscious as entertainment, as a disengaged flood of images, like TV or Internet. Jung has the old-fashioned view that we have to extend moral responses toward the images we encounter. Hillman finds this antiquated, intrusive and moralistic.

Amorality, disengagement and entertainment

From the 1970s, Hillman rejected Jung's notion of individuation as too pedestrian, too human and workmanlike, and he advocated a project of 'Dehumanizing or Soul-Making' (1975: 167). Hillman was not interested in Jung's 'relations between the ego and the unconscious' (1928), but was advancing a method of soul-making that involved simply being-in-the-soul. Hillman had abandoned the Jungian interpretation of images in favour of aesthetic delight in images. Instead of moral or spiritual development, Hillman sought aesthetic satisfaction, and the amplification of images by linking one's inner iconography with the history of art, especially the Renaissance. The international interest sparked by Hillman's work was absorbed by art critics, literary scholars, poets and visionaries. The everyday world of psychic life, and the problems of clinical practice, had been ignored.

Hillman introduced into American Jungian thought the idea of the unconscious as a kind of Disney theme park. He renamed the collective unconscious the 'Underworld' (1979), and felt that we could go on fantastic tours into this exotic region, emerging from it without being morally transformed and without having any impact on the exotic creatures whom we encountered there. One day we could visit the amazing sites of Adventureland, another day it could be Fantasyland, and the next day Tomorrowland. But as in Disneyland, what we saw and witnessed would have no direct bearing on ourselves, and would not transform us. It would all be 'out there', one character talking to another character, one God to another God, but without any moral connections to ourselves.

Hillman ignored moral problems and ethical dilemmas. Questions such as how to live in the presence of mystery, how to wrestle with archetypes, how to 'be' as human beings in relation to the Gods and Goddesses, were questions he no longer engaged. At one early stage, he was interested in the idea of an 'imaginal ego' (1972), but this was lost as the fascination with the unconscious increased. He argued that by remaining disconnected in this way, by refusing to become morally involved, we allow the archetypes to express themselves more fully and thus prevent them from being colonised by the ego.

> Part of the movement to demoralize psychology is disowning responsibility. We have come to believe that responsibility, commitment, standing for our every word and deed are psychological notions, whereas they are moral ideologies.
>
> (1975: 179)

In such writings we are told not to import moral attitudes into psychology. However, Jung believed that everything human involves us consciously or otherwise in moral choices and in ethical discernment. The human domain is a moral domain, and to overlook this is to go down a very dangerous road, for the individual and for society.

In a move which runs parallel to New Age ideology, Hillman arrives at the view that the human psyche is not human, and therefore not ethical. 'Our essentially differing human individuality is really not human at all.' He continues:

> It is not my individuation, but the daimon's; not my fate that matters to the Gods, but how I care for the psychic persons entrusted to my stewardship during my life. It is not life that matters, but soul.
>
> (1975: 175)

'It is not life that matters' seems to be an odd position, opening the door to all sorts of destructiveness in the name of 'soul'. Fascists would agree with Hillman that life 'doesn't matter', only the great ideals matter, to which everything must be considered subordinate, and to which everything must be sacrificed. Hitler felt that life did not matter, only the Third Reich. If life doesn't matter, then what does matter? Who is to determine what matters most? To avoid ethics, in the name of keeping psychology pure of the ethical, is not to avoid 'ideologies', as he argues, but to expose oneself and society to all manner of ideologies and 'isms', which claim to be representing the great principles. Life must be considered sacred, and we must morally and legally work to protect life from debasement, defilement and destruction.

The inhumanity of the New Age is neatly portrayed by the popular belief that we are not human beings having spiritual experiences, but rather 'spirit-beings' having human experiences (Faber 1996). Since we are not fully human, we cannot always be expected to act in humane or compassionate ways. Sometimes, we have to be cold, aloof and ruthless, to ensure that we 'transcend' the ordinary and leave behind the merely mundane. This sense of spirit is chillingly cold and remote, and it is little wonder that people possessed by this spirit long for isolation and detachment. There is very little soul in this position, if by soul we mean warmth, containment and engagement.

Hillman claims that even his own writings on the archetypal figures have no moral weight or value, but must be discarded as casually as we wave good-bye to the figures who have entertained us. In his 'Processional Exit' to *Re-Visioning Psychology* he writes:

> All that is written in the foregoing pages is . . . to be disavowed, broken, and left behind. By holding to nothing, nothing holds back the movement of soul-making from its ongoing process, which now like a long Renaissance processional slips away from us into memory, off-stage and out of sight.
>
> (1975: 229)

It is clear that for Hillman the unconscious is little more than a passing parade of semi-anonymous forms and mysterious figures. But all great religious paths teach us, contra Hillman, that *the sacred makes claims on us*. We are not the same after the encounter with an archetype or God as we were before. Transformation takes place, both within ourselves and even, according to Jung, within the archetypes and Gods themselves. This was Jung's great insight: that the ego and the archetypal figures are both transformed by these encounters. In *Answer to Job* (1952a), Jung writes that Yahweh, seemingly remote and aloof in his heaven, is influenced and transformed by the sufferings of humanity. But Hillman is reacting against Jung's Jewish-Christian theology, preferring an earlier revelation of the sacred in which Gods were remote and untouchable, and where humans sat idly by while the Gods went about their play.

Hillman claims that this amoral attitude prevents us from falling prey to hubris:

> Disowning [the Gods and archetypes] prevents the psychological sin of identification.
>
> (1975: 180)

If we respond morally to the archetypes, we 'commit the sin of satanic selfhood, the ego who owns what is archetypal'. The logic is seductive, but again this is not true. The reverse is true: if we refuse to have moral dealings with archetypes, we leave ourselves open to possession and unconscious identification. The casual, New Age approach of not being involved, of just letting things happen, of not being morally responsible, makes us more prone than ever to inflation and godlikeness. It is precisely in our conscious engagement with archetypes that we discover our humanity and realise that we are not the Gods.

For me, further proof of this was found in observing the behaviour of the followers of Hillman in Dallas, during my own time spent there as a research scholar. Hillman's students employed his rhetoric about egolessness and the 'disowning of responsibility', but many of them showed a distinct tendency to identify with the archetypes, sometimes referring to themselves and to each other as Aphrodite, Artemis, Dionysus or Hermes. This seemed to me to be closer to New Age culture than to Jungian culture. The students would discern traits in their behaviour that resembled aspects of the Gods, and then the 'great sin' would indeed be committed. There would be a consequent blurring of identities, and they would claim to be inspired by the Gods in this or that kind of behaviour.

The immorality of this became quite clear, since certain patterns of behaviour became justified by naming the God or Goddess who was ultimately responsible for these patterns. An amorous adventure or sordid affair, for instance, could be justified by saying that 'Aphrodite made me do it', and in this way the person is magically relinquished of all responsibility. Or stealing another student's ideas was justified by invoking the name of Hermes, the thief. Suddenly we are back thousands of years in the ancient past, before the development of the human subject as we know it today.

At the time, I wondered what the Texas law courts or the American legal system would have to say to practitioners of archetypal psychology. Would invoking the Gods stand up in court? I once complained to Hillman about the behaviour of his students, and he agreed, admitting that some of them could not resist the temptation of archetypal identification. But I noticed he failed to make any general announcement about the problem, and seemed to assume that it was just an unfortunate quirk among some of his students. But my point is that this kind of behaviour is to be expected, and is not quirky. Unless we protect ourselves against inflation, we will be assailed by it in one form or another, and a psychology that vigorously eschews the development of a higher authority in the psyche is more prone to inflation than most. Perhaps this is what Aryeh Maidenbaum meant when he said, 'If you take Hillman symbolically, he's meaningful. If you take him literally, you're a basket case' (Yoffe 1995: 48).

Formal entry to the New Age

When Hillman departed from the exclusive atmosphere of post-Jungian thought in the late 1980s, and entered the American New Age, many scholars were shocked by his descent from former intellectual heights. Certainly, his shift in gear seemed astounding. Instead of speaking to an educated, sophisticated audience about the phenomenology of archetypes, he was now addressing a large, mixed, often uneducated audience about life and psyche. But clearly Hillman's turnaround was not as dramatic as many supposed. He had already thrown out Jung's individuation process, with its struggle and strife, in favour of a quietistic, relaxed, effortless method of psychic life that asked us to 'stick to the image'. Although his early style was hyperintellectual and difficult, the actual message was simple, relaxed, uncomplicated. Like American poet Walt Whitman, he could sing:

> I lean and loafe at my ease . . . observing a spear of summer grass.
> (Whitman 1855: 32)

Observe the image, but do nothing about it, was Hillman's message.

Divested of its intellectual trappings, this message was ripe for marketing. Millions of people like to do nothing and be rewarded for it. Millions long to become what Marie-Louise von Franz called 'soul-tourists', that is, people who are attracted to the realm of psyche, but who do not expect to be challenged by it, and who avoid the discomfort of change at all costs. The only problem Hillman faced, as an intellectual writer with much erudition, was how to de-school himself so that this message could be delivered to the masses. In one of his New Age books he writes: 'Please, we're not in a classroom and I am not your instructor' (1995: 20).

In the late 1980s, Hillman reinvented himself as a New Age guru, public commentator, co-leader with Robert Bly of the American men's movement, writer of newsy columns and calls to public action, ecological polemicist, chat show celebrity and media figure who famously appeared on the Oprah Winfrey Show, making this famous TV star cry before an audience of millions. Suddenly, all the marks of the New Age begin to appear, such as flattering his readers, offering visions of splendour and grandeur, while the author adopts the position of shaman or seer. Hillman's writing suffers from this sudden inflation. He makes grand gestures and portentous claims at the beginning of books, and yet by the end the reader feels let down, because the promised boon has not been delivered. Inflated rhetoric and cliché abound in such works as *Kinds of Power* (1995), *The Soul's Code* (1996), and *The Force of Character* (1999), as well as the lamentable, *We've Had a Hundred Years of Psychotherapy and the World's Getting Worse* (1993).

Inevitably, Hillman turned to the subject of power, and to America's obsession with it. As if America needed reminding of its eternal lust for power, and its need to revive and renew its claim to be the 'most powerful' in the world, Hillman joins the New Age movement, he says, to facilitate 'the recovery of a sense of power in American society' (1995: 13). Where has the man gone who wanted to break the corporate power of the establishment and advocate the simple values of receptivity to the soul? We are cured, he said in 1972, when we abandon the power-hungry ego and accept the feminine. I would argue that the power and strength that ought to have been acknowledged as part of the ego's rightful domain has now returned with a vengeance, and yet it is still 'out there', upon the face of the world. By the late 1990s, Hillman writes to make America more powerful, to make men feel stronger, and to subdue the dragons of radical feminism. The internal drama of the psyche has been externalised, because it is being acted out unconsciously.

In *Kinds of Power*, his first move, as in Deepak Chopra's *Seven Spiritual Laws of Success*, is to flatter his readers and tell them that great things are at hand, if only we can reach out and grab them. Rather than critique or challenge corporate America, he tells this brash establishment that they have the best minds in the world:

> As a writer on psychology, I am turning to business for my audience because that is where I believe the most daring and challenging minds are at work and where issues of power are most central.
>
> (1995: 1)

The insincerity of this is obvious to all readers, and most likely to the author as well. This is Hillman's naked bid for power and publicity. The back cover tells us that 'If you like the ideas in this book and are interested in learning more, become a member of the Currency Connection' simply by emailing or dialing a free 1–800 number. A former leader of the Jungian avant-garde has become a full participant in New Age capitalism, a burgeoning economy based on large promises, inflation and soul-tourism. The most insightful analysis of this spiritual materialism is found in Kimberly Lau's *New Age Capitalism: Making Money East of Eden* (2000).

One aspect of New Age economics, according to Lau, is to tell readers what they already know, and to present their ordinary activities in a portentous light, offering inflated perspectives on the mundane. But New Age writers must not call for personal change or make difficult demands, because this economy is all about 'spiritualising' what we already do. We are already being spiritual, but we don't know it. The New Age writer must be sure to make no separation between Caesar and God, to present greed as good, and represent materialism as spiritual search:

We might like to believe love determines our destiny or that the deep dreams and passions of the soul, or the advances of the technological sciences, are the truly formative factors that direct our lives. In actual living, however, only the ideas of business are always with us, from driveway to desk, from dawn to dusk.

. . .

Our contemporary civilization is held together neither by ideas of beauty, truth, justice, or fate, nor by military force like the *pax romana*, nor by common laws, divinities, language or shared beliefs. Only the ideas of business are actually universal. The ideas of business, such as trade, property, product, exchange, value, profit, money, are the ideas that consciously or unconsciously rule the planet's human life.

(Hillman 1995: 1–2, 6)

Whereas authentic spirituality involves us in change, challenge and sacrifice, false spirituality works according to the 'add-on' principle which is basic to consumer capitalism: we can simply add on a mystical perspective to what we already do. The comfort zone in which we live is already a mystical experience. There is no need for renunciation, salvation or change, because we are already holy. Capitalism does not have to change, simply get better and more efficient, and America does not have to renounce its power, just get more powerful.

Hillman remains to the end an enigma and a collection of contradictions. Loyal friends and followers close their eyes to his recent activity and remember the Hillman of the 1970s. But we have to notice what has been taking place over the last twenty years, during which all the 'post-Jungian' developments have been reversed, and the refused or repressed heroic elements have been acted out publicly in popular and corporate culture. Hillman resisted the hero's approach to the inner world, preferring to 'wed' the primordial unconscious in a mystical marriage. He did not slay the dragon, but decided to ride it into the Underworld. Jung wrote:

Anyone who . . . lets himself be devoured by the monster, and vanishes in it, attains the treasure that the dragon guards, but he does so in spite of himself and to his own greatest harm.

(Jung 1928: 261)

Hillman seems to have won the treasure, the insight into the unconscious, but he certainly did this 'in spite of himself and to his own greatest harm'.

The human element ends up the victim of insight, rather than the master of it. Significantly enough, the individuation process that was refused kept going anyway, without conscious involvement or participation. Jung often declared that if individuation is rejected, it keeps moving ahead at an unconscious level and in symptomatic ways. Individuation is not just Jung's 'theory', but a psychobiological process to be reckoned with. Hillman systematically rejected ego, hero and self, only to become a father figure and a hero for 'soft' or 'feminine' American men who claimed to need a boost to their flagging masculinity. Hillman rejected progress and development in the psyche, only to become an advocate for progress and empowerment in corporate America. The individuation process indeed appears to be archetypal, and if we do not co-operate with it, it runs its course without our assistance, coming to the aid of external forces that do not need our bolstering.

Thomas Moore: the return of moral proportion to popular psychology

At the same time as Hillman struggled to reinvent himself as a popular figure, another phenomenon was brewing close to home and close to Hillman's heart. His student and long-time associate Thomas Moore was achieving outstanding commercial success with the release of his book *Care of the Soul* (1992). This book was on the *New York Times* bestseller list for an extraordinary length of time, and it was followed by several other popular titles, including *Soul Mates* (1994), *Meditations* (1995), *The Education of the Heart* (1996a), *The Re-Enchantment of Everyday Life* (1996b), and *The Soul of Sex* (1998). It was Moore who seemed to lead his teacher Hillman into the popular domain, giving Hillman the confidence and the expectation that he too could become popular.

Some commentators and journalists assumed the worst when *Care of the Soul* became a runaway commercial success (Yoffe 1995). Was Moore 'selling the soul' in the sense of reducing his field to psychobabble for financial gain? Was he making the impossible promises to readers that had so often destroyed the credibility of Jungian bestsellers? Was he inviting them to identify with archetypes, to avoid the pain of self-scrutiny by running away with Iron John or running off with wolves? My response is 'no' to these questions. Moore is not successful because he has betrayed the soul; he is successful because he has tried to put the inarticulate longings of the soul into ordinary, everyday language.

To my mind, Moore is the most successful of all Jungian popularisers, because he does not sell the field short or distort its precepts to win popular appeal. Moore refuses to indulge excess. He does not make excessive claims, does not summon the Gods so that they can work wonders for us, but gently introduces readers to the domain of soul and the interior world. Moore explains his approach:

> You can see that care of the soul is quite different in scope from most modern notions of psychology and psychotherapy. It isn't about curing, fixing, changing, adjusting or making healthy, and it isn't about some idea of perfection or even improvement. It doesn't look to the future for an ideal, trouble-free existence. Rather, it remains patiently in the present, close to life as it presents itself day by day, and yet at the same time mindful of the realms of religion and spirituality.
>
> (1992: xiii)

Importantly, his book is not about 'cure', but 'care' of soul. He is not advocating a spiritual quick-fix, because his work 'has to do with modest care and not miraculous cure' (1992: 6). Moore actually confronts the arrogant human need for the quick-fix directly in his book:

> My cautious definition has practical implications for the way we deal with ourselves and with one another. For example, if I see my responsibility to myself, to a friend, or to a patient in therapy as observing and respecting what the soul presents, I won't try to take things away in the name of health. It's remarkable how often people think they will be better off without the things that bother them. 'I need to get rid of this tendency of mine', a person will say. 'Help me get rid of these feelings of inferiority and my smoking and my bad marriage'. If, as a therapist, I did what I was told, I'd be taking things away from people all day long. But I don't try to eradicate problems. I try not to imagine my role to be that of exterminator. Rather, I try to give what is problematical back to the person in a way that shows its necessity, even its value.
>
> (1992: 6)

Moore shows how we can popularise Jungian thought not by exaggerating its claims or by advocating miraculous results, but simply by explaining its tenets, precepts and goals by using ordinary language, and by avoiding the in-house jargon that professional Jungians use. Moore is talking directly to the reader about the modest goals of Jungian therapy, and about the process of befriending alien symptoms and annoying neuroses, without employing the technical jargons that turn the uninitiated reader away. Moore writes eloquently about 'honoring symptoms' rather than getting rid of them, and his entire approach is not businesslike and egotistical, but contemplative and poetic.

I think what saves Moore from New Age excess and narcissistic grandeur is the religious approach he adopts to his subject. It is religion, historically, that has protected us from the distortions of spiritual inflation and from the grandiosity of egotistical claims. It is not that I am such a fan of dogmatic theology or mainstream religious practice, but it is the *religious attitude*, as Jung advised, that protects us from the 'perils of the soul' that attend any direct encounter with extremely dangerous archetypal forces. Where religious morality is absent, there the New Age effects its most corrosive and dangerously distorting influence. If we are unprepared for such encounters, they immediately inflate us beyond human proportion, and madness is set loose in the name of spiritual experience. Moore declares that he follows the Renaissance example of 'not separating psychology from religion'. In this, he parts company from the anti-religious Hillman and returns to the model of Jung.

Jungian scholars often refer to Moore as 'Hillman Lite' (Yoffe 1995: 46), but I think they miss an essential difference between them. Moore had a Roman Catholic background, and spent several years as a priest in a Marist order. Although he was a man of the American New World, he had allowed the religion of the Old World to shape and inform his spiritual life. Hillman's natal religion was Judaism, but he renounced this as soon as his enquiring mind could not make sense of it. I would expect Hillman to recover his Judaism eventually, but meanwhile he experiences enormous alienation from his spiritual roots. Although Moore's journey took him outside and beyond the church, he remained loyal to important aspects of his spiritual formation, including the need to bear witness to a higher authority above the personal ego. That authority was not always named 'God', but Moore's spiritual compass always pointed to true north, whereas Hillman's spun around in a perpetual giddy motion.

Moore was attracted to Hillman's mind and inspired by his vision, yet it seems to me that Moore went beyond Hillman in his attachment to religious spirituality, his historical interest in the Renaissance, and in his psychological return to Jung. Moore's attitude is in fact remarkably close to Jung, although Jung's background was Protestant. But like Jung, Moore treads carefully and lightly across religious ground. He adopts a religious attitude without being piously religious. He is informed by Christianity without being stridently 'Christian':

Here is another major difference between care of the soul and psychotherapy in the usual sense: psychology is a secular science, while care of the soul is a sacred art. Although I am borrowing the terminology of Christianity, what I am proposing is not specifically Christian, nor is it tied to any particular religious tradition. It does, however, imply a religious sensibility and a recognition of our absolute need for a spiritual life.

(1992: xiii)

I agree with Moore about these matters. The Jungian work will flounder and remain marginalised in society until such time as it drops the pretence of being a secular science, and declares itself to be a psychology of religious experience. This is a failure found also in Jung, who protests to the end that his work is scientific and empirical, although in *Memories, Dreams, Reflections* he drops the stance of empiricism and speaks openly about his religious convictions. Jung felt that his contribution would only be acceptable if conducted in the context of science, but ironically it is this claim that has prevented him from being recognised as a major contributor to mainstream psychology.

Is Jung's work 'psychology' or not? It is not psychology as that discipline is defined today by academia, but it is certainly psychology in the sense of a *logos* of psyche. Jung's work is the science or art of life integration, and to the extent that life involves us in more than the rational, Jung's work is a science of life. However, I believe this work only gains full cultural importance when viewed as part of the unfolding history of Western religious thought. Jung's work offers us a psychology of religious experience, and that is what we need today. It seems that the vast problems that threaten to engulf popular Jungian literature, and thus serve to destroy the credibility of Jung, such as hubris, arrogance, inflation and grandiosity, are all fundamentally religious problems, and can only be addressed by referring to the religious contexts in which these problems can be resolved. It is here, I think, that the American passion for direct contact with the numinous achieves its most sane and interesting resolution. When the American passion for close encounters accepts certain religious lessons from the more conservative Old World, then the New World passion becomes grounded and does not lead to destructive spiritual experiences.

Chapter 5

Jungian fundamentalism and cultural regression

> Men desire to hear good tidings; and the masses listen to those who bring them.
>
> Tillich (1949: 17)

Related to the problem of popular inflation is the problem of popular fundamentalism. There are many kinds of fundamentalism on offer in today's spiritual supermarket, and Jungian fundamentalism is a recent addition to the stock-in-trade. 'Fundamentalism' may not be the right term, because it suggests that Jung's psychology is being literally and concretely applied, whereas we are often referring to a popular New Age movement that has never adequately read or understood Jung in the first place. I assume, for instance, that many fundamentalist Christians actually read the Bible, or selected passages of it, whereas I do not think we can assume that fundamentalist Jungians actually read Jung. I have met New Age people for whom the notion of 'archetype' is an article of faith, and for whom 'psychological types' and the 'four functions of consciousness' are undisputed blueprints of human nature, and yet these people have not read Jung's volumes on the archetypes or the types, and feel no compulsion to do so. Fundamentalist Christians often have the Bible beside their bed, but fundamentalist Jungians have the latest bastardised version of Jung at their bedside table, and they only approach Jung at second- or third-hand, that is, after he has been put through a New Age wash that makes him almost unrecognisable to serious readers of Jung.

Prophecy and science in the search for truth

Before reviewing the nature of Jungian fundamentalism, I would like to review the problem of fundamentalism *per se*, and in particular Jung's own views on this subject. In his essay 'The Spiritual Problem of Modern Man' Jung acknowledges that,

> Everything has become relative and therefore doubtful. And while man, hesitant and questioning, contemplates a world [of flux and change], his spirit yearns for an answer that will allay the turmoil of doubt and uncertainty.
>
> (1928/31: 177)

Since the so-called 'death of God', the collapse of Christendom and the overthrow of the old religious certainties, the modern person, or the person who is cognisant of the realities of the present, as distinct from the reactionary, the ignorant or the uneducated, is forced to live with a colossal existential and philosophical burden. The modern person lives in a time in which nothing can be taken for granted, everything is subject to questioning and doubt, and this plunges him or her into an existential anxiety which Jung assumes as the hallmark of the 'modern' condition.

We must endure this difficult critical period, and not terminate it falsely, artificially or prematurely with new or old answers. Living in the present requires a certain negative capability, and the normal ego is not good at this art, because of its innate need for security, or for illusions of security. And yet, quite fairly and reasonably, Jung acknowledges in the above passage that it is not just our ego that longs for security, but that our 'spirit' also 'yearns for an answer that will allay the turmoil'. There is, presumably, a right answer to be discovered, and truth to be encountered in the chaos of the times. Jung writes:

> We want to have certainties and no doubts, results and no experiments, without even seeing that certainties can arise only through doubt and results only through experiment. The artful denial of a problem will not produce conviction; on the contrary, a wider and higher consciousness is required to give us the certainty and clarity we need.
>
> (1930: 751)

Jung is not the radical relativist or open postmodernist that some scholars would like him to be. He clearly believes there is a way through and beyond the turmoil of the modern condition, but this way is not easy to find, and the dogmatic statements of any conviction or faith position will have to be rigorously tested by experiment, and refuted and denied if found wanting. However, he often indicates that a deep security can be found by 'a wider and higher consciousness'. Similarly, in his auto-biographical narrative he writes:

> To some extent I perceive the processes going on in the background [of the psyche], and that gives me an inner certainty.
>
> (1961: 355)

In statements such as this, Jung the scientist gives way to Jung the prophet, but this is no woolly prophecy, because prophecy and science have to work together in the pursuit of truth, to keep each other honest.

But the way to truth cannot be imposed by the wilful ego or super-imposed by outside authorities or institutions. Nothing can be trusted, for in a time of crisis, false prophecy is rife. Instead, we have to look for guidance from, and trust the direction of, the unconscious psyche, from whence true prophecy arises. But anyone claiming to have discovered the way must be greeted with healthy scepticism and doubt:

> When therefore a prophet appears at a moment's notice, we would be better advised to contemplate a possible psychic disequilibrium.
>
> (1928: 262)

The modern 'prophet' is as likely to be a madman as a prophet, precisely because the atmosphere of anxiety and uncertainty produces many curious specimens for the psychiatrist's consulting room. In our time, we are peculiarly vulnerable to the eruptions of the unconscious, and what first arises from this realm may be pathological and tortured, rather than prophetic and truthful. But Jung offers this very helpful clarification:

> I would not deny in general the existence of genuine prophets, but in the name of caution I would begin by doubting each individual case; for it is far too serious a matter for us lightly to accept a man as a genuine prophet. Every respectable prophet strives manfully against the unconscious pretensions of his role.
>
> (1928: 262)

Once again, this passage shows that Jung is an interesting mixture of prophet and scientist, or believer and sceptic. He believes there is 'genuine' prophecy to be found, but he is not especially confident about our ability to capture or articulate it. Genuine prophecy is possible, and we can live our lives in the hopeful expectation of receiving it, but it is rare, difficult to discern, and we must not smugly assume that it will always spring forth just because we are in desperate need.

Living with uncertainty and the necessity of problems

Meanwhile, Jung writes, we are saddled with many problems of a personal, social and cultural kind, and we have to remain faithful to these problems and not avoid them through fundamentalism or any other 'ism' that offers instant relief from our difficulty:

> The psychic life of civilized man is full of problems; we cannot even think of it except in terms of problems. Our psychic processes are made up to a large extent of reflections, doubts, experiments, all of which are almost completely foreign to the unconscious, instinctive mind of primitive man.
>
> (1930: 750)

Our naivety and childlikeness, however, would have us cling to unconsciousness, and refuse to encounter life's difficult problems and choices:

> Everything in us that still belongs to nature shrinks away from a problem, for its name is doubt, and wherever doubt holds sway there is uncertainty and the possibility of divergent ways. And where several ways seem possible, there we have turned away from the certain guidance of instinct and are handed over to fear. . . . Every one of us gladly turns away from his problems; if possible, they must not be mentioned, or, better still, their existence is denied. We wish to make our lives simple, certain, and smooth, and for that reason problems are taboo.
>
> (1930: 750–1)

Fundamentalism is the chief culprit here. It attempts to make our lives 'simple, certain, and smooth'. It erects taboos against the questioning mind and asks us to accept ready-made answers. It promotes fixed opinions and rigid stereotypes, and avoids change by adopting programmes which screen out the real problems. As such, fundamentalism must be considered anti-Jungian, since for Jung the pursuit of truth must always transcend the ready-made formula, including his own. Responding to problems, dealing with complexities and making hard decisions are the very things, according to Jung, which build human character and give vitality to our consciousness:

> It is the growth of consciousness which we must thank for the existence of problems; they are the Danaan gift of civilization. It is just man's turning away from instinct – his opposing himself to instinct – that creates consciousness. Instinct is nature and seeks to perpetuate nature, whereas consciousness can only seek culture or its denial.
>
> (1930: 750)

Avoiding cultural and personal regression

Jung concedes that at difficult times in history the temptation to revert to the past, to return to old patterns and stereotypes, is enormous. But such temptations, delightful or easy as they may be, must be resisted. Facing difficulties and problems is not glamorous and not comforting, but we are saddled with them and must accept the fate that comes with them. We have been thrust forward in history, away from the innocence of the primitive or primal state, and away from the pure instinctuality of early humanity. We cannot go back, but must move forward with the evolutionary thrust of history:

> Problems draw us into an orphaned and isolated state where we are abandoned by nature and are driven to consciousness. There is no other way open to us; we are forced to resort to conscious decisions and solutions where formerly we trusted ourselves to natural happenings. Every problem, therefore, brings the possibility of a widening of consciousness, but also the necessity of saying goodbye to childlike unconsciousness and trust in nature.
>
> (1930: 751)

Jung goes on to suggest that our plight in the midst of problems, doubts and fears is actually the existential and human experience of our Fall from Eden. To want to rid ourselves of problems is to want to recover that first, original Eden, but this is neither possible nor desirable. We must battle onward and accept the fate that has befallen us.

> This necessity [of saying goodbye to childlike unconsciousness] is a psychic fact of such importance that it constitutes one of the most essential symbolic teachings of the Christian religion. It is the sacrifice of the merely natural man, of the unconscious, ingenuous being whose tragic career began with the eating of the apple in Paradise. The biblical fall of man presents the dawn of consciousness as a curse.
>
> (1930: 751)

According to Jung, there is something driving us onward which has to be honoured and respected. In the name of this future vision, this teleological goal, pain and difficulty in the present must be endured. To avoid pain or to abandon difficulty is to abort the future and to stifle its development. We suffer so that the unknown that is drawing us onward can be realised. The present uncertainty is a kind of holy uncertainty, an uncertainty willed by fate and compelled by destiny. Humanity may experience this difficulty as a curse, but it is merely the limitations of consciousness that compel us to this negative assessment of the evolutionary current of the human spirit.

It therefore seems appropriate that a New Age movement that calls for a return to Eden, a going back to the womb-state of unconsciousness, a return to bliss and ecstasy, should promote a simple fundamentalism as its basic intellectual position. If its goals are effortlessness and ease, reduction of tension and heightening of comfort, then this would manifest philosophically as a return to 'trust in nature' and 'the security of instinct which knows no problems'. To realise this trust, and to consolidate this security, 'Jung' will be seized upon, appropriated and misrepresented. Ironically, the thinker who is himself opposed to fundamentalism will be used in the service of the New Age vision to promote a new kind of fundamentalism. Jung's theory of archetypes will be adopted and adapted to make the longed-for cultural regression possible. The archetypes will be the new laws or commandments, written in stone, as a sort of modern-day equivalent to the Mosaic laws which were brought down from Mount Sinai. Only the new laws will not be brought down from on high, but dredged up from below, from the unconscious.

In this way, Jung's provisional and experimental researches are constructed as articles of faith, and his open and ongoing theories are interpreted as final, revealed truths. Jung himself anticipated such dogmatic and inflexible uses of depth psychology:

> Modern thought has had to come to terms with Einstein's relativity

theory and with nuclear theories which lead us away from determinism and border on the inconceivable. Even physics is volatizing our material world. It is no wonder, then, in my opinion, if modern man falls back on the reality of psychic life and expects from it that certainty which the world denies him.

(1928/31: 182)

In some New Age and other Jungian groups around the world, to suggest that Jung's work contains many fascinating insights, but is hardly the last word on either the archetypes or the structure and dynamics of the psyche, is met with incomprehension or emotional resistance. In local Jung clubs and societies everywhere, a kind of inflexible Jungian fundamentalism has grown up which is completely antithetical to the spirit of Jung. To introduce intellectual criticism and an atmosphere of doubt or questioning is to risk ostracism. To contradict received opinions, or to challenge belief in the 'solidity' of archetypes, is regarded as heretical. But Jungian fundamentalism is itself the true heresy.

Elements of Jungian fundamentalism

In the literature to date, only Andrew Samuels has employed the term 'Jungian fundamentalism', and he has used it in the context of clinical identity and professional training. A kind of fundamentalism, he says, is evident in some of the training programmes, in the structures that control who and what is in or out, and in the unreal idealisation of Jung. For Samuels, fundamentalism is expressed in a narrow-mindedness that promotes Jungian thought at the expense of other psychodynamic theories, and in an exclusive emphasis on 'the Jungian way', which serves as an excuse to ignore 'the worlds of ideas, politics, the arts or religion' (1998: 21). This could also be called professional chauvinism or tunnel vision. But because my concern here is not with professional Jungian culture, but with the use and dissemination of Jung in the wider public domain, I seek to broaden the term 'fundamentalism' to refer not simply to narrowness of outlook or partisan vision, but to conceptual rigidity and epistemological arrogance.

I think the term 'Jungian fundamentalism' is appropriate in several ways. First, it suggests America, from whence most, but not all, popular Jungian fundamentalism derives. America is the home of Protestant fundamentalism, a movement that literalises scripture and insists on the historical inerrancy of the statements of faith. American national psychology will be the subject of the following chapter.

Second, 'fundamentalism' is appropriate in terms of the dogmatic and inflexible use of various Jungian terms, even if these terms have been transmitted mainly through colloquial assumptions, hearsay, and gossip, rather than close reading of the collected works. This popular discourse asserts that key Jungian terms such as 'archetypes' and 'the collective unconscious' are somehow bedrock, written-in-stone concepts, rather than useful or working terms that were put forward by Jung in the spirit of scientific adventure and endeavour, and which, in the spirit of science, were intended to be updated, revised or even discarded upon further enquiry and investigation. Fundamentalism reifies the Jungian terms and concepts, elevates them far beyond their experimental status and employs them as *de facto* articles of faith.

Third, 'fundamentalist' is appropriate in terms of the abolition of all uncertainty, openness and mystery in Jung's writings. The fundamentalist voice is a voice of insistence and stridency, and a voice particularly assertive about the supposed spiritual rewards that must result from following Jung's path of self-realisation into the realms of wholeness and holiness. If we are to go down this path, the fundamentalist must feel completely assured that he or she will 'get something out of it', that 'it will be worthwhile', and that 'you can depend on it'. He or she will want to be more than adequately compensated for their trouble, for their reading, their commercial investment in the tapes, books, workshops, therapy sessions. There is always a 'value for money' component in the popular dissemination of any philosophy, outlook or worldview. There is little room for experimentation, for trying out, for waiting and seeing, for admitting that some parts, even the whole framework, could be wrong.

Fourth, and following from this, we find the popular Jungian discourse 'fundamentalist' in the sense of obliterating all poetry, metaphor and symbol from Jung's thinking and constructions. Jung prefaces most of his conjectures and conclusions with a metaphorical 'as if'. In his writing he speaks 'as if' a God or Goddess were erupting from the psyche and seeking recognition and respect from the human person. It is 'as if' this myth or that legend were insinuating itself, revealing itself from the depths of psyche. This 'as if' dimension is sometimes overtly stated, but at other times it is absent, although implied in the context of his writing. The fundamentalists erase the metaphorical 'as if' and replace it with definite assertions about the concrete existence of psychic and archetypal contents, which are viewed as 'hard wiring' or 'genetic codes'.

Significantly, both Jung's academic enemies and his popular admirers tend to get rid of the metaphorical 'as if' – the one to condemn him for impossible mysticism, the other to elevate him to messianic status. Either way, Jung's terms are treated like literal things, and their supposed 'presence' is seen as evidence of unfounded essentialism by intellectuals, and of reassuring spirituality by popular readers. In the New Age, it is important that the constructs of psyche are viewed as literally real, so that we can be buoyed up by them when we feel down. The psychic figures must be 'there' to greet, meet and support us. Thus, any intellectual challenge to this belief system is regarded as an act of psychological vandalism, and responded to with high levels of aggression and emotion. The Jungian fundamentalist despises the Jungian intellectual because he or she takes the fundamentalist out of the comfort zone that is used as a defence against real thought.

It is typical for New Age Jungian literature to capitalise all the Jungian nouns, including archetype, collective unconscious, active imagination and so on. The capitalisation of these nouns gives the pleasant sense that they are solid, reliable and real. We can rely on them in a kind of false or phony way, as soon as they are reified and capitalised. One example almost at random is the following description of active imagination by the American populariser Robert Johnson:

> The essence of Active Imagination is your conscious participation in the imaginative experience. This kind of imagination is active because the ego actually goes into the inner world, walks and talks, confronts and argues, makes friends with or fights with the persons it finds there. You consciously take part in the drama of your imagination.
>
> (1989b: 140)

This sounds exciting to untrained ears, mostly because it seduces us into believing that the human ego can make its presence felt in the unconscious, and rearrange the situation there to suit the ego's needs and dreams of power. This dream of power needs to believe that it is making a difference with 'real' psychic existents. The idea of the ego 'going into the inner world' is a Jungian metaphor, to be grasped at the metaphorical level. The inner world is a fluid, ambiguous concept, but in the popular literature it loses all fluidity and becomes as real, and as do-able, as an excursion into a Disney theme park. Johnson capitalises Active Imagination, so that we can be sure that what he is talking about actually exists.

In actual practice, active imagination is extremely difficult, often messy, and rarely works well, mainly because the ego gets inflated by the possibility of involving itself with the inner world and moving things around to its own satisfaction. The usefulness of active imagination in the service of individuation and life integration is still problematical, yet Johnson presents it as a sure-fire winner. In my experience, active imagination attracts the same kind of people who are interested in 'lucid dreaming', another technique where the ego is encouraged to impress its own will upon the unconscious, rather than learn from it and be directed by it. Hillman advocates an entirely passive response to the unconscious, while Johnson suggests that the ego must impress itself upon the unconscious. Neither approach approximates to the subtlety and complexity of Jung, where the ego and the unconscious interact with each other and change each other irrevocably.

Typical of New Age Jungian writing is the confident tone that compels us to buy the idea or concept because we are being shown how to take control of our inner lives: 'You consciously take part in the drama of your imagination.' Johnson's book has the subtitle *Using Dreams and Active Imagination for Personal Growth*. But personal growth consists partly in growing beyond the ego that believes it knows best. The ego that enters the inner world like a tourist, seeking to walk and talk, adventure and roam, is often destroyed by the unconscious because it is a fraud. Personal growth has been Americanised to mean that the ego always wins, that our innate powers are realised, that the dangerous animals are behind bars, that the Disney officials are always standing by to help us, and that the animals we 'fight' are the ones we can beat. Above all, the journey is always entertaining, an encounter with real monsters and forces who know their own names, who are designated with capital letters, who remain the same, and who can always be successfully integrated. I often enjoy reading what Johnson writes, because he strives so hard to be understood by many people, but in his simplification and packaging of Jung for general consumption he runs into the typical problems.

Fundamentalism and Jung's conservatism

Most importantly, the fundamentalist sensibility is used to promote a backlash against modernity, and especially against feminism, and to support a project of cultural regression. Once we have the so-called 'fundamentals' that can assert what the psyche or society is 'really like', or should be like, and even a metaphysical base to support these assertions, we then set about to prop up the psychological structures, political forms, gender categories and social stereotypes that modernity has challenged and that are (often quite rightly) collapsing around us. The anxiety that asserts the need for fundamentals is the same anxiety that asserts the need to return to the past, to go back to times which were apparently more stable, to recover periods of history where men and women knew their place, and acted confidently in accordance with that knowledge.

If Jungian psychology is perceived to be offering psychological building-blocks and archetypal foundations, then it is a veritable goldmine for people who feel uneasy about change, and who wish to provide 'spiritual' support for outmoded ways of being. This point is especially significant, because with so much popular Jungian activity in this backlash mode, social commentators and scholars have come to assume that 'Jungian equals conservative', and that Jungians are by definition opposed to social change. Gender studies scholar Kenneth Clatterbaugh asks, if Jungian work is made to put the seal of approval upon conventional social forms, how can Jungian work ever support or promote social change (1990: 101)? Commenting on the political damage done in Australia by Jungian books on men's spirituality, Terry Colling writes:

> most of these popularist [Jungian] books seem to point men in a regressive direction, calling upon them to reconnect with archetypal male images that have little relevance to modern society or to issues of gender equality.
>
> (Colling 1992: viii)

Andrew Samuels, writing in the post-Jungian field, finds himself driven to assert that:

> Those in the men's movement who look to classical Jungian psychology to provide a theoretical underpinning for what they do and feel will be as disappointed as those in the women's movement were to find that Jungian psychology can often be ahistorical, essentialist, confused between contemporary description and eternal definition, and profoundly conservative.
>
> (1993: 191)

I agree with Samuels that in the fields of gender and sexuality Jungian categories and understandings can be ahistorical, confused and eternalist. I have written elsewhere about this problem, where I explore confusions in Jung's writings between rigid stereotypes and sacred archetypes (Tacey 1997). But my own view is that 'archetypal theory' itself need not necessarily lead to conservative attitudes or backlash programmes, and that such uses of the theory may be profoundly misguided, as I will explore in a moment.

As Samuels often argues, and as I explore in *Remaking Men*, Jung is most conservative in matters of sexuality and gender identity. Jung acknowledges this in his memoirs, in a curious admission:

> By way of compensation, I think, I am conservative to the bone.
> (1961: 358)

Although the theory of archetypes is not necessarily conservative, since it allows for variation and for the influence of the world and experience on archetypal formations, it may be the case that Jung has applied his own theory in conservative ways. I believe he may have misused the theory of archetypes whenever he wanted to lend weight or 'scientific' support to his deeply conservative views on sexuality, gender and society. We therefore need to rescue the theory from its author, as the theory appears to be bigger and broader than its author. If Jung's conservatism has provided a basis for the fundamentalism of New Age Jungians, then a work of deconstruction is called for, to divest the basic theory from the social prejudices or biased attitudes that have hitherto been attached to it and presented to us as a package deal. Archetypal theory today is in an appalling state, and a major task of future research is carefully to unpack and examine the entire field of archetypal discourse, which has been made muddy and unclear by popular misrepresentations.

Saleable Jungian commodities and hard-wiring

The field of gender and sexual identity is favoured by American New Age Jungian fundamentalists. This immediately suggests that in our gender and sexual identity we are most desperately uncertain, vulnerable and in need of mythological reinforcement. The fundamentalists generally assert that only the male Gods are for men and boys, whereas Goddesses are the models for women and girls. This neatly sexist categorising flies in the face of history and cosmology, since it is known that the devotees of Dionysus, for instance, were both men and women, and the followers of the Goddess Athena were mostly men. But fundamentalists like to be definite about their boundaries, and so the Gods are tied with blue ribbons and presented to men, and the Goddesses are adorned with pink and presented to women. But archetypes are by definition universal, which means they are found everywhere where psyche is present. The Gods do not stop at an artificial boundary called 'gender', and they pay no homage to artificial and culturally constructed boundaries. As Samuels has rightly discerned, 'The nostalgia, the yearning . . . for this orderly world in which men and women have their place, is a totalitarian longing' (1993: 191).

I do not know what Robert Bly's intentions were when he wrote *Iron John: A Book About Men*, but the effects of this book were, I believe, ultimately regressive for men, and harmful to the Jungian field. This book offers men the vain hope of becoming bigger, stronger and firmer than they are. Reading *Iron John* is like swallowing Viagra: it gives the mental phallus, the male mystique, a sudden erection. For men with flagging self-esteem or a confidence which has been battered by life or challenged by feminism, it gives the reassuring boost of confidence, and all backed up by powerful archetypes and the theories of Jung. Bly uses archetypal discourse as a way of avoiding the psychological and emotional dilemmas of the modern male, who is faced with the difficult task of learning how to live without the masculine props and mystique that have supported the traditional male of the past.

The spiritual challenge that confronts men today is to take off the male mask of prestige, power and strength, and to experience the 'weaker' side of their character, which contains feeling, emotion, sentiment and insight. Unless men can manage to disidentify from the masculine persona, there can be little healing of the wounds that have been inflicted on themselves, women, the earth and indigenous cultures. Just at the point where men are beginning to sense the terrible inadequacy of their artificial masculine protest, and – at the same time – where feminism is beginning to bite and to have real impact on male culture, Bly comes up with a narrative about Iron Hans that lifts men out of their vulnerability and suffering, and shows them a way back to traditional masculine 'health' and well-being. Bly sees men 'hurting' across the Western world, and he arrives on the scene with a Jungian balm that will stop the pain and link men again to their 'real' natures, to the so-called inner masculine or 'deep male'.

In this way, Jungian archetypal theory can be used as a way of restoring patriarchy and of avoiding social change. The archetypal dominants of our time are working to dislodge the oppressive and tyrannical patriarchal structures that have ruled Western consciousness for hundreds of years. Progressive forces in society and in psyche have been striving to overturn rigid structures and to release the archetypal feminine into consciousness and culture. Jung, Neumann and von Franz write continually of the need for change and transformation, of the potential wholeness and healing that can arise if the repressed and unconscious forces of Western history are admitted into our lives. Jung believed that our 'civilisation is in transition', and that

We are living in what the Greeks called the *kairos*, the right moment, for a 'metamorphosis of the gods', of the fundamental principles and symbols. This peculiarity of our time, which is certainly not of our conscious choosing, is the expression of the unconscious man within us who is changing.

(1957: 585)

One could hardly wish for a more resounding endorsement for social change. Jung is virtually announcing that his psychology exists partly to help us to understand social change and to come to terms with it. Knowledge of the archetypes and of the self-regulatory function of the psyche can help us make sense of our situation, and approach times of difficulty with some nobility and self-respect. For change naturally brings uncertainty, doubt and stress. Change forces us to walk away from what we already know, and to embrace what we do not yet know.

Contrary to this spirit of experiment and enquiry, the New Age Jungian literature teaches us to sink back into the forms and stereotypes we already know. Bly restores men to their 'true' nature, and co-workers such as the Jungian analyst Robert Moore and writer Douglas Gillette offer men Jung's theory of archetypes as a way of returning to the past and of feeling supported by metaphysical entities:

As students of human mythology, and as Jungians, we believe there is good news for men. It is our experience that deep within every male are blueprints, what we can also call 'hard wiring', for the calm and positive mature masculine.

(Moore and Gillette 1990: 7–9)

New Age Jungianism constructs Jung as a benevolent Santa Claus, with good news and candy for all readers of the popular literature. The good news is that we do not have to worry too much about the confusing mess we are in with regard to gender and sexual identity. We can forget the mess and just sink back into the unconscious and recover the 'hard-wiring' that is already there for our use and support. Society has simply forgotten that this hard-wiring exists, and the task of Jungian psychology is to make it available and accessible again.

In *Women Who Run with the Wolves*, Clarissa Pinkola Estes invites women to develop a similar kind of faith in invisible supports:

To find the Wild Woman, it is necessary for women to return to their instinctive lives, their deepest knowing. Let us shed any false coats we have been given. Don the true coat of powerful instinct and knowing.

(1992: 21)

This is wonderfully seductive and attractive to modern readers. Books that offer this kind of illusory solace sell hundreds of thousands, and even millions, of copies. Such commercial success makes the authors of these books rich, but it makes the Jungian field itself very poor. Because Jungian psychology is not just about illusion, but about psychic reality. The reality is that life is never this easy, and never has been this easy. Jung insists that 'the certain guidance of instinct' is no longer within reach of civilised humanity. We cannot simply relax back into the arms of instinct, because consciousness has thrown up many problems and obstacles that have to be dealt with. Jung's psychology is adamant about this point: there can be no easy way out of the modern dilemma, and yet here we have a Jungian analyst telling us to abandon ourselves to the realm of instinct.

Typically in the New Age literature, the knowledge of the frail and merely human ego is seen as 'false' knowledge, while that which comes from the instincts is seen as 'true' knowledge. Estes invites us to *return* to our instinctive lives and deepest knowing, but what could 'return' mean in this context? Jung has said that there was never a time in history when we had hold of all the answers and were possessed of a 'deepest knowing' that liberated us from the pain of choice, tension, error and brokenness. Not since we were expelled from Eden have we had the option of collapsing like a child into the arms of an adoring sacred parent. Clarissa Pinkola Estes, along with the New Age for which she speaks, is asking us to return to Eden. This is the primary fantasy of New Age philosophy: the belief in the recovery of a golden age, a former time when men and women knew themselves, their place in society, and thus had little stress or tension to cope with.

The call to such a 'return' is not only anti-Jungian and illusory, but it is also anti-social and even anti-human. Jung argues that our human destiny forces us to face 'the necessity of saying goodbye to childlike unconsciousness and trust in nature' (1930: 751).

He writes of the necessary 'sacrifice of the merely natural man', and of the importance in accepting, even embracing, 'an orphaned and isolated state where we are abandoned by nature and are driven to consciousness'. 'There is no other way open to us; we are forced to resort to conscious decisions and solutions where formerly we trusted ourselves to natural happenings' (1930: 751). This side of Jung is completely overturned and thrown out by the American New Age Jungian fundamentalists, who make their fame and fortune precisely by advocating that a return to Eden is possible, that abandoning ourselves to Mother Nature is still viable, that avoiding the pain of rupture and the agony of brokenness is an option, if only we could hand everything over to the collective unconscious and the archetypes. This is delusional thinking, and my guess is that the writers of this literature know it is delusional.

American fundamentalism and the conservative backlash

Everywhere we turn today we see the same story: the false idealisation of the collective unconscious, the idealisation of instinct, the romanticisation of the past as a time of security and wellbeing, the nostalgic return to old patterns, old habits, old stereotypes, and above all, the spiritualisation of the old patterns and stereotypes. In today's society, people are prepared to give consciousness away, because it seems only to saddle us with problems and confusions. We are losing our nerve, and in this climate, all sorts of dangerous things become possible. One option is to seek the dissolution of our painful consciousness in drugs and mind-altering substances. If consciousness is not being valued or respected, then dissolving consciousness becomes a very real and dangerous option. But also we notice that the disregard for consciousness leads to an infantilisation of the individual and society. We do not accept responsibility for ourselves, but are all too willing to hand over responsibility to 'parental' entities, forces and powers (Adorno 1964).

It often seems to me that the popular Jungian attitude could well be smoothing the way for a future outbreak of fascism and mindless conformity. If the archetypes and instincts are anything at all, they are, as Jung so often stated, the opponents of individuality and free expression. It is astonishing to consider why so many American popularisers of Jung should represent the instinctive state as an ultimate one to strive for. Isn't America supposed to represent the ideals of freedom, liberty and democracy? Why should it be advocating the abolition of these hard-won values and freedoms? Why should it want to destroy the very thing that makes freedom and liberty possible? Jung wrote that 'The free sway of instinct is not compatible with a strongly developed consciousness' (1927/31: 55). In 'Instinct and the Unconscious' he said that instincts are resistant to education, opposed to change and generally intransigent: 'We must admit that the element of learning is sometimes totally absent.' Putting it even more directly, he wrote:

> Instinct is an essentially collective, i.e., universal and regularly
> occurring phenomenon which has nothing to do with individuality.
>
> (1919: 270)

We therefore arrive at some astonishing contradictions. The New
Age spiritual movement purports to be about individual expression,
spiritual freedom and self-realisation, but its deepest impulses are about
the abolition of individuality and freedom, and the dissolution of the self.
Similarly, the American nation is meant to stand for freedom, liberty,
fraternity, but among its deepest impulses is the desire to extinguish
individuality in the acid-bath of collectivity. Hence the terrible, even
nauseating idealisation of the 'Collective Unconscious', about which Jung
has this to say:

> I call the collective unconscious 'collective' because it is not made
> up of individual and more or less unique contents, but of those which
> are universal and of regular occurrence.
>
> (1919: 270)

Perhaps it is in America, the Land of the Free, where people experience
most acutely what Jung called the 'orphaned or isolated state of consciousness'? Perhaps it is in America, where individuality is consciously and
forthrightly espoused, where people are most sorely beset by the nostalgia
for Eden, for lost innocence, for the ancient past – for anything, other than
the difficult present. With one part of its mind, the American psyche puts
forward and advocates the values of the independent will and the
individual spirit. These are the 'advertised values' of the American ideal.
But with another part of its mind, there is a radical compensation. It is as
if the values of the individual spirit and the independent ego call forth
opposite values in the soul: the values of collectivity, conformity and
standardisation. The nation which dedicates itself consciously to freedom
longs to be bound, grounded, unfree, because of the dreadful isolation and
alienation that the independent spirit brings.

Jung sensed this during one of his few trips across the Atlantic. In
'The Complications of American Psychology', Jung wrote about the
astonishing 'defencelessness of the individual against the onslaught of
[collective forces]'.

> In America, the overwhelming influence of collective emotions
> spreads into everything. If it were possible, everything would be
> done collectively, because there seems to be an astonishingly feeble

resistance to collective influences. It is true that collective action is always less laborious than an individual attempt. The momentum of collective action carries much further than even concentrated individual effort, since it makes people unaware of themselves and heedless of risks.

(1930: 957)

Given these facts, it is difficult to know whether in the popular Jungian literature we are being presented with Jungian psychology or with American psychology. I think we are being presented with American psychology, with its characteristic idealisation of collectivity, its romanticisation of instinct, its high regard for conformity and its nostalgic attachment to Eden and the Garden, and that all of this is being dressed up as 'Jungian thought', simply because it is being presented in Jungian terms and concepts. American psychology is merely using Jungian psychology to promote and further itself.

What we have to ask the American popularisers of Jung is this: How do we know that instinct would run the psychological show better than our confused consciousness? At least consciousness struggles to be ethical, even if this lapses at crucial moments. Instinct, however, is nonethical, or as it were, pre-ethical. Ethics are simply not on its mind. As Jung has said, 'Instincts share with reflexes their uniformity and regularity as well as the unconsciousness of their motivations' (1919: 270). Instinct seeks its own ends, smoothly and automatically, and this takes us back, historically, to the brutality and unconsciousness of pagan times. No matter how much confusion and doubt consciousness affords us, we have to continue to support it, because it has been willed by fate, and we finally have no choice but to affirm it, and to refuse the simple romance of 'returning to our instinctive lives'.

The regressive restoration of the patriarchal persona

In the American Jungian literature on the psychology of men and masculinity, we notice an astonishingly powerful backlash against feminism, and a desire to champion the 'masculine mystique' almost as if patriarchy were a sacred rite that feminism is attempting to desecrate. I have already referred to the profoundly conservative works by Robert Bly, Robert Moore and Douglas Gillette, but in their wake have emerged a new tradition of books that celebrate the patriarchy as if it were a sacred cult to be preserved at all costs. This new tradition includes works such as *Like Father, Like Son* (Vogt 1991a), *Return to Father* (Vogt 1991b), *Absent Fathers, Lost Sons* (Corneau 1991), *At My Father's Wedding* (Lee 1991), and *Fatherson* (Collins 1994), all of which represent the father in a wildly idealising light. Of course it is true that men need the father to complete their individuation. But somehow men cannot separate their individual psychic needs from the needs of society and the world. When men feel the need to connect with the father archetype, they tend to want to see the father idealised and promoted in society at large. James Hillman is engaged in this same process, and it is deeply disturbing and socially dangerous.

It is far too early, historically, to call for a 'Return to Father' (Vogt 1991b). We have hardly begun to separate ourselves and our society from this most oppressive and difficult archetype, when some Jungians are calling for the dignity of the father to be restored. We have hardly begun to open ourselves and our society to the feminine, before 'archetypalists' are calling for a restoration of the stability of the past. What we must learn to do at this critical time is separate archetype from social stereotype. It is fine for men to yearn for a connection with the father, but as soon as this becomes a desire to reconstitute the past or to restore the cult of patriarchy, we can say that this yearning is regressive, has become literalised, and is psychologically derailed.

We are losing our nerve and long to be embraced again in father's arms. We have glimpsed a new world, and desire to go back to the old. Jung says that a typical human reaction to the revelation of the unconscious is to deny that we have seen it at all. He speaks of this as a 'regressive restoration of the persona', and he roundly condemns this timid and escapist approach to psychic reality, in which outmoded appearances are restored. It seems that today's society is attempting a regressive restoration of its patriarchal persona, because it hardly knows how to cope with the powerful archetypal and feminine forces that have recently been unleashed. Jung speaks of a terrified man who seeks to pretend that his encounter with the unconscious never took place:

> If he tries to patch up his social reputation within the confines of a much more limited personality, doing inferior work with the mentality of a scared child . . . then, technically speaking, he will have restored his persona in a regressive way. He will as a result of his fright have slipped back to an earlier phase of his personality; he will have demeaned himself, pretending that he is as he was *before* the crucial experience.

(1928: 254)

This could be a description of the late modern world, which has been profoundly shaken by several major revolutions: black rights, women's rights, indigenous rights, children's rights, civil rights, post-colonial rights, all of which have necessarily worked to destabilise the ruling patriarchal dominants of collective consciousness. But the social-political patriarch has weathered these and other storms, and is seeking to make a come-back. He asks us, like Clinton or Nixon, to forget his misdemeanours and to remember him as he was *before* the crucial experiences. He asks us to take him back into our confidence, to accept him on trust, to admire his good looks and charisma, and to believe in his capacity to unite and inspire the community. There is a flag-waving, celebratory, forgiving mood in the community, which has had enough of change and would like to return to the way we were. Samuels writes of 'the nostalgia that has swept America . . . and Germany' (1993: 190), and this nostalgia is not innocent, but is thoroughly dangerous, because so much social reality and experience is being swept aside, repressed, forgotten or ignored.

When the father re-emerges with his old charisma and his 'father knows best' appeal, we can forget about the revolutionary struggle against oppression and dictatorship. When the archetype takes on a new, rosy glow, we forget about the heinous crimes of the historical-social father and his systematic mistreatment of blacks, women, children, the indigenous, the land, colonial societies and earth's natural resources. The father re-packages himself as ecologically sensitive, politically correct, caring for others and regretful of past wrongs, but actually little or nothing has changed. The Pope in Rome apologises for the misdeeds of the ancient past, but meanwhile a thousand new or continuing crimes go undetected and unrecognised. It is simply that the media advisers and the spin doctors have spruced up the external image of the political or religious patriarch, and have given him good advice about how to be 'in touch' with the times. When the archetype becomes reactivated, there is a great temptation to idealise the father as all-knowing, wise, benevolent, but the temptation must be resisted, lest we lapse back into a fiercely rigid conservatism where everything patriarchal takes on a mystical shine just because it is traditional and therefore stable.

Political fascism depends upon the mystical glow of socially engineered archetypes. Fascism usually takes on the role and demeanour of the all-knowing, all-powerful sacred parent, and submission to this sacred parent, like submission to instinct or archetype, is constructed as a sacred task and national or racial duty. By renouncing human responsibility and choice, we are drawn back into an ancestral-spiritual vortex, we are suddenly reconnected with the spiritual roots of our nation, our gender, our race, or whatever force or thing is being mythologised, and we are willing to commit any crime or act on behalf of the mystical-ancestral symbol, whether this be conceived as Fatherland, Motherland, or any other primitive construct of the mythic imagination. How incredibly easy, it often seems to me, it would be to enlist popular, fundamentalist Jungian psychology in an outbreak of fascism, to use this theory as an excuse for massive cultural regression.

Reification of archetypes and magical thinking

I want to return now to the New Age interpretation of Jungian archetypes, since so much of the confidence and optimism at the heart of the new fundamentalism is based on the belief that the archetypes are simply 'there' to hold us when we fall, to support us when we are down, and to rebuild our personalities when we are broken. All New Age versions of Jung engage in the reification and idealisation of archetypes. The need for moral and spiritual absolutes is such that we have to be 'absolutely' certain about the existence of archetypes. Men are offered the archetypes as 'hard-wiring', a useful, practical, 'real man's' metaphor, while women are introduced to them as if they were top models or show girls in an American beauty pageant. Jean Shinoda Bolen, for instance, can confidently assert in her *Goddesses in Everywoman*:

> Archetypes exist outside of time. . . . The Greek Goddesses are images of women that have lived in the human imagination for over three thousand years.
>
> (1985: 22–3)

What marvellous news to the New Age consumer! We can simply go shopping in the collective unconscious, and pick up the Greek Goddess who most suits our needs for sexual and human identity. The fantasy is that they have been held in suspended animation for over three thousand years, just waiting for me to pick one up, take her home and introduce her to my friends.

It is true that the archetypes 'as such' exist outside of time, but according to Jung these archetypes are, for this very reason, completely inaccessible to us and outside the range of human experience. All we can know are the 'effects' of the archetypes in time and culture, and these effects, contrary to New Age ideology, are shaped by history and conditioned by culture and time. The Gods and Goddesses are simply not available to us today as useable models, as if all we have to do is add water, stir, and then they come to life for us again. For Jungian analysts to insist that they can be employed in this way represents a deliberate travesty of the work, for popularity and financial gain.

Jung's archetypes are presented in the popular literature as useable 'things' which are reliable, solid, predictable and secure. But in Jung's writings, the archetypes are numinous, liminal, fluid and extremely difficult to grasp. They are not fixed or solid objects, but are mercurial, tricksterish and indeterminate. If we compare this situation to theoretical physics, we might say that for Jung the archetype is close to the descriptions of quantum mechanics: it is imponderable, complex, processual and dynamic. At one moment, the smallest element of matter can be described as a wave, and at another moment it is just as surely described as a particle. In the realm of microphysics, as in the realm of the psyche, relativity holds sway, there is an 'Uncertainty Principle', and what is perceived is itself determined by the perceiver and shaped by the act of perception.

By contrast, New Age discourses try to pretend that the archetypes are like Newton's predictable building blocks of matter. New Age spirituality is not modern or postmodern, but rather it hankers after a premodern cosmology which is out of date and of merely nostalgic or illusory usefulness. Newton is preferred to Einstein, because Newton gives the illusion of absoluteness and solidity, even though we know today that all that is metaphysically solid often melts into air. For the New Age, history does not exist, and nor does geography exist. Time and space are equally illusory, so that it is easy to imagine that the modern woman in California can seriously contemplate basing her personality on 'archetypes' that are derived from an ancient Greek civilisation that is three thousand years old. For the popular discourses, the archetypes are frozen in time: they are the same today as they were in ancient times, and they will be the same in the future.

The archetypes are widely believed to be in a state of suspended animation, in a remotely eternal dream-state, removed from the exigencies of time or space. They are the same in Australia as they are in China; they are the same in ancient Greece as they are in modern America. This is why the archetypes can be 'collected' in handbooks based on the Gods and Goddesses of ancient Greece, and then sold to the reading public as viable models. The New Age believes that the archetypes are non-incarnational and do not participate in the world of creation. Therefore they are not influenced by the march of time or the revolutions in society, because they issue forth from a metaphysical realm which knows nothing of time, change or relativity. Clearly, such unhistorical and anti-incarnational archetypes are oblivious to social mores, tastes and changing moral values. This is why 'spiritual' people in the New Age movement can afford to be so ignorant of history and so uninterested in political realities, because the reality that they are linked to is perceived as eternal, unhistorical and apolitical.

Jung distinguishes between the pure archetype *an sich* (as such), as a numinous, borderline concept, and the 'archetypal image', which refers to the manifest expression of the archetype in human and cultural experience. Following Kant, his philosophical mentor, Jung differentiates between a noumenal and a phenomenal world, and he argues that the noumenal is ultimately metaphysical, about which we can know little and assert even less.

> The archetypal representations (images and ideas) mediated to us by the unconscious should not be confused with the archetype as such. They are very varied . . . and point back to one essential 'irrepresentable' basic form. The latter is characterised by certain formal elements and by certain fundamental meanings, although these can only be grasped approximately.
>
> (1947/54: 417)

We certainly cannot rely on our descriptions of the noumenal, or depend on their accuracy, because they are at best shots in the dark, ways of encompassing or articulating mystery. We can only 'know' what takes place in the phenomenal world, and therefore much of our investigation of the archetypes has to be confined, rather modestly, to this world. However, like Kant, Jung did not wish to erase the noumenal just because reason could not understand or grasp it. Rather, the noumenal, in this case the pure archetype, remains as a 'regulatory ideal' (Kant), an ideal which can be postulated but never taken for granted. According to this philosophical view, life might work better if we assume the functional reality of these entities, even though their 'existence', in any material or even metaphysical sense, can neither be proved nor disproved.

The New Age production of Jung ignores the Kantian complexity of his theory of archetypes, and cares little for academic distinctions between 'archetypes' and 'archetypal images'. According to the popular view, archetypes are archetypes, and no qualifications are accepted or entered into. The 'myth' of archetypes is already well established, and no amount of scholarship is going to convince people that archetypal theory is infinitely more complex than they realise. When Jung makes statements about archetypes, there is a metaphorical 'as if' dimension that qualifies everything he says, and this 'as if' dimension, which situates Jung in the modern and even postmodern intellectual traditions, and which prevents him from regressing to magical or premodern thinking, is simply jettisoned by the New Age, which wants the ease and delight of magical thinking.

The New Age ignores the theory of the 'archetypal image' because this theory places too much emphasis on culture, history and time, and detracts from the absolute and pristine authority of the archetype as eternal law. The New Age would be bitterly disappointed by Jungian theory if it took the time to find out more about it, because it is too individual, too relativist, for New Age taste. The totalitarian element in the New Age is wary of individuality; it likes its Gods in uniform, and it likes metaphysical things to work to predictable formulae. Samuels writes in *Jung and the Post-Jungians* that at first glance Jungian theory appears to offer a regimented and predictable view of the psyche. It may seem that 'the enormous stress laid on what is held in common [in Jung's theory] could limit individuality'. However, he says, there is a 'balance between the innate and the unique'. 'From the very beginning of archetypal theory, there is a concern for individuality and for personal experience' (1985: 25–7). The archetype does not annul personal experience and substitute for it the miraculous imprint of the divine mind or Platonic Idea. Rather, according to Jung, the archetypal and the numinous can only make itself manifest and felt through the particularities of individual and historical experience. This is a life-friendly theory, and not otherworldly. Jung's archetypal theory is a psychological answer to Blake, who wrote: 'Eternity is in love with the productions of time' (1793: 151). In the New Age movement, however, things work in reverse: time is in love with eternity, and time does not see the 'point' of itself, and longs to dissolve itself in the archetypal embrace of the eternal.

The archetypal 'image' concedes that the eternal 'archetype' is always radically modified and conditioned by history and society, and the eternal can only be known, ultimately, through its phenomenal manifestations in time, place and history. This is too intellectual and difficult for the New Age, which likes to believe that the eternal is a pristine, formed 'reality' which simply punctures the veneer of time and space and hands us models and values as if written on tablets of stone. In Jung, the idea of a fixed, unchanging, eternal inventory of archetypes and Gods is an impossibility; at best a convenient or lazy fiction, at worst a delusional system of thinking. Jung insisted that the content of archetypal images is not inherited, not mystically passed across the threshold from eternity into time, but that the content 'is variable, subject to environmental and historical changes' (Samuels 1985: 25). This means that Jung's theory of archetypes is more worldly and less mystical than the New Age can understand, and more worldly and historical than many of his critics are prepared to realise.

Chapter 6

American expansion and the limitless self

I chant a new chant of dilation or pride.
Whitman (1855: 53)

I am larger, better than I thought,
I did not know I held so much goodness.
Whitman (1855: 159)

America, power and the unholy hunger for God

Finally, it is worth enquiring more specifically into the relationship between America and power. Why are all the popular, grandiose, inflated versions of Jungian psychology American? One simple response is to say that Americans invented the New Age, so America would necessarily give us the New Age production of Jung. Another is to say that America popularises every idea or theory that is capable of popularisation, and Jung's attractive vision necessarily gets caught up in this process. However, why is Jung twisted specifically toward the production of spiritual power and personal empowerment in America?

The great American pathology, it often seems to those of us who are not Americans (and perhaps to those who are), is its intoxication with power, with being the first at everything and the best in the world. From the beginning of its formation, America has been strongly attached to fantasies of greatness, and to dreams of power, which have become integral to its sense of purpose on the world stage and to its sense of destiny. As Jung wrote in his 1930 essay, 'The Complications of American Psychology':

America is perhaps the only country where 'greatness' is unrestricted, because it expresses the most fundamental hopes, desires, ambitions, and convictions of the nation.

(1930: 976)

In the same essay, Jung said that 'many Europeans are infected by feelings of inferiority when they contact America and meet her heroic ideal' (977). But the heroic ideal readily turns ugly if it is not checked or balanced, if it is not self-limiting, and if boundaries are not drawn around it. This point, about the potential ugliness and danger of the heroic mode, and its need to be curtailed for the sake of wholeness and civilisation, is the point that Joseph Henderson made well-known in his famous analysis of the hero cycles of the Winnebago Indian myths in Jung's *Man and His Symbols* (1964). That essay, written before the phenomenon of the American New Age, becomes all the more important from the historical and prophetic point of view. When heroism becomes unlimited and endless, it spills over into pathology and inflation. The taste for greatness can rapidly degenerate into grandiosity if this greatness is not counterbalanced by a keen sense of social responsibility, human compassion and political reality.

But from the beginning of its settlement by Pilgrim Fathers in search of the New Jerusalem, America has had an extraordinary hunger for God. One could argue that the search for God, for Ralph Waldo Emerson's transcendent plane, for Whitman's cosmic sacredness, for William James's religious experience, is more primal to the American psyche than power itself. In America, God comes before power, and human power is merely an offshoot of divine power. This is the perspective which is overlooked by James Hillman in his *Kinds of Power* (1995), but it is grasped fully by Harold Bloom in his major work, *The American Religion: The Emergence of the Post-Christian Nation* (1992). Harold Bloom argues, like William James before him, that Americans do not want second-hand religion. As Walt Whitman sings to his American readers:

> You shall no longer take things at second or third hand . . . nor look through the eyes of the dead. . . . nor feed on the spectres in books.
> (1855: 33)

Americans do not want to know God at second or third remove, from Jerusalem, Rome, Dublin, Canterbury, Iona or Athens. They do not even want to know God from churches or authorities in New York or Chicago, because they have a real hunger to know God in their hearts and personal lives. They do not want their spiritual knowledge from priests or books, but want to know the sacred immediately and to apprehend it directly.

They want to know God intimately and personally, and if they are to have gurus at all, they must be American gurus. This, I think, is part of the creation myth of America that forces people like Joseph Campbell and Hillman to forget their debt to Jung and Europe, and to pretend that they are the originators of their own ideas. In contrast to this heroic American usurpation of Jung, is the humble style of Robert Johnson, who constantly defers to Jung, telling the reader that virtually every idea came to him while working with 'Dr. Jung' in Zurich.

It is from the 'unholy' hunger for personal or direct experience of God that the American inflation or grandiosity arises, as it were, as a by-product of the religious hunger. As Harold Bloom realises, the true American religion is closer to *gnosis* than to traditional systems of religious faith or devotional worship. Christianity in America goes through an 'in-spirational' shift of focus, which is why so much American Christianity is Pentecostal, charismatic and experiential. It is not just about believing in the dark, but about experiencing in the light of a higher power. The gnostic urge to direct experience can often cloak itself in conventional form and costume, but underneath, at its core, such religiousness is mostly highly personal and individualistic. Americans cry out for dramatic conversion and transformational experiences, not just for routine Sunday gatherings. Clearly, this hunger for personal experience has a double effect. It makes religion vital, personal, unique, and gives it a distinctively cogent flavour, even if those outside the circle of transformational life find the experience distasteful, fanatical or bizarre.

Dissolving into the divine

But the American ego, desperate for first-hand contact with the sacred, has a tendency to lose its moorings in consciousness and to be dissolved in the fluid realm of the collective psyche. This dangerous tendency toward self-dissolution in the archetypal matrix is all the more real and actual because, as a New World nation, America lacks the historical grounding in reality that is experienced in older, more established nations, such as the European countries. The zest for the divine has a disorienting and destabilising effect, and this fluidity creates a lack of inner security and groundedness. My own sense is that Americans actually compensate for this lack of inner security by developing large and grandiose dreams of power, status and strength. American largesse and grandiosity is to some extent a product of what Alfred Adler called the 'masculine protest', a tell-tale, compensatory reaction-formation to felt but barely understood inner weakness.

Most of these internal dynamics are projected outwards upon the face of the world, precisely because they are so profoundly unconscious. Hence American politics, economics and foreign policy is always preoccupied with identifying and tracking perceived enemies, saboteurs or destroyers. The American ego is always sure that someone or something is bent on destroying it, if only this someone or something could first be found out. An enormous amount of energy and capital is directed into national security, international policing and surveillance organisations, and the great national task is to search for and destroy the public enemy.

Jung captured this dilemma in a memorable passage:

> Always he imagines his worst enemy in front of him, yet he carries the enemy within himself; a deadly longing for the abyss, a longing to drown in his own source, to be sucked down to the realm of the Mothers.
>
> (1912/52: 355)

America's worst enemy is not Russia, or Cuba, or Nicaragua, or Iraq, or Islam, or spies from overseas or aliens from outer space, but itself. Its enemy is its own lack of self-definition, its disregard for psychological and spiritual borders, limitations, restrictions and barriers.

Dissolving into collectivity and responding to New World space

In its rush toward the archetypal and numinous field, America throws itself headlong into the matrix, and has to suffer the terrible consequences of dissolution into 'collectivity', which is the distinguishing character of the collective unconscious. In his 1927 essay 'Mind and Earth', Jung comments on the lack of boundaries and proprieties in American public life:

> The almost total lack of privacy and the all-devouring mass sociability remind one of primitive life in open huts, here there is complete identity with all members of the tribe. It seemed to me that American houses had their doors open all the time, just as there are no hedges round the gardens in American towns and villages. Everything seems to be street.
>
> (1927: 95)

Some of this detail strikes me as incorrect, but the point is taken. The lack of proportion or boundary, Jung argues in his 1930 essay on America, 'is positively terrifying' (1930: 957). Jung does not, somewhat surprisingly, go on to make a psychological analysis of the absence of boundaries, but confines his remarks to the social and political arena. But he does suggest a lack of definition in the psychic structure of this young country, and remarks that, 'A nation in the making is naturally a big risk, to itself as well as others' (1930: 980).

In human development, the problem of not respecting boundaries or borders is the problem of the infant, not of the mature adult. Hence Count Keyserling's pronouncement, which Jung quotes, is peculiarly apt to this discussion: 'America is fundamentally the land of the overrated child' (cited in Jung 1930: 932). In his *America Set Free*, Keyserling comments on the vastness of the American land-mass, and he speaks about the vastness and greatness of the American human spirit that has moved into and filled out these spaces:

> America's very spirit is one of width and vastness. The spirit of width and vastness is similar to that of Russia and Central Asia, and entirely different from that of Europe.
>
> (cited in Jung 1930: 927)

The vastness of American geographic and psychic space has the double or paradoxical effect of creating openness, boundlessness and freedom, and yet of crushing the human element in this same open space. There are few moorings for the psyche to hold on to, as most of the moorings of the old world have been rejected or overcome in the enthusiasm to enter a New World of unlimited opportunity. There is the freedom to do what you like, but one cannot do as one likes, because of the fact that the human ego, the agent of free will, loses its definition in the vast primal sea, and gets swept along willy-nilly in the currents. In America, writes Jung,

> The overwhelming influence of collective emotions spreads into everything. If it were possible, everything would be done collectively, because there seems to be an astonishingly feeble resistance to collective influences.
>
> You are simply reduced to a particle in the mass, with no other hope or expectation than the illusory goals of an eager and excited collectivity. You just swim for life, that's all.
>
> You feel free – that's the queerest thing – yet the collective

movement grips you faster than any old gnarled roots in European soil would have done.

(1930: 957)

Here Jung's comments on the American psyche echo in sentiment, and even in precise wording, D.H. Lawrence's comments on his Australian experience:

You feel free in Australia. And so you do. There is a great relief in the atmosphere, a relief from tension, from pressure. But what then?

(1923: 24)

Jung comments that the collectivity of America

has a decidedly flattening influence on people's psychology.

(1930: 957)

D.H. Lawrence writes that in Australia,

The instinct of the place was absolutely and flatly democratic.

(1923: 18)

These great masters of literature and psychology, both writing in the early decades of the twentieth century, are making exactly the same analyses of the psychic problems of New World countries. Here in Australia, we know the 'American' problem only too well: limitless space, openness, freedom, and yet the human psyche cannot take full advantage of this freedom because it loses form and definition in the face of it (Tacey 1995: 35–50). The human person feels free, and imagines himself to be free, and the evidence of his surrounds tells him he is free, but in fact the forces of collectivity and conformity cut across our so-called freedom, and the human will is driven to the wall.

We Australians subscribe to a cultural mythology that says we are rebels and battlers, that we despise authority and desire to go it alone, but the facts show that the reverse is true: we are probably among the most conformist and standardised people in the world. We have a vast and distant land, with open horizons extending in every direction, but we choose to huddle together in mega-cities around the coast. We celebrate the bush but rarely go there, we sing folk songs about rebels, bush rangers and roaming swagmen, but rarely question authorities when we are told what to do.

America and Australia: taking-over, or over-taken by, psychic space

Yes, the American problem is also the Australian problem, which is partly why I am so fascinated by these issues. But I am also fascinated by the opposite nature of the national responses. Faced by the infinity of psychic and geographic spaces, the typical Australian response is to become despondent and depressed, to feel crushed or over-taken by the psychic spaces that yawn before the human ego like an unfathomable abyss. On the other hand, the typical American response is to be buoyed up and elated by this same expansiveness, to see it as a great opportunity for human development and enterprise. Australian literature is mostly a literature of despondency, nihilism, despair and tragedy. American literature, however, is optimistic, positive and richly affirmative of the human endeavour. In his 'Phenomena Resulting from the Assimilation of the Unconscious', Jung speaks about these opposite kinds of human responses to the unknown. In some patients, he writes, the encounter with the unconscious

> produces an unmistakable and often unpleasant increase in self-confidence and conceit: they are full of themselves, they know everything, they imagine themselves to be fully informed of every-thing concerning their unconscious, and are persuaded that they understand perfectly everything that comes out of it.
>
> (1928: 221)

But then,

> Others on the contrary feel themselves more and more crushed under the contents of the unconscious, they lose their self-confidence and abandon themselves with· dull resignation to all the extraordinary things that the unconscious produces.
>
> (1928: 221)

These typical responses, Jung argues, reflect a lack of human stability and a loss of balance and equilibrium in the relations between the ego and the unconscious.

> The former, overflowing with feelings of their own importance, assume a responsibility for the unconscious that goes much too far, beyond all reasonable bounds; the others finally give up all sense of

responsibility, overcome by a sense of the powerlessness of the ego against the fate working through the unconscious.

(1928: 221)

Jung acknowledges that these two modes of reaction represent 'crude extremes', and that a 'finer shading would have been truer to reality'. The same can be said for my attempt to apply these modes to the national psychologies of Australia and America. Obviously, I am making huge exaggerations in order to develop an argument, but I think the exaggerations are worth considering. Jung's model is all the more exciting for our national typologies, when he asserts that each mode of reaction secretly hides the opposite mode within itself.

> If we analyse these two modes of reaction more deeply, we find that the optimistic self-confidence of the first conceals a profound sense of impotence, for which their conscious optimism acts as an unsuccessful compensation; while the pessimistic resignation of the others masks a defiant will to power, far surpassing in cocksureness the conscious optimism of the first type.
>
> (1928: 222)

Here is an interesting key to some of the complexities of the national characters. America has a 'conscious optimism' and a very visible and robust self-confidence, but it conceals 'a profound sense of impotence', for which the assertive optimism acts as an 'unsuccessful compensation'. In the United States, the popular New Age hype and human potential discourse is certainly an unsuccessful compensation against the epidemic of depression, inertia and chronic fatigue found everywhere in America today. The New Age spirituality movement cannot be fully understood outside the American psychosocial context in which it first emerged. Part of the reason why it appears so overweening, so over-the-top, so devoid of psychological balance and human grounding, is because it is a kind of spiritual protest against the barely articulate but nevertheless felt sense of human impotence. The New Age movement is a spiritual antidote to American depression, and as such the soaring optimism can only be understood as an attempt to get America out of the doldrums, where it so often finds itself. I will return to this theme in a moment.

On the other hand, Australian despondency and negativism is also a kind of mask, as Jung suggests. It masks a 'defiant will to power, far surpassing in cocksureness the conscious optimism of the first type'. Although consciously espousing a basically downcast, resigned or negative view of the world, Australians secretly long to become the biggest and the best at everything, especially at competitive team sports and the Olympic games. The great delight of Australians is to beat the Americans at their own games: at baseball, football, netball, motor racing, tennis and so on. At times, the laid-back, casual, no-worries Australian psyche can suddenly burst forth with an astonishing will to power which can terrify even the Americans. Hence the Australians present a puzzling picture to the rest of the world: the literature and high culture is imbued with values of resignation and despair in the face of apparently impossible odds. The landscape is 'bigger' than we are, and frequently defeats us in elemental outbursts of flood, drought, fire and natural calamities. The Australian humour is the opposite of the American humour. Ours is down-beat, ironic and often self-deprecating; American humour is assertive, bold and self-confident. But the Aussie battler is secretly a superman beneath his bush disguise, and he sometimes shows this in almost irrational bursts of heroic achievement and high striving.

Jung correctly diagnoses boundary-problems in relation to his own patients:

> The arrogance of the one and the despondency of the other share a common uncertainty as to their boundaries. The one is excessively expanded, the other excessively contracted. Their individual boundaries are in some way obliterated.
>
> (1928: 225)

Although developed, fostered, manufactured and devised in America, as a product of American soaring optimism, the New Age movement is doing very well in Australia, and is far more successful here than many realise. Consciously and outwardly, most Australians berate and despise the New Age, but after bad-mouthing it they find themselves ineluctably drawn toward it. All major bookstores in Australia report significant and growing sales in New Age books, music and products. Most stores now have entire sections devoted to the optimistic discourses of the Mind/Body/Spirit movement. Many cultural commentators are dumbfounded and confused by this. It seems so profoundly un-Australian, as we pretend to be down-to-earth, pragmatic, practical and not in the least spiritual or cosmic in our attitude. But, as Jung recognises, this is merely an external mask, which belies the fact that, inside our shrunken rationalism, Australians are hungry and desperate for an expansion of the spirit that they recognise as quintessentially American.

Mental health, boundaries and borders

The counter-side of American optimism is discovered even in the inspirational New Age literature which is designed to boost American confidence. After flattering corporate America by declaring that it contains the best minds in the country, and that it has a finely differentiated and intense sense of power, James Hillman bursts out with the unexpected news that Americans are suffering from powerlessness and impotence. He writes:

> At the other end [of the spectrum] we find that hapless dejected disempowerment felt by so many in our nation who cannot find the words for their aimless despair, beyond vague mumblings about 'empowerment'. Empowerment has become the major catchword for barking people into the self-help and recovery booths at the therapeutic carnival.
>
> (1995: 13)

This is unexpected, because only moments earlier Hillman was telling his audience that it is the most powerful country in the world, and that in America 'power rules the roost'. 'Power is the invisible demon that gives rise to our motivations and choices', he said. But suddenly, power is more invisible and elusive than anyone could imagine.

> So many people today feel 'disempowered'. What is it they, and we, are asking for? Where and why has the power gone that once filled the dream of better times in a better land? Is psychology the place to go to be reempowered? Can individual citizens together with their support groups in sessions taking place all over the country by the hundreds of thousands every evening of the week 'find the power'?
>
> (Hillman 1995: 13)

Having raised these problems and questions, Hillman drops them immediately, because he senses that they will depress his readers, who may not dial his Currency Connection, or buy his inspirational tapes and future books, if they tire of his voice. His job as a New Age writer is to keep the readers high and buoyant on big ideas, great insights and amazing possibilities. The New Age writer must keep the reader entertained, stimulated and away from morbidity. The American power-complex wants to be told how big and wonderful it is, not how small and impotent it is.

All Hillman will concede is that 'the soul is desperately seeking the power of mind to be applied to the powerlessness it experiences' (1995: 18). He then devotes the remainder of *Kinds of Power* to 'the recovery of a sense of power in American society'. Having expressed the problem for a moment, just long enough to scare readers with the prospect of their own impotence, he goes on to talk about cure, recovery and the way back up. A Jungian analyst who had not joined the New Age would have a different approach. He would point to the way down, into the unconscious, away from the defence mechanisms that keep psychic reality at bay. He would not seek to pander to the illusions of omnipotence, recovery and invulnerability. But Hillman knows that America has no desire to face its own internal psychospiritual nightmare. To tell the truth has little or no market value, because people prefer to hear flattery and lies about themselves. As Jeremiah rages: 'The prophets prophesy falsely, and my people love to have it so.'

The cure of depression and powerlessness is not to encourage mania and escapist fantasy, but to go down deep into the depression, and to shore up the ego against the inundating tide of the turbulent unconscious. The cure of chronic depression is to recover our sense of human boundary, and to live comfortably and realistically within the human limits that have been allotted to us. This is what the Old World can still teach the New World: not to be so greedy, lustful and ambitious. Life is lived properly when it is lived humbly within certain realistic limits. When that takes place, we neither soar off into the ether in manic transcendence, nor do we sink into the terrible and soul-destroying depths of the collective unconscious. To be unbounded in joys and ambitions means also to be unbounded in despondency and despair. The hypermania of New Age spiritual fantasy is simply the flip side of depressive psychosis. To know our own limits, to remember our humanity in the face of the infinity of psychic space, is to recover our sanity and restore our mental health.

Walt Whitman, an American, a kosmos

> I dilate you with tremendous breath, I buoy you up.
> (Whitman 1855: 81)

It could be that to find the true father of the American New Age, we should look not to Jung or Gurdjieff, but go further back in time, and remain on American soil, to consider the case of Walt Whitman. I once asked the poet Robert Bly, who was visiting Australia, what he thought the real difference was between Australia and America. He said: 'We have Whitman, and you do not.' It is a poet's answer, yet I accepted it as insightful and useful.

The nearest poet to Whitman we have in Australia is Les Murray, who is cautiously celebrative, affirmative and at times incantatory. But many of the nineteenth-century Australian poets, such as Lawson, Boake, or Adam Lindsay Gordon, lost themselves to depression, despair, alcoholism, suicide and self-torture. The vastness of the land and the hugeness of the psychic space had a disintegrative impact upon their consciousness. Australian poets, until recently, were not able to reach out into the vastness and contain it, or even cope with it.

Walt Whitman, on the other hand, in his classic 1855 volume *Leaves of Grass*, was able to announce to his fellow Americans that they were to expand themselves to correspond to the size and proportion of the continental land-mass. If they could not reach beyond themselves to encompass an equivalent greatness, then the greatness of the land would be experienced as negative or monstrous. Whitman wrote in his prose introduction:

> The largeness of nature of the nation were monstrous without a corresponding largeness and generosity of spirit of the citizen.
>
> (1855: 6)

'The United States themselves are essentially the greatest poem,' he declared, and the poets that would arise in this nation would be the 'greatest poets' on earth (5). Whitman gave precise indications about how the citizen and the poet were to expand to include such greatness:

> The poet's spirit responds to his country's spirit, he incarnates its geography and natural life and rivers and lakes. . . . When the long Atlantic coast stretches longer and the Pacific coast stretches longer he easily stretches with them north or south. He spans between them also from east to west and reflects what is between them.
>
> (1855: 7)

The poet is to include worlds and realms of experience that are vast and complex. If the poet is forced to contradict himself, it is because he is not confined to rational logic, but stretches to include the teeming life of creation:

> Do I contradict myself?
> Very well then, I contradict myself;
> I am large, I contain multitudes.
> > (1855: 96)

This poet announced himself confidently, as

> Walt Whitman, an American, one of the roughs, a kosmos.
> > (1855: 56)

Whereas the Australian response to vastness was to be over-taken by it, to feel weak and helpless before the infinity of new space, the American response was to 'take-over' psychic space and to declare themselves the masters of it. The human person would expand to become a cosmos; he would swell to fill the greatness that was manifest in the continental land-mass. But these spaces were not just physical, they were powerfully metaphysical as well. Most of Whitman's metaphors are spatial, but he is not simply mapping the geography of the American coastline, but the geography of the cosmos and of heaven and hell:

> Have you reckoned a thousand acres much? Have you reckoned
> > the earth much?
> Stop this day and night with me, and you shall possess the origin
> > of all poems,
> You shall possess the good of the earth and sun,
> there are millions of suns left.
> > (1855: 33)

Whitman has an almost intoxicating sense of plenitude and entitlement: 'there are millions of suns left'. There are worlds and realms of space just waiting for the taking. This is the opposite of restraint, propriety or humility. Whitman is giving full permission to the human being to take what he desires. Whitman is not concerned about existing ownership of these worlds, about indigenous entitlement to American land, nor about the prior claim on psychic space by God and the sacred. Restraint and proportion are merely hang-ups of the Old World, because people in the New World can have it all. Americans can become intimate with the infinity of God, as they become intimate with the land they have occupied. Whitman writes that

> The pleasures of heaven are with me, and the pains of hell are
> > with me,

The first I graft and increase upon myself, the latter I translate into
a new tongue.

(1855: 53)

The self 'grafts' upon itself the cosmic realms of heaven and hell, and as
a result it 'increases' in size and stature, or in other words, it becomes
American. The self or ego, as Jung would say, loses its human boundaries
and becomes God-like in its proportions. In fact, the self in this scenario
becomes bigger than God, and Whitman boldly announces the onset of
the American struggle with hubris and arrogance:

And nothing, not God, is greater to one than one's self is.

(1855: 93)

As no Australian could do, or would dare to do, Whitman takes leave of
normal human boundaries and is cast aloft on the wings of hubris:

I chant a new chant of dilation or pride.

(1855: 53)

I am larger, better than I thought,
I did not know I held so much goodness.

(1855: 159)

In 'Song of Myself', Whitman expands the self to include everything
in Manhattan and North America. The long, incantatory poem literally
dilates to include an inventory of all American history and all American
peoples, landscapes, events, things and objects. Stylistically, the sense of
abundance and fullness is expressed in the long, overflowing lines of
poetry, which can barely be contained on the printed page. America is vast,
and Whitman is the poet of that vastness, who deliberately seeks to inflate
himself to include it all. Whitman's method is to wander through the streets
of Manhattan, and the pathways of imagination, and to identify himself
with everything he sees. He knows the world by assimilating it to himself.
This means that his own form becomes ambiguous, fluid, amorphous:

To be in any form, what is that?
Mine is no callous shell,
I have instant conductors all over me whether I pass or stop,
They seize every object and lead it harmlessly through me.
I merely stir, press, feel with my fingers, and am happy.

(1855: 96)

The human self befriends and knows the world by taking it inside itself. 'Instant conductors' take hold of every object and 'lead it harmlessly through me'. This, once again, reminds us of infantile behaviour and psychology. The infant knows the world by putting its objects into its mouth, by testing, ingesting, devouring. Whitman knows the world by absorbing it: objects are befriended by being assimilated.

In this connection, a great many American pathologies become more understandable. American obesity and overweight is the bodily conse-quence of trying to take the world inside the self. American consumerism is the art of gaining power over the things and objects of the world. American excess is the art of expanding to include the world. American imperialism and foreign policy is the political consequence of expanding beyond the borders of the self and home territory. The American space programme, and the conquest of the moon, of Mars, of the galaxies, is this same centrifugal movement: forever expanding beyond the known to include and encompass the unknown. The American version of Descartes is this: I consume, therefore I am.

Who need be afraid of the merge?

Whitman enjoins Americans to lose their innate, human fear of merging with the divine. We have an innate fear of inflation, and it expresses itself as conscience (realising we are merely human), as guilt (Promethean shame in face of our theft of what does not belong to us), and as common sense (realising our mortality and our death as ultimate limitations). Whitman says these fears and resistances should be cast aside. He holds out his hand to Americans, and asks them to join him in his cosmic dance, in which he enters into the life of the divine:

> Who need be afraid of the merge?
> Undrape, you are not guilty to me, nor stale nor discarded.
>
> (1855: 38)

Inevitably, the classic image of the sea arises, as in New Age spirituality today, and spiritual endeavour is regarded as an immersion in the oceanic feeling:

> You sea! I resign myself to you also.
>
> (1855: 54)

In another poem from *Leaves of Grass*, Whitman confronts more directly the fear of death that underpins our fear of the sacred:

> Do you suspect death? If I were to suspect death I should die now,
> Do you think I could walk pleasantly and well-suited toward
>   annihilation?

> (1855: 114)

In one part of my mind, I find Whitman's invitation to enter into the divine inspirational and ecstatic. In another part of my mind, I read it as Satanic and demonic. He is actually playing the role of the serpent in the Garden of Eden. He is whispering into the ear of Americans, telling them to forget their learning and education and hang-ups. Forget what European religion and the God of their forefathers has told them. He is asking them to cast aside their puritanism and their fears of the body, of sexuality, and of personal cosmic expansion. Americans inhabit a New World now, and it is as if they are back before the Fall, and can have another go at relationship with the divine. Whitman is calling for a new religious dispensation. He is asking Americans to leave their state of exile and enter into full-bodied communion with God, as if the post-lapsarian state or the New Jerusalem were merely a thought away.

Whitman passionately believed that the American experience would give rise to a completely new experience of God. No longer other-worldly, up there, or beyond the clouds, God was to be experienced in the very material dimensions of all creation, especially in the human person. Just as the self was to be exalted in the image of God, so God would be felt in the lowliest and most ordinary places, even in the formerly taboo or indecent regions of bodily, excretory and sexual parts.

> Through me forbidden voices,
> Voices of sexes and lusts, voices veiled, and I remove the veil,
> Voices indecent by me clarified and transfigured.
> Divine am I inside and out, and I make holy whatever I touch or
>   am touched from;
> The scent of these arm-pits is aroma finer than prayer,
> This head is more than churches or bibles or creeds.

> (1855: 57)

Here we see very strongly the sense that personal experience is the true ground of religious experience for the American nation. The American sacred was to be revealed through immediate, personal, first-hand experience. This primal religious ground boasts that it is better than the old religiousness, it is 'finer than prayer', 'more than churches or bibles or creeds'. Jung would agree that direct experience of the sacred is more important to us today than second-hand knowledge through creeds or hereditary belief. But, and here is the curious twist in Jung's thought, he would say that creeds present a purer version of the sacred if the ego is in danger of contaminating the direct experience with its own power urges. If the ego subsequently imagines itself as divine, then personal experience is not finer than prayer or churches, but indeed it becomes considerably less than these traditional forms. If the direct experience becomes contaminated, Jung would advise against the personal journey and suggest that the individual return humbly to the life of the church.

Whitman's vision is clearly not Christian, for he does not see the need for a Redeemer or Messiah. The individual does not need Christ, for he has become like Christ, '[making] holy whatever [he] touches'. Today the world is clearly at the beginning of a post-Christian era, in which the traditional religious forms are no longer valid or attractive. We can make a leap into the Christification of the individual, where the individual can experience a personal relation to the sacred. But there are so many problems with this new religious dispensation that the old religious forms are starting to look very attractive once again. There are simply no guarantees against contamination and pollution of the immediate experience. It is one thing to affirm the radical presence of God in creation and in our lives, but quite another to lose altogether the vital distinction between ourselves and God. We have the hunger for intimacy with God, but not, it seems, the understanding or theology to make this intimacy viable. There is nothing in Whitman that gives me the confidence to believe that the new religious dispensation is actually workable.

At times, Whitman seems to be struggling to make a distinction between his human self, or ego, and his cosmic or mythopoetic self. For instance, he writes:

> My dinner, dress, associates, looks, business, compliments, dues,
> . . . or ill-doing . . . or loss or lack of money . . . or depressions
>   and exaltations,
> They come to me days and nights and go from me again,
> But they are not the Me myself.

(1855: 35)

These are interesting moments psychologically and philosophically. At times the sense of reality intrudes into the dream of cosmic expansion, and some distinctions are drawn. But overall I think Whitman fails dramatically in the task of separating the human from the divine, or the ego from the supraordinate Self. He has become intoxicated by largeness and excess, and in this mood, he cannot make a very compelling case for the maintenance of human boundaries.

In most of his later writings, for instance, such boundaries are collapsed, and the dark, morbid and pathological side of his vision becomes clearly apparent. In the 'Calamus' poems of the 1860s and beyond, his poetry becomes fatuous, portentous and flatulent. The poet is unable to distinguish any more between God and man, between the sacred and the profane, between sexuality and divine worship. His emphasis on the immanence of the divine leads ultimately to a cult of sexuality, and to a poetic imagination that can only be described as lavishly porno-graphic. The mood of the later poems is often one of orgiastic frenzy, indicating that Dionysus, the loosener, has seized hold of the poet, and that Christ, the restrainer, has been abandoned. Also, Whitman is unable to distinguish any longer between himself and God, and he makes claims for himself and his poetry that are simply embarrassing, if not downright sacrilegious. After the climactic heights of 'Song of Myself', the passage is mostly downhill for Whitman, except for a few rare gems and lyrics amid a sea of bad writing.

Inflation and Godlikeness is not just an existential or human problem, but a literary and artistic problem as well. Inflation destroys art by blowing it up with ridiculous claims and hopelessly unrealistic fantasies. Since inflation encourages formlessness, the art inspired by inflationary energies loses form and restraint. Whitman becomes virtually a parody of himself in his later poems, and his celebration of the body and the erotic becomes monotonously one-sided and unrelieved. The force that would withhold, restrain, hold back, has been swept aside in the mad rush toward oceanic bliss and the false holism of self-dissolution. But when the cosmic frenzy subsides, Whitman feels, predictably, hollow, empty and powerless. In his early preface to *Leaves of Grass*, he announced himself as belonging to the company of the world's greatest poets, and his self-expansion seemed limitless. But by 1888, in 'A Backward Glance O'er Travel'd Roads', we find a vastly different personality, one which is shrunken in size and import:

> That I have not gain'd the acceptance of my own time, but have fallen
> back on fond dreams of the future – anticipations – 'still lives the

song, though Regnar dies' – That from a worldly and business point of view *Leaves of Grass* has been worse than a failure – that public criticism on the book and myself as author of it yet shows mark'd anger and contempt more than anything else – And that solely for publishing it I have been the object of two or three pretty serious special official buffetings – is all probably no more than I ought to have expected.

(1888: 297)

The fierce turbulence of the cosmic tides has left him feeling washed up on the beach of life. Far from being the greatest poet ever, he feels unloved, humiliated and misunderstood. Despondency, inertia and depression is the flip side of overweening arrogance and hubris. The poet or person who expands to supernormal proportions has this terrible fate in store for him. When the cosmic high subsides, the person or poet feels less than human, and to be sure is less than human insofar as the normal ego has been wiped out by the intoxicating flood of energy. One could speak of a 'Whitman complex' in the American psyche, namely, a fierce swing from highs to lows, from cosmic pride to self-loathing, from great power to powerlessness and impotence. We find the Whitman complex in virtually every American guru or would-be guru. In every case, the problem is the same: the flaunting and mocking of the very boundaries that provide sanity and refuge from the cosmic storm. This is the fatal American disease.

All of us have to remember, I think, that the ego is itself archetypal, and it will always strive to separate itself from the cosmic sea and to dry itself out. In response to Whitman's question: 'Who need be afraid of the merge?' we could respond: the ego needs to be afraid of the merge. The ego is not only the representative of human life, and therefore the receptacle of our instinct for survival, but it is also divinely ordained and a symbol of the 'son' of God. It is important to God, therefore, that the ego is not drowned in the ocean of bliss. The ego is the psychological bearer of the task and responsibility of the incarnation.

Longing for return to the World Mother

But there are clearly different visions of the divine character. Insofar as God is 'father', the idea of dissolving in the cosmic sea is repugnant and abhorrent. God the Father does not condone an addiction to bliss, but enjoins us to work toward our salvation by enduring the trials and tensions of life in the world. The symbol of life under the authority of God the

Father is not the cosmic dance but the cross and crucifixion. But Whitman's God is not God the Father. This, I think, is why American Christian high culture could not condone his vision, and could not accept it as its own. Whitman's vision is clearly a vision of God as orgiastic Mother. It is a vision of God as ocean and infinity. His task is not the preservation of form through the maintenance of boundaries, but the dissolution of form through the abolition of boundaries. Whitman's vision is compensatory to Christianity, to puritanism, to propriety and restraint.

Given all this, it is understandable that American Christian high culture in the nineteenth century would view Whitman as an alien, an outsider, a danger to the social establishment. Whitman desperately wanted to be accepted as the poet of his nation, but his nation was clearly divided about his status. At the end of 'Song of Myself', he sang:

I too am not a bit tamed, I too am untranslatable,
I sound my barbaric yawp over the roofs of the world.

(1855: 96)

His 'barbaric yawp' is the cry for the Great Mother, in a world which was still consciously and overtly aligned with the Heavenly Father. Hence, mainly the counter-cultural impulses would take Whitman seriously and identify with his mission. The American puritanical consciousness would find him repugnant, and some clergymen went so far as to publicly burn and destroy his works. It was the visionaries and the ecstatics, the bohemians and drop-outs, who would adore Whitman and adopt him as their own. In the twentieth century, it was the beat generation who championed Whitman, including Allen Ginsberg, Jack Kerouac, and the 'dharma bums' of the west coast. Later, in the 1960s, the hippies discovered Walt Whitman and saw in him a leader of the generation that sought to drink the intoxicating milk of the Great Mother. Then, in the 1970s and 1980s, the New Age recognised in Whitman the voice of its own aspiration.

Whitman was perhaps the first New Ager, who sat facing west from California's shores, looking longingly across the Pacific ocean toward the majesty and exoticism of the mystic East.

Facing west from California's shores,
Inquiring, tireless, seeking what is yet unfound,
I, a child, very old, over waves, towards the house of maternity,
    the land of migrations, look afar,

> Look off the shores of my Western sea, the circle almost circled;
> For starting westward from Hindustan, from the vales of
>   Kashmere.
>
> (1860: 186)

This poem, 'Facing West from California's Shores' was written in 1860, precisely a hundred years before the hippies would sit on Californian beaches and dream of their passage to India (Toolan 1987). It was in the 1960s and 1970s that the Mother religions of Hindustan and Kashmir would be imported into America, packaged to suit New Age interests, and smelling of sandalwood and patchouli. But like Whitman, the Age of Aquarius would sample the Indian delights and discover, to their amazement, that they do not completely satisfy the Western spiritual need.

> Now I face home again, very pleas'd and joyous,
> (But where is what I started for so long ago?
> And why is it yet unfound?)
>
> (1860: 186)

I don't think I have ever met an American hippy or a cosmic New Ager who was able to say that he or she was satisfied, that he or she had found what they were looking for. There is always a shimmering goal ahead, which is not quite grasped and never really attained. The goal bobs out of reach, on the sea of cosmic bliss, because the goal is not attainable in human terms. The goal of this striving is full immersion into the womb-state of cosmic bliss and harmony. The drive is toward oneness with the Cosmic Mother, who becomes synonymous with India in the Western imagination. Whether India conforms to our Western projections is hard to discern, but for the Westerner, India becomes the carrier of the image of the Great Mother, it is the 'house of maternity', as Whitman announces. In the poem 'A Woman Waits for Me', written during the same period, Whitman writes:

> A woman waits for me, she contains all, nothing is lacking,
> I will go stay with her who waits for me.
>
> (1855: 167)

The Cosmic Mother 'contains all' and in her presence 'nothing is lacking'. Yet this embrace does not satisfy us and cannot satisfy us, because the Western task is to bring the Mother and the Father together into a greater whole, not merely to exchange one cosmic parent for the other.

America has come close to a great truth, but it has not come close enough. America realises that a new revelation of the divine is at hand. It realises that this revelation is incarnational and earthly, material and physical, sexual and immediate. It realises that this revelation exalts the human being as never before, and that we are to bear witness to God, eyeball to eyeball, in intimate and passionate contact, an encounter that radically transforms ourselves and God. And yet if we do not maintain our humanity in the midst of this intimate encounter with the sacred, our own potential divinity is lost as well. There is something profoundly wrong about the democratic spirituality which places humanity and God on the same level. We are not ready for this radical democracy of the spirit, and never will be ready insofar as we are part of the creation and not Gods.

Conclusion
The choice of wholeness

My conclusion to this work will be in two parts. The first will concern itself with the conflict between the archetypes of spirit and matter, or, in personified terms, God and Gaia. The New Age represents an untutored outburst of Gaia energy and interest at the end of the Christian era. All of us will have to attend carefully to the uprising of Gaia, and not simply leave it to exploitative and commercial forces in popular culture to attend to her. I do not believe, however, that Gaia is a completely separate deity, uniquely different from the Western God. For me, at least, Gaia is the feminine/immanental face of the divine, a face repressed and lost through patriarchal culture, and always present in the original experience of the Godhead.

In the second part of this conclusion, I will turn to the relation between the ego and the soul, and explore the present and future consequences of their encounter. In this context, I will explore the mythological idea of apocalypse, and the eschatological idea of a new age, as symbols of the state of human consciousness 'after' the encounter with soul. The New Age spiritual movement is a kind of parody of the post-egoic consciousness, a consciousness where ego has been displaced by soul, and where the human being is in deep relation to the cosmic substratum of reality. It remains to be seen whether the uprising of the sacred will cause the human ego to obliterate itself in the ecstasy of the cosmic source, or whether the ego can hold out against this seduction, and work toward a post-egoic state in which ego and soul become partners in dialogue and wholeness.

THE FUTURE MARRIAGE OF GOD AND GAIA

> Perhaps it would not be too much to say that the most crucial problems
> of the individual and of society turn upon the way the psyche functions
> in regard to spirit and matter.
>
> (Jung 1937: 251)

Going back to move forward

The New Age movement is in one sense a religion of nature. The
New Age merges almost effortlessly with ecospirituality, the worship of
nature spirits, paganism, pantheism and wicca (Crowley 1989). It is
also profoundly connected to the spiritual rediscovery of the body and its
energies and powers, as demonstrated in herbalism, naturopathy, acupunc-
ture, therapeutic massage, crystal healing, nutritional medicine and sacred
sexuality (B. Campbell 1980). In mythic or archetypal terms, it is a new
expression of the ancient religion of the Great Goddess and of Mother
Nature (Lovelock 1988). The New Age presents itself as an earthy or
holistic corrective to the disembodied, disconnected and transcendentalist
directions of mainstream patriarchal culture. Its 'holism' may be partial,
inadequate and expressive of an opposite kind of dualism in which
(spiritualised) matter reigns supreme, but it is nonetheless a real attempt
to compensate for what it perceives as a serious and debilitating one-
sidedness in Western culture and its major institutions (M. Ferguson
1981).

The New Age speaks for what has been repressed and denied in the
West. It correctly observes that our various religious traditions, including
Catholicism, Protestantism, Judaism and Islam, have become chiefly
identified with the sacred symbols and images of patriarchy, and that this
privileging of the masculine God has been detrimental to the Mother and
to the feminine face of God. For long periods of history, the West has
celebrated the Sky God, the Heavenly Father, the Word or Logos, the Law
of the Father, and, in the case of Christianity, the revelation of the Father
through the person of the Son. To some extent Catholicism has avoided
the problems of extreme one-sidedness by maintaining its tradition of the
Blessed Virgin Mary, and thus the image of an original wholeness or unity
has remained a distinct possibility. Protestantism has often intolerantly
claimed that Catholicism is idolatrous in its adoration of the Virgin,
thereby missing the point altogether of this vital religious tradition.
However, all Western religions have been alienated from sexuality, the
body and nature, i.e. from the earthly or non-celestial side of the Mother,

and to this extent even the Marian Catholic traditions have remained patriarchal. All Western religions have become dangerously imbalanced, and our religious future clearly lies, as the New Age correctly discerns, in a resacralisation of the natural realm, of the body, nature, matter, sexuality and instinct.

The New Age reflects a counter-cultural reaction against the abstractions, intellectuality and otherworldliness of patriarchy's symbolic order. As such, it has real legitimacy insofar as it expresses the life that has been confined to the collective unconscious while patriarchy has dominated the attitudes and style of our consciousness. However, the New Age goes wrong to the extent that it advocates a new one-sidedness to heal the old one-sidedness. It correctly reads the spirit of the times, the need to divinise nature and to reveal the sacred within the natural, but it lacks a guiding philosophy or an inclusive theology that might enable it to bring spirit and nature, God as Father and God as Mother, Logos and Eros, into a right relationship or an integrative wholeness. The New Age runs counter to the patriarchal symbolic order, but all it does, in one sense, is replace this with a matriarchal symbolic order. Historically speaking, it takes us back to the Great Mother religions of pre-Christian times, in search of a healing answer to patriarchy's desecration and despoliation of the natural realm. The Father God is overturned and discarded, while Mother Gaia is celebrated and revered.

To this extent, the New Age must be counted as a regression, but it is a 'sensible' regression, given the fact that patriarchy in its exploitative and progressive mode appears set to destroy the earth, its ecosystems and its biodiversity, unless the patriarchal juggernaut is arrested and checked by a conservative and environmentally defensive counter-will. In the face of such potential devastation and havoc, the appeal of the matriarchal religions of the past is enormous, and one can understand why the worship of the Great Goddess is gaining huge popular appeal, not only in eco-feminism and feminist spirituality, but also in popular environmentalism and the spirituality movement in the wider community. But we do not need to go back in time, we need to press forward and ahead, to move beyond patriarchy and not retreat to a pre-patriarchal era. We need to recover the ancient or primal perception of the world, but in an entirely new way, so that we might marry God and Gaia, or integrate the realm of nature and the realm of the spirit.

D.H. Lawrence put it memorably when he said that our civilisation needs to make a 'detour' back to the past, to recover the mysteries of nature and the sacredness of the body, but that this detour is for the sake of advancement, not for the sake of regression: 'We must make a great swerve in our onward-going life-course now, to gather up again the savage mysteries.' Lawrence insisted that this movement must not be a full-blown cultural regression, but must be a guided and fully conscious 'return' for the sake of revitalisation and wholeness. He was emphatic about this point: 'But this does not mean going back on ourselves. We can't go back' (1924: 144–6).

Christendom's inevitable demise: what we leave out will destroy us

Religions that identify with an exclusively transcendental concept of spirit, and subscribe to a negative view of nature and the body, are destined to be destroyed by history and time. Life moves naturally toward balance and wholeness, and nature will simply tear down and undermine whatever is constructed in opposition to it. If Western culture in general, and Christianity in particular, is currently being overwhelmed by the forces of instinct, sexuality, desire and materiality, this is only because Western culture decided to promote a concept of spirit that was antagonistic to nature rather than inclusive of nature. We have backed a spirituality which is bogus and ultimately self-destructive, since it leaves out more than half of creation from its view of the world.

Whatever is left out is relegated to the realms of the unconscious, where it gathers a kind of negative or demonic power, and eventually the repressed returns with a force that is as irresistible as it is destructive. Our patriarchal religious tradition has not only demonised nature, earth, body and sexuality in this way, but women and the feminine have also been demonised insofar as they have been constructed as opponents of the patriarchal experience of spirit. It is difficult for me not to assign gender categories to these archetypal forces, although I realise that some feminists find this practice objectionable. But gender is given with the very structure of these archetypes, and at this level we are not providing prescriptions about human behaviour, about how men and women ought to behave, but rather we are describing universal forces, mythic figures, or Gods.

In Western culture, masculine spirit and feminine nature are falsely constructed as antagonists or opponents in the field of the soul, and our culture is a battleground in which these forces constantly slog it out. This provides the archetypal background for the famous 'battle of the sexes' that dominates the social and political environment of Western societies.

Patriarchal religious traditions in the West consider themselves to be endangered by the feminist movement, the clerical ordination of women, the popular spirituality movement, and by the presence of homosexuality and unconventional sexual styles in the clergy. These popular political forces and movements not only exert social pressure on the patriarchal institutions, but they also carry enormous archetypal and spiritual authority as well, because they threaten the beleaguered structures of patriarchy with the authority of the repressed and what has been excluded. When nature is left out, it exacts its revenge by intensifying its instinctual claims on the human soul, and by forcing people, especially the clergy and 'men of God', to take on or express burdens of eros that are wholly unacceptable to the prevailing patriarchal standards and the ruling moral canon.

But nature also claims its revenge by making the patriarchal or traditional spirit appear suddenly 'irrelevant' to ordinary people's lives. Nature brings our human perception 'down to earth', and it makes the patriarchal spirit seem otherworldly and supernatural. When forced into a defensive posture, nature makes spirit seem so lofty, high and remote that ordinary people lose interest in it, sensing that it can no longer be connected to the ground of their experience. Because vast numbers of people have already decided that traditional spirituality is irrelevant to their lives, that they can throw off the encumbrances of religion as so much unnecessary baggage, we can justifiably claim that nature is winning its fight against spirit. Paganism ousted and reviled has returned triumphantly, and Christianity is now on its knees, having to admit not only that its flock has gone astray, but that some of its own clergy and ministers have been made victims of unintegrated sexual desires and unregenerate claims of the repressed body.

Our transcendental concept of spirit has peaked and is now in tragic but inevitable decline. Its climax was discovered in the late medieval period, but already in the Renaissance we witnessed the return of the pagan realm of nature and desire, which was responsible for the revitalisation of the arts and culture in that period. Nature and desire made a second great comeback in the Romantic movement, but it was contained and warded off by the advancing patriarchal consciousness. Possibly the last great peak of the transcendentalist and patriarchal spirit was found in nineteenth-century Victorian morality, an extreme social backlash against nature and eros which did incredible damage to the integral relationship between spirit and nature, and from which we are still suffering today. But in the twenty-first century, we can no more support our rarefied concept of spirit than we can hold back the tides of desire that sweep over and through our culture.

Jung and the emergence of the archetypal feminine

Jung died in 1961, some years before the New Age movement and its cult of nature had gained international momentum, and so he could not be expected to comment directly upon this social phenomenon. But Jung had already noted that the archetypes of the Mother, the feminine and nature were gaining enormous power in the collective unconscious, that this vast realm had been forcibly repressed under patriarchal consciousness, and that these archetypes were becoming actively constellated, as if in anticipation of a cataclysmic change (1912/52). Jung saw that the times demanded new and immediate focus on what the Christian tradition had neglected, repressed or thrown out (1928; 1933b). He was, after all, a Freudian for some years, whose psychology was preoccupied with the repressed forces of nature and eros that had been building up in the Western psyche. He had foreseen the rise of paganism in the Western psyche, and he had already identified this resurgent paganism as the archetypal source for twentieth-century fascism and national socialism (1946).

Jung had a positive mother complex, and this inclined him to many of the matriarchal arts and sciences that had been banned by the patriarchy, but which were already becoming available to the public in Jung's own day. Jung's interest in astrology and divination is well known, and he virtually single-handedly recovered the ancient art of alchemy to modern scientific and psychological scrutiny (1944). Jung was also ecological and romantically attached to landscape, earth, trees, long before these attitudes became celebrated and entrenched in popular ecology (1927/31). In Jung's time, ecological awareness was politely referred to as 'conservation', and this was generally the province of the politically conservative, not, as with the 'Aquarian Conspiracy', the counter-cultural and those interested in opposing the capitalist economy.

Perhaps more than Jung himself, his leading follower Erich Neumann was steeped in the awareness that the archetypal feminine was about to displace and challenge the archetypal foundations of patriarchy, as we can see especially in his classic work *The Great Mother* (1955) and also in *The Origins and History of Consciousness* (1949b). Neumann also wrote important essays on Leonardo and the mother archetype, on 'The Moon and Matriarchal Consciousness', and on the rise of the earth archetype in modern times, all of which bear prophetic testimony to the imminent emergence of the feminine face of the divine. More recently, Jungian analyst Edward Whitmont has devoted an entire volume, *Return of the Goddess* (1982), to the phenomenon of the awakening of the archetypal feminine and her phallic son-lover in the context of modernity and postmodernity.

Jung could see that the old, pre-Christian Gods and Goddesses were stirring to new life in the Western soul, and that these archetypes were often discovered in the psyche as the core nuclei of complexes and psychoneuroses. Jung was interested in the pre-Christian, the non-Christian and the post-Christian, but unlike the New Age he was not anti-Christian (1938/40). He did not suffer from anti-Christian prejudice, nor did he feel obliged, like James Hillman after him, to sing the praises of ancient Greece while denouncing the Jewish-Christian heritage. Jung was committed to the task of restoring the Christian God to cultural dignity and to human understanding. Jung could see that the one-sidedness of patriarchal religion and culture would constellate the awakening of compensatory matriarchal and feminine archetypal figures, but his response to these figures was always ambivalent. He felt we must encourage the archetypal feminine to present itself after centuries of neglect and repression. However, we can ill afford to allow the feminine to take possession of consciousness; it must be integrated and not allowed to dominate in a new, equally extreme and undesirable one-sidedness.

Jung would be critical if he felt that a new cult of Gaia, or the so-called Gaia hypothesis, would come at the expense of God the Father, the masculine principle, and the spirit. What would be the point, he would ask, of two thousand years or more of differentiation of the archetypal masculine, if we are prepared to throw it all out in a panic response to the plight of the feminine? Why must we head for a cultural *enantiodromia* (a swing from one extreme to another), when we have the opportunity to consider both sides of the archetypal spectrum? Why settle for a new one-sidedness when our deepest imperative, to ourselves and to our culture, is to struggle towards wholeness and unity? By all means bring on Gaia and bring back Demeter, but let us engage these archaic personalities in a meaningful dialogue with Christian spirituality and Western religion. While we are at it, let us also work toward a recovery of the lost feminine dimension within the Jewish-Christian God (as Shekinah, Sophia, Lillith, Mary, Wisdom and Holy Spirit). But in tossing out our cultural bath-water, Jung would warn that throwing out the baby Jesus would lead to full-blown repression of the masculine spirit, and to dangerous repercussions and consequences from the neglected or banished realm of the masculine.

Can Christianity be redeemed?

The history of Christianity is in one sense the history of our catastrophic failure to bring spirit and nature together, accompanied by unreal idealisations of spirit and heaven on the one side (as all-good, sublime, angelic), and equally unreal demonisations of nature and embodiment on the other side (as all-bad, demonic, satanic). Only some of the mystics and heretics struggled valiantly within the Christian tradition to resolve the warring dualities in their inward and contemplative lives, and these lives are now crucial and exemplary for the future development of religious life in the West. This is why so much creative scholarship is now being focused on figures such as Hildegard, John of the Cross, Meister Eckhart, and others who attempt to discover the divine in this reality, spirit in the mysteries of nature, and religious transcendence in the ordinariness of daily life.

This is also why there is such widespread public interest in Celtic Christianity, because the Celts refused to subscribe to the dualisms of official religion, and they adopted the view, inherited from their own pre-Christian pagan cosmology, that if the divine could be found anywhere at all it could be found in the mysteries and wonders of the natural world. But the public face of the church, and the institution of Christendom, upheld the so-called 'triumph' of spirit over matter, of the transcendent over the immanent, leading to the desacralisation of nature and the diminishment of the physical world's holy presence. The Christian concept of spirit remained otherworldly, unnatural and outside nature, impatient with embodiment, and squirming nervously to break free from the embrace of *matter* (which derives from the Latin *mater*, or Mother).

Jesus did not appear to be radically dualistic, but his culture, society and religious context were so, and when Paul took hold of the Jesus story, he recast it into a strongly dualistic mould. In Paul's letters and epistles, we find the meeting and coalescing of two cultural traditions of dualism: firstly from the Jewish world, with its radical separation of God and fecund nature, and secondly from late Greek philosophy, with its strongly patriarchal separation of mind and body, *nous* and *physis*, and *logos* and *eros*. Paul's message, however, may have been distorted by mistranslation and misconception of his meaning. Scholars of the New Testament assure me that Paul has been misrepresented by church traditions. Paul was attempting to contrast the life which is turned toward God in hope and faith with the life which is turned away from God in self-enclosure and narcissism. The state which is turned away from God, and which is overcome by sin, became identified with 'the flesh' and our libidinal or bodily nature. I believe that a sophisticated consciousness can deconstruct Paul's message in such a way as to preserve his essential point about the necessity of being turned toward God, without demonising the body in the process. The fallen or sinful element is clearly the hubristic or arrogant ego, and not the body and its sexual functions. Christianity urgently needs psychological insight to liberate it from its own dreadful literalism.

If Christianity is to have a future, it must attempt to represent itself as holistic and positively oriented toward creation. Wholeness must start at home by attempting to bridge gaps between sectarian traditions. Western Christianity will have to take the best of Protestantism and the best of Catholicism as it maps its future course. We will need a tradition (Catholicism), but we will also need a critique of that tradition (Protestantism). We will need Catholic substance, ritual and sacramentalism, but also Protestant principle, dynamism and vigorous criticism. It could be that the way forward is also, paradoxically, the way back. No religion that is entirely patriarchal can ever hope to speak to an age which is in dire need of ecological re-enchantment (Moore 1996b).

The way ahead will be simultaneously a recovery of the adoration of the Madonna and a return to the central importance of the feminine, not just in the virginal Mary figure, but also in the sensuous and transgressive Mary of Magdalene. The mystics and heretics will be rediscovered as exemplary figures who attempt in their own spiritual journeys an integration of the warring opposites that continue to conflict and rage within the official structures. And the mysteries of Celtic Christianity can be re-explored to suggest ways in which spirit and nature can coexist in an immanental Christianity that is not a mere regression to paganism (pantheism), but a genuine integration of the forces at work in the psyche and in the cosmos (panentheism).

The paradox of wholeness: the mystical marriage of Father and Mother

The secret of the present situation lies in paradox. We cannot persevere with patriarchy, not even for nostalgic or sentimental reasons, for patriarchy without checks or balances is lethal, as history and ecology has shown. We must aspire toward a higher condition of integration or wholeness, in which the advances of the patriarchal spirit are brought into a new relation with the natural realm. Wholeness, as Jung knew, is based on a dialogue or conversation between pairs of opposites, and in this case the so-called opposites are those of spirit and nature. Jung's method always involves breaking down the violent antagonism between the opposites and drawing them into a liberating state of interplay, dance or dynamism. This is his notion of how wholeness can be achieved, as we move from the stalemate situation of 'either/or' to the transformative position of 'both/and', an inclusive and revolutionary wholeness.

However, to shift from the stalemate of either/or to the possibilities of both/and requires archetypal support, and Jung feels that this shift is never achieved by human capacity alone. The archetype of the Self, the figure of wholeness, needs to be constellated, to facilitate a coming-together of the warring opposites. The Self, in turn, achieves its work by way of the 'transcendent function' (1916b), that function of the psyche that allows the opposites to be brought together and reconciled. Christians might say that the indwelling Christ allows them to gather together the pieces or fragments of life, so that they are made whole in the spirit. Jung's Self is also a divine or sacred force, which cuts across the human tendency toward splitting and dissociation, and institutes a new ethos or mode which is governed by wholeness and made possible by love. By way of a transforming love or eros, the various conflicting parts of the psyche are brought together and experienced as different parts of an indivisible and mysterious whole.

In terms of the development of our civilisation, clearly the Self has to become activated to allow us to go down the paradoxical path that Jung and Lawrence envisioned for us. If left to our own devices, we would move endlessly 'between the opposites', shifting from a patriarchal spirit that resists the natural to an entirely 'natural' condition in which the transcendent spirit is nowhere to be found. When we gain hold of one, the other is lost, and vice versa. At present it seems that we are losing hold of the patriarchal spirit, and entering into a New Age in which nature will be revered and adored. So long as we are subject to the laws of compensation and opposition, we will drift eternally between the opposites of spirit and nature, never managing to strike a creative balance between these archetypal perspectives.

But Jung's radicalism, his modern or revolutionary thinking, was always held in check by a healthy conservatism and a high regard for the Judaeo-Christian symbolic order that needed to be compensated by the forces of nature. I often feel that Jung's saving grace, and what protected him from the excesses of modernity, was this deeply conservative element, which prevented him from throwing out the old order to champion and extol the new. Jung could never have been a New Ager because I have been defining 'New Age' as a deliberate or unconscious championing of those archetypal forces and complexes that Western culture has left out.

Because Jung thinks in terms of paradox he would insist that there is no point in exploring and elevating the Mother unless the Father is preserved, conserved and brought back into the psychic and spiritual economy. He would insist that the emergence of the Mother religions from the collective unconscious only makes sense if the Father and his Spirit are 'present' to greet and embrace the newly emerging matriarchal elements. Jung would introduce a psychotherapeutic standpoint here, emphasising that the Father can only be cured of his sickness and his spiritual isolation if his partner the soul, or nature, is 'restored' to him. The Father of the West is languishing and dying because he is alienated from nature and the feminine, hence his suffering can only be redeemed by the spontaneous appearance and uprising of the missing partner or bride. If we forget the Father's suffering and concentrate solely on the celebration and adoration of the Goddess (wicca, herbalism, paganism), we have forgotten the very archetypal process that has willed this change into existence in the first place. Our task and fate is to encourage, foster and facilitate the mystical marriage between spirit and nature, heaven and earth, Father and Mother.

THE APOCALYPTIC ENCOUNTER OF EGO AND SOUL

Having reviewed the problem of the encounter between spirit and nature, I would now like to consider the relations between ego and soul. Managing the relations between these archetypes and contents of the psyche will determine whether there is to be an authentic new age of humanity, or whether we are to destroy ourselves in a conflagration. The encounter between ego (human construction) and soul (sacred reality) is in fact the psychological basis for the ongoing myth of apocalypse or Armageddon, the explosion that takes place at the end of time, when God and the world collide. From a psychological perspective, the only way to avoid the tragic consequences of the apocalypse is for the ego to face voluntarily the reality of the soul, that is, to seek consciously its own transformation. The ego can either choose wholeness through conscious union with the soul, or it can be unconsciously and fatally united with the soul in a fiery conflagration. The art of conscious trans-formation is the common goal shared by religion, alchemy and Jung's individuation.

In the New Age movement, I have argued, wholeness is sought but rarely achieved. The problem is that the ego and the soul do not achieve a positive equilibrium, because one is often championed at the expense of the other. When the ego is infantile or poorly developed, it is readily seduced by the soul, and loses its own ground, in which case the sacred triumphs but the ego is effectively annulled, resulting in manic or depressive psychosis. This does not fulfil the goal of religion because it is not incarnational, and does not bring creator and creation together in a new unity. On the other hand, the greedy ego can seek to appropriate the realm of the soul to itself, partly because it misunderstands its own limitations, and has no understanding of the 'third thing', the Self, Christ, Buddha or Atman, which alone can reconcile creator and creation. When the ego consumes the soul, the result is megalomania, inflation, tyranny and addiction to power.

We pay a high price for the infantilism of the ego and for the narcissism of its claims, especially when an unprepared or unformed ego goes in search of spirituality. To counteract the seductive attractions of Hillman's archetypal psychology (where ego is dissolved in the soul) or the excesses of Whitman's cosmic grandiosity (where ego appropriates and overtakes the soul), we need to know more about the psychology of wholeness and the theology of incarnation. Moreover, as I keep emphasising, the art or science of linking ego and soul (*religio*) is of immediate public concern, so we are obliged to express difficult psychological and spiritual problems in language that can be understood by many people.

Between two worlds: a diversity of morbid symptoms

Antonio Gramsci, the Italian Marxist, wrote:

> The old is dying and the new cannot be born; in this interregnum there arises a great diversity of morbid symptoms.
>
> (cited in Gordimer 1981: 1)

Gramsci was talking about society and its economic systems, but this wonderful quotation can just as readily be applied to our psychological and spiritual lives. There is a general sense today that the old world is dead, even though the old clings on for as long as it can, especially in our religious, economic, educational and political systems. Something new wants to be born, but what is it? A cloud of uncertainty hangs over us, as we await whatever it is that is supposed to happen. Samuel Beckett saw our waiting as tragic and absurd in *Waiting for Godot*, and in his *Endgame* there is a haunting mixture of metaphysical enigma and painful uncertainty: 'What's happening, what's happening?' Hamm asks, and Clov replies enigmatically, 'Something is taking its course' (1958: 17).

We are witnessing the 'individuation' or development of Western consciousness, yet we are at a point in history where the new development is being resisted. The psychosocial drama of the day, as of any time, is being played out between the ego and the soul. The old ego is like the Old King in a fairytale, a king who no longer rules with the authority of the psyche (or the 'kingdom'), but he clings onto power and tries to fend off the new by denying its existence. Meanwhile, the new, split off from mainstream consciousness and denied entry into society's formal institutions, develops its own separate culture and thus the 'New Age' is born.

But the New Age is not the new age that we are waiting for. The New Age is almost a parody of the new values of soul and spirit that want to be born, and as such it is one of the 'morbid symptoms' that Gramsci refers to. Precisely because it has been forced to lead a split-off, separate existence, the New Age movement has been dealing with repressed spiritual values in an atmosphere of general unconsciousness and lack of clarity. It has not benefited from the guiding light of consciousness, and is not illuminated by the revelation of sacred scripture or the evidence of religious history or theology, and so there is tremendous murkiness and muddiness in its thinking. Its motivating forces have been personal longing, instinctive desire and instant gratification. It is a response to spiritual need which is largely a product of our consumerist society and its attempt to satisfy human craving. In this movement, the values of spirit and soul are distorted, and often out of balance with, and poorly related to, ego and society.

The wily Old King, the ruler of the old consciousness, looks across at the New Age and laughs. He sees a series of spiritual activities that look parodic, false, vulgar, gauche, awkwardly imported or artificially 'added on' to society. These activities, he pronounces, do not 'belong' to our society, and he tries to banish them. Is this, he sneers, what wants to challenge my hegemony? Is this the pathetic thing that would like to seize control of society and lead us into the future? From where he stands, the New Age looks ridiculous, hopeless and embarrassing. There is no grandeur in it, just a collection of spiritual bric-à-brac which has no apparent value, nor aesthetic appeal. Beside the classic art works of the Old King, and his mansions full of artistic and spiritual treasures, the New Age looks like so much scribbling in the sand.

I am in regular contact with two institutions of the Old King, one is the church and the other is the university. The church is the King's sacred shrine and throne, and the university is his seat of knowledge and learning. Because one is sacred and the other is secular they seem to be opposed, but they are not. Both are products of the Old King's mind and part of his hegemony. Both look at the New Age and laugh with scorn and derision. The church says the New Age is pagan regression, gnosticism, narcissism and witchcraft. Therefore, because the church sees only these things, it feels justified in rejecting it. In fact, the more vehement the rejection, the more convinced it is that it is thereby bolstering the great traditional values of religious culture. Hostile defensiveness becomes associated with a just stance for truth in a chaotic and fragmented time.

The university cannot integrate or educate the New Age impulse because it cannot agree with its assumptions. It laughs with scorn and derision at the students who want to study astrology, wicca, meditation, sacred ecology, cosmology, spirituality and self-realisation, because it does not understand what this is all about. Is it some barbaric assault on human reason? Is it a regression to pre-medieval mentality in an institution that is still committed to the project of Intellectual Enlightenment? Is this the poisonous effects of Jungian psychology in a popular culture that seems to have swallowed whole the unlikely idea of a Collective Unconscious and its swag of Archetypes? As with the church, hostile defensiveness becomes associated with a just stance for truth in a society given over to superstition and credulity.

The institutions of the Old Age are right to defend themselves, but unless they can learn to integrate aspects of the New Age they will not survive, much less thrive. People are leaving the old institutions in droves, draining the Old King of his power and leaving him without subjects to govern. For many people involved in the search for wisdom and self-realisation, the church and the university are already irrelevant to their lives, their journeys and their investigations. There is now a widening gap between an education system committed to reason and a New Age committed to personal spirituality. A university that I will not embarrass by naming was recently offered several million dollars by a sporting champion who had been helped by a Jungian therapist, to establish an academic chair in Jungian psychology. The President of the university set up a committee to look into the viability of the chair, but the committee decided to refuse the funding to protect its intellectual reputation. The Psychology Department had advised that Jungian psychology was a flaky, mystical, New Age discourse, and the university could not support it.

The Old King is a tyrannical ego who refuses to have truck with the living reality of the soul. His hegemonic ego will cling to what it knows, to its version of reality, which it is convinced is the only one. This ego likes to imagine it is in control of the personality and in charge of the world. It establishes itself as the sole psychological authority and attacks other authorities that challenge the illusion of its own omnipotence. More morbid than the symptomatic activity of the New Age is the paranoid aggressiveness of the Old Age as it attempts to ward off the new and defend itself against the future.

The dangers of close encounters with the soul

The Western world is experiencing a kind of midlife crisis, or a moment of deep transition, and our turn to the spiritual is in many cases forced upon us by necessity. Like the sporting hero who wanted to endow a chair in Jung, we often have to break down before we 'break through' to a new way of seeing and perceiving the world. We are not heading toward spirituality because we are the willing inheritors of a religious culture; we are being hounded toward the spiritual as an urgent response to the mess we have got ourselves into. Those who resist this development are merely frustrating the evolution of consciousness, or are preventing us from growing into our cultural maturity. Modern society is not allowing itself to grow up, because age brings wisdom beyond the rational ego, and such wisdom is not wanted by secular society. Jung argues that as we mature we grow beyond the confines of the limited self, and sometimes the ego must break, collapse or painfully fracture before we can accept our own spiritual growth. Life shatters the cocoon-like encasement of the ego, and this can be a terrifying and anguished experience. As scripture says, 'It is a terrible thing to fall into the hands of the Living God' (Hebrews 10.31).

The more tightly sealed the envelope of the ego, the more violent and upsetting will be the involuntary experience that seeks to jolt us out of our condition. This leads to another paradox: the more often we can have a numinous experience of the Wholly Other, the not-self, the less likely we are to be plagued by shocking events and disturbing revelations that turn our heads to the larger life. Again, we can understand scripture in the light of this psychological truth: 'He who has his life shall lose it, and he who loses his life for my sake shall find it.' When the ego clings onto everything, it will most likely lose everything, but if it sacrifices to a larger life, it will be allowed to live, and live abundantly.

Nature, fate, destiny or God – however we like to conceptualise the Wholly Other – will simply cut off the supply of vitality and life to the inflated creature who does not consciously live the sacramental and devotional life. Western consciousness must now sacrifice something of its ego-boundedness and its ego-security for the sake of greater growth. To the extent that it resists this process, it is contributing to what Jung calls the 'frustration of archetypal intent' and delaying the necessary transformation of society.

The person who spiritually matures is the person who grows into a sense of the Other, into an awareness of the importance of other people, of social needs beyond my needs, of the centrality of nature and the environment, and of the divine imprint in all things. An egocentric culture makes us oblivious to the life of nature and the delicate ecological balances in the environment, it makes us ignorant of our social responsibility, and disrespectful of age and ageing. We have not learned the lesson which is basic to all ancient and tribal cultures: that the personal self is a working fiction, and deep down we are coterminous with the social collective, the ancestors, and even the cosmos itself.

In tribal cultures, initiations took place not only to mark the beginning of puberty and adolescence, but also to begin the transition whereby human identity shifts from the personal ego to the collective or transpersonal soul. This process of spiritual transformation needs rituals and cultural support to further it along, and in this regard so-called 'primitive' societies are far in advance of our 'sophisticated' society. In initiations, the neophyte is urged to identify with a totemic symbol, with the life of the whole tribe and the strivings of the ancestors, and in this way the personality is weaned away from the ego and directed toward the life of the soul. Ancient initiations enable persons to pass from narcissism to wisdom, from ego-centredness to eco-centredness.

Our culture patently fails to teach us how to pass from the condition of ego to the condition of soul. Our culture is Luciferian in its insistence that we stick to the ego and continue to deny the great world of the sacred. Instead of encouraging age and wisdom, our culture encourages continued youth and endless selfishness. Because wisdom cannot be conceptualised, age is viewed merely as the absence of youth, the loss of the ability to live recklessly and passionately from the personal ego. Today, age simply means that we are forced to slow down, to enjoy fewer diversions offered by our culture; therefore, it is decided, old age is a bore. But age should mean that we are more able to enter the larger life beyond the ego, and to shed many of the personal ties, affectations and idiosyncrasies that prevent us from participating in the universal life of the creator.

The person or culture who is caught inside the ego often longs for a kind of negative or symptomatic transcendence. We find that, despite our conscious commitment to maintaining the ego, we are unconsciously addicted to this or that activity or substance that holds out the possibility of release. The illusions offered by drugs, alcohol, consumerism and other forms of affluent indulgence seem irresistible to the ego that cannot or does not want to discover the natural path to transcendence. It is tragically ironic that a culture that refuses the open and available path of natural transcendence ends up destroying itself in pursuit of a negative or artificial transcendence. Human life has been ordained by nature to transcend the ego, and if it lacks the guts to negotiate this transformation consciously, it will become the victim of transformation gone wrong. If we do not consciously grasp wholeness and choose it as our goal, there is the likelihood that the human experiment will blow up in our faces, due to the massive accumulation of everything that has been rejected by the ego.

The psychodynamics of apocalypse

Religion and theology have long imagined a future apocalypse, an Armageddon, or the end of time. Our task today is to translate these puzzling ideas and concepts into terms that have existential importance and psychological immediacy. If we leave the idea of the apocalypse in theological space, it remains mute, dead and untouchable; it fails to speak to us. By translating these ancient ideas into the modern language of ego and soul, we can rescue our religious heritage from its present state of social irrelevance.

The message that every true prophet delivers is: Repent, for the end of time is at hand. 'Repent' simply means to reconsider, to think again. The human ego has to reconsider its own identity, its responsibility and task in the larger picture, and its instrumental relation to the sacred. 'The end of time', in psychological terms, is the end of the ego's reign in profane time, as distinct from eternal life in sacred time. The secular mind naturally recoils from such prophecies, and denounces them as the morbid products of doom and gloom. But the prophetic voice is right: humanity must either recover its sense of the sacred, or bust.

Apocalypse means the revelation of the sacred, which could be seen as that process by which the ordinary self is displaced, revealing the larger eternal life that stands behind the ego and is blocked by its separateness. Apocalypse is the revelation of the Other, at the expense of the ego. If one has not developed a relationship with what stands behind the ego, then when the ego is swept aside or displaced, one is plunged into a void and becomes nothing. This, I take it, is what religion means by casting unbelievers into hell. 'Unbelievers', in my own psychological reading of religion, means those who have failed to develop a relationship with the non-egoic realm, and 'hell' is a mythological place which expresses the torturous condition of relating to nothing outside the ego and its own desires.

Scripture often announces that the End is Nigh, that the end of time is at hand. Like everything else in scripture, this is usually interpreted literally and concretely by the rational intellect, as pointing to an actual end of the world, and when the prophesied end does not come, people say: Look, it didn't happen after all; it is an empty myth or fantasy, we are still here and we have survived. So the prophecy is deemed to be wrong or baseless. However, the prophecy is only wrong if it is interpreted literally in this way. The idea of the End of Time refers symbolically to the overcoming of our profane state in normal time. It refers to the end of our alienation from God, and it suggests that the overcoming of this alienation is always 'at hand', always imminent. Psychologically, there is the possibility that we can terminate our egoic separation and begin a new life in restored relationship with the sacred. This is the eschatological dream of a new age of the spirit, and Paul's vision of new life in the spirit.

For very good reason, traditional religion imagined that this restoration of sacred unity between man and God would not take place in this life, but would be reserved for the afterlife. In this life, we could only achieve glimpses of such unity, especially in the ritual of the Eucharist and in the holy sacraments of reconciliation. The church would look upon the New Age movement today and rest assured that its historical antipathy to the achievement of sacred unity in this life has been vindicated. The church has long believed that terrible inflationary consequences can arise when man pretends to have personal intimacy with God, and some of the seven deadly sins reflect this anticipation of inflation, including satanic pride (Lucifer), power and avarice (Mammon), and all-devouring hunger (Beelzebub).

So the eternal life is always projected beyond this life into a life after death, and ordinary people would assume that the phrase 'at hand' signified a stern warning about imminent death, cataclysm and divine judgement. But mystics, visionaries and poets have always recognised that this is a kind of metaphor for the availability of the eternal at any point in time, including now. By definition, eternity is operating at every moment, and not just after our physical death. Eternity is present in time, and as such is available to us in subtle and yet important ways, as the ever-present cosmic background of everything we do. The seeing of this eternity is an act of imagination and seeing-through, a way of seeing that makes the usually opaque world transparent and illumined. As Jung and Blake knew, we see through to the sacred by the art of symbolic perception, that is, by seeing the things of this world as sacraments or analogues of the sacred reality.

If we develop a living relationship with the sacred, the end of time won't destroy us, but will radically transform us. This, in theological language, is called salvation or redemption. Salvation is renouncing the illusion of our independence, or overcoming our orphaned selfhood. If we have the courage to make that transformation, to follow through with that *metanoia*, then the sacred won't destroy us, but will transform us into an aspect of itself. By accepting that relationship in faith, we effectively annihilate the opposition between self and sacred, ego and soul, time and eternity, and take on the eternal dimension that is given with the sacred.

It is here that a transforming symbol or figure becomes crucial, such as Christ, Buddha, Atman or Holy Spirit. We cannot resolve the tension between ego and soul unless there is a third thing which is capable of uniting the opposites. Without the third thing, ego devours soul (Whitman), or soul devours ego (Hillman), and we end up incapacitated and unable to carry forward the creative process of the universe. Incarnation requires that a third thing that is neither God nor man, but both, comes into being. Jesus of Nazareth willingly and consciously took on this identity upon himself; in other words, he sacrificed himself so that we could move beyond profane time. Or, as we are told in church, he died so that we could live. The frustrating thing is that the church does not explain what this extraordinary statement means, and we are often none the wiser, even after decades of diligent church-going.

Here, as everywhere in religion, we meet the possibility of distorting and ugly literalism: eternal life does not mean that my separateness, my orphaned selfhood, goes on living for eternity. This is a sentimental corruption of the idea of eternity and a product of false or concrete thinking. The saved or redeemed self only goes on living to the extent that it has entered into relationship with the sacred, and therefore participates in the continuity and eternity of the sacred. By forming a relationship with the sacred, we not only transform ourselves, but we also transform the sacred. It is no longer an enemy or tyrant, anxious to overwhelm us with its apocalyptic force, but it becomes friend or lover, taking us into its bosom for eternity. This is why, for Christians, God is not wrathful or destroying, but takes on the demeanour of a loving and redeeming God, since those who have faith in the Messiah, and in the abiding presence of the Holy Spirit, will not perish but have everlasting life.

Whether our personal apocalypse is experienced as positive or negative depends largely upon the condition of our personality, and upon our preparations for the end of profane time. If we are completely identified with the separate selfhood of the ego, which is the normal, natural and as it were 'unredeemed' condition of humanity, then apocalypse can only be seen as dreadful, destructive and horrifying. However, if we have come to experience and know the 'second self' behind the ego, which is variously referred to as the spirit or soul, then apocalypse is not a devastation, but a fulfillment of spiritual yearning and prayerful longing. It would be wrong to assume that the apocalypse is something that an outside, supernatural God does to the human person, but rather it is a total transformation that springs from within the personality itself. We can gain a deeper insight into these 'external', mythological events if we accept that we have two selves, or two lives, and that creativity and health involves finding a balance between these selves.

The appearance and ambivalence of the child archetype

Western religion claims that we have to become as little children before we enter the kingdom (Matthew 18.3). However, scripture does not ask us to 'remain' as a little child, but to become as a child, that is, grow into a second innocence, and grow out of adult rationality and cynicism. The appearance of a second innocence and childlike qualities would herald the awakening of the spirit, and allow the reality of the soul to break through the rigid defences of the ego and the hard walls of rational thought.

The New Age is very much about the awakening of the child within, of the archetype of the child. New Age workshops, books and seminars all encourage us to find the child within, which is seen as the essence of our creativity and spiritual renewal. If we are viewing Western culture in a developmental sense, it would seem that the child archetype would arise after the intense rationality of scientific enquiry, as it were, as a compensation for our intense rationality. The child archetype would herald the dawning of a new era of culture, an age in which the language of spirit can be heard again, in which poetry and scripture makes sense again, in which we are no longer imprisoned by the structures of thought.

If the New Age can be seen as an eruption of the child archetype, this perhaps accounts for why so many learned, responsible adults become infuriated, baffled and embarrassed by this movement. Our adult consciousness does not want to know about a new age of the spirit, but merely wants to continue on its present course, becoming more and more rational, productive and 'successful' in its own terms. The child motif is perhaps activated by way of compensation to our obsessive rationality and common sense. As Jung has said:

> The child motif . . . is not just a vestige [of the distant past] but a system functioning in the present whose purpose is to compensate or correct, in a meaningful manner, the inevitable one-sidedness and extravagances of the conscious mind.
>
> (1940: 276)

But what arises spontaneously is most often rejected by consciousness:

> The symptoms of compensation are described, from the progressive point of view, in scarcely flattering terms. To the superficial ego, it [compensation] looks like a retarding operation, [and] people speak of inertia, backwardness, fault-finding . . . and so on.
>
> (1940: 277)

Herein lies the problem of our moral and ethical response to this movement. The whole movement is too easily dismissed by common sense. Our common sense sees only the infantilism and the silliness. For it, the New Age is viewed as bugbear and irritant. The rational persona, enjoying its modern and sanitised consciousness, is infuriated by the sudden appearance of a dirty, wild, uncouth child, who rushes into the secular spaces of the world, bringing apparent disorder and mental chaos in its wake. The compensatory process activates what Jung calls a 'retarding ideal', which, he says, 'is always more primitive, more natural (in the good sense as in the bad)' than the existing psychic condition it is compensating (1940: 277). It takes an unusual, symbolic or prophetic kind of awareness to see the redemptive element in this upsurge of chaos, to see the message in the mess, or the deeper wisdom that is operating through the compensatory process.

The compensatory child motif is always double-sided. On the one hand, it is childish, infantile and messy, but on the other hand it is childlike, magical and wondrous. It brings bad and good news, and the problem for consciousness is to discern both elements at once, to realise that beneath the infantilism are some important magical elements which may harbour the elixir of life, and the possibility of redemption. Jung often argues that redemption comes from the rejected element, from the stone rejected by the builders, from the very thing which is devalued. The saviour, he writes, 'is either the insignificant thing itself, or else arises out of it' (1940: 267).

However, much discernment is required at this stage, so that we do not overvalue the so-called 'retarding ideal'. There is always the danger that we can become identified with the compensatory elements, in which case the positive aspects of the compensatory process are overemphasised, the child is crowned as king, and the infantilism, vulgarity or crudeness are ignored or swept aside. An unreal idealisation of the New Age, found in many fans and supporters of this movement, represents a defensive resistance to its infantile or incomplete aspects, while hostile rejection of the New Age represents a defence against the compensatory process that needs to be integrated.

If we are either too accepting or too condemning, this archetype's compensatory task cannot be fulfilled. The whole point of compensation, according to Jung, is to bring the existing situation and the uprising content into meaningful relationship. This means that the New Age and the Old Age have to interact with each other, since 'viable progress only comes from the co-operation of both' (1940: 277). Such interaction is bound to be difficult, due to the contradictory nature of what is being brought together. Such tension is necessary and important, and is in fact the precondition for the birth of the reconciling symbol, the 'third thing' that can arise from the conflict of these opposites. The psychological goal is to dissolve both the New Age and the status quo, to find a Third Way beyond the retarding ideal of the New Age and the ideal of society, and allow the third position to be born from the clash of opposites. The child archetype, Jung says, 'anticipates the figure that comes from the synthesis of conscious and unconscious elements in the personality'. The appearance of the child motif 'paves the way for a future change of personality' (1940: 278).

In 'The Futurity of the Archetype', Jung stresses the importance of the child in its prophetic and prospective role. We must not just see the child for what it appears to be, but realise that it carries the seeds of the future, that the child is a symbol of the developmental process, and of the need for a pathway through the present impasse. So too in our cultural theme, the New Age cannot be viewed merely as it seems, but must be viewed as an anticipation of a future kind of consciousness. It is an anticipation of our post-secular and post-rational future, and is not just a sign of regression to infantile stages of society, as Mel Faber argues (1996), but also a symbol of an as-yet-unrealised cultural and spiritual future.

One of the essential features of the child motif is its futurity. The child is potential future. Hence the occurrence of the child motif . . . signifies as a rule an anticipation of future developments, even though at first sight it may seem like a retrospective configuration.

(1940: 278)

The child is both beginning and end, an initial and a terminal creature. The initial creature existed before man was, and the terminal creature will be when man is not. Psychologically speaking, this means that the child symbolises the pre-conscious and the post-conscious essence of man.

(1940: 299)

The child archetype is Janus-faced, looking backward to the past and forward to the future, and is prophetic of the future direction of consciousness. I would prefer to call this future post-egoic, rather than 'post-conscious', as in the above quotation.

Like an infant, the New Age grasps for this and that, often not knowing the differences between major world religions or esoteric spiritual traditions. One day it prefers North American indigenous mythology and vibrational medicine, and the next day it develops a taste for Zen Buddhism, Taoism or Confucianism. Three days later, the Australian Aboriginal Dreaming is all the rage, to be replaced soon after by New Zealand Maori animism or Papua New Guinea shamanism. Like an infant, it consumes everything; religious products go into its mouth, are sucked for a while, and are often spat out undigested. Like an infant, the New Age thinks that God exists as a source for its own pleasure; it is something to grasp, acquire and manipulate.

The religious impulse reborn like a child in a secular time has no memory of its past, no recollection of its historical traditions, and no awareness of its grand cultural heritage. Like Plato's conception of the soul, it loses all this background as it traverses the Plains of Forgetfulness on its way toward rebirth. It emerges into the present world as a *tabula rasa*, an innocent, naive impulse with no history or cultural background. In its infantile or childish aspect, the New Age symbolises the incoherence and illiteracy of the spirit in a secular age. It is the religious impulse learning again how to walk, taking a few faltering steps forward, and learning again how to talk, moving toward a new, revelatory style of discourse. It urges us to talk about spirit, where before we spoke only about facts and events.

Enduring the embarrassment of the new is perhaps what will make any future religious high culture possible. The infant spirit must be nurtured and allowed to grow up, so we might discover the important clues and directions that lie within it. There is a genuine post-rationalist age ahead on the cultural horizon, but we may have to tolerate a good deal of psychobabble and discordant noise before the authentic new age reaches us. The new age dawns gradually, slowly, and if we are too harshly critical about the early stages we may be rejecting important aspects of our future, or refusing the crude matrix out of which the pearl of the future will be produced. It is too early to determine the shape or outline of the new age, and for the time being we are stuck with the New Age. We have to acquire a certain patience or negative capability, so that the authentically new can be born.

References

All references to the works of Jung are to paragraph numbers, not to page numbers, in accord with scholarly practice.

References to the writings of Jung are indicated by the essay or chapter, followed by *CW (Collected Works)*, and the volume number. All references are to *The Collected Works of C.G. Jung*, translated by R.F.C. Hull, edited by H. Read, M. Fordham, G. Adler, and William McGuire, and published in England by Routledge, London, and in America by Princeton University Press, Bollingen Series XX, 1953–1992. There are 20 volumes in the collected works, plus four supplementary volumes.

With regard to the Holy Bible, several editions and translations have been consulted and compared, including *The English Revised Version* (1885), *The Revised Standard Version* (1952), *The Jerusalem Bible* (1966), and *The New International Version Study Bible* (1995).

Adler, Alfred 1964: *The Individual Psychology of Alfred Adler*. New York: Basic Books.

Adler, Margot 1986: *Drawing Down the Moon: Witches, Druids, Goddess-Worshippers, and Other Pagans in America Today*. Boston: Beacon Press.

Adorno, Theodore 1964: *The Authoritarian Personality*. New York: John Wiley.

Age, Mark 1970: *How to Do All Things: Your Use of Divine Power*. Tennessee: Age Metacentre.

Albanese, Catherine 1977: *Corresponding Motion: Transcendental Religion and the New America*. Philadelphia: Temple University Press.

Allison, A.W. (ed.) 1983: *The Norton Anthology of Poetry*. New York: Norton.

Batchelor, Stephen 1994: *The Awakening of the West: The Encounter of Buddhism and Western Culture*. London: Aquarian Press.

Beckett, Samuel 1958: *Endgame*. London: Faber, 1982.

Bednarowski, Mary 1995: *New Religions and the Theological Imagination in America*. Bloomington: Indiana University Press.

Bellah, Robert 1991: *Beyond Belief*. Oxford: University of California Press.

Besant, Annie 1897: *The Ancient Wisdom*. Adyara: Theosophical Publishing House, 1939.

Bishop, Peter 1994: *Dreams of Power: Tibetan Buddhism and the Western Imagination*. London: Athlone.

Blake, William 1793: 'The Marriage of Heaven and Hell', in Geoffrey Keynes (ed.), *Blake: Complete Writings*. Oxford: Oxford University Press, 1976.

—— 1794: 'Europe: A Prophecy', in Geoffrey Keynes (ed.), *Blake: Complete Writings*. Oxford: Oxford University Press, 1976.

Bloom, Harold 1992: *The American Religion: The Emergence of the Post-Christian Nation*. New York: Simon & Schuster.

—— 1996: *Omens of Millennium*. London: Fourth Estate.

Bloom, William (ed.) 1991: *The New Age: An Anthology of Essential Writing*. London: Rider.

Bly, Robert 1990: *Iron John: A Book About Men*. Reading, MA: Addison-Wesley.

Bolen, Jean Shinoda 1985: *Goddesses in Everywoman*. New York: Harper Colophon.

—— 1989: *Gods in Everyman*. New York: Harper Colophon.

Bowman, Catherine 1992: *Crystal Awareness*. San Francisco: Llewellyn.

Button, John, and Bloom, William 1992: *The Seeker's Guide: A New Age Resource Book*. London: Aquarian Press.

Campbell, Bruce 1980: *Ancient Wisdom Revived*. Berkeley: University of California Press.

Campbell, Eileen, and Brennan, J.H. 1990: *The Aquarian Guide to the New Age*. Wellingborough: Aquarian Press.

Campbell, Joseph, and Moyers, Bill 1988: *The Power of Myth*. New York: Doubleday.

Capra, Fritjof 1976: *The Tao of Physics*. London: Fontana.

—— 1983: *The Turning Point: Science, Society and the Rising Culture*. London: Fontana.

—— 1989: *Uncommon Wisdom*. London: Flamingo.

Capra, Fritjof, and Steindl-Rast, David (eds) 1992: *Belonging to the Universe*. New York: HarperCollins.

Carroll, John 1993: *Humanism: The Wreck of Western Culture*. London: Fontana.

Casey, Caroline 1998: *Making the Gods Work for You*. New York: Three Rivers Press.

Chopra, Deepak 1993: *Creating Affluence: Wealth Consciousness in the Field of All Possibilities*. San Rafael: New World Library.

—— 1994: *The Seven Spiritual Laws of Success: A Practical Guide to the Fulfillment of Your Dreams*. San Rafael: Amber-Allen.

Christ, Carol, and Plaskow, Judith (eds) 1992: *Womanspirit Rising: A Feminist Reader in Religion*. New York: HarperCollins.

Clatterbaugh, Kenneth 1990: *Contemporary Perspectives on Masculinity.* Boulder: Westview Press.

Colling, Terry 1992: *Beyond Mateship: Understanding Australian Men.* Sydney: Simon & Schuster.

Collins, Alfred 1994: *Fatherson.* Wilmette, IL: Chiron.

Corneau, Guy 1991: *Absent Fathers, Lost Sons.* Boston: Shambhala.

Crowley, Vivianne 1989: *Wicca: The Old Religion in the New Age.* Wellingborough: Aquarian Press.

Daly, Mary 1979: *Gyn/Ecology: The Metaethics of Radical Feminism.* London: Women's Press.

Das, Surya 1999: *Awakening to the Sacred.* New York: Bantam.

Davis, Oliver 1988: *God Within.* London: Darton, Longman & Todd.

Drury, Nevill 1987: *The Shaman and the Magician.* Harmondsworth: Arkana.

—— 1989: *The Elements of Human Potential.* Shaftesbury: Element Books.

—— 1999: *Exploring the Labyrinth: Making Sense of the New Spirituality.* Sydney: Allen & Unwin.

Edinger, Edward 1972: *Ego and Archetype.* Baltimore: Penguin, 1974.

Eliade, Mircea 1957: *The Sacred and the Profane.* New York: Harcourt, Brace & World, 1977.

—— 1969: *The Quest: History and Meaning in Religion.* Chicago: University of Chicago Press, 1975.

—— 1976: *Occultism, Witchcraft, and Cultural Fashions.* Chicago: University of Chicago Press.

Eliot, T.S. 1942: *Four Quartets,* in *Collected Poems.* London: Faber, 1965.

Estes, Clarissa Pinkola 1992: *Women Who Run With the Wolves: Contacting the Power of the Wild Woman.* London: Rider.

Faber, Mel D. 1996: *New Age Thinking: A Psychoanalytic Critique.* University of Ottawa Press.

Faludi, Susan 1991: *Backlash: The Undeclared War Against Women.* New York: Crown.

Ferguson, Duncan S. (ed.) 1993: *New Age Spirituality: An Assessment.* Louisville, KY: Westminster/John Knox Press.

Ferguson, Marilyn 1981: *The Aquarian Conspiracy: Personal and Social Transformation in the 1980s.* Los Angeles: Jeremy P. Tarcher.

Fox, Matthew 1983: *Original Blessing: A Primer in Creation Spirituality.* Santa Fe: Bear.

—— 1991: *Creation Spirituality: Liberating Gifts for the Peoples of the Earth.* San Francisco: Harper & Row.

Freud, Sigmund 1930: *New Introductory Lectures on Psycho-Analysis. Standard Edition,* vol. 22. London, Hogarth Press, 1974.

Frey-Rohn, Liliane 1984: *Friedrich Nietzsche: A Psychological Approach to his Life and Work.* Zurich: Daimon Verlag, 1988.

Gordimer, Nadine 1981: *July's People.* Harmondsworth: Penguin.

Green, Martin 1992: *Prophets of a New Age.* New York: Scribners.

Griffin, David Ray (ed.) 1988: *Spirituality and Society: Postmodern Visions.* Albany: State University of New York Press.

—— (ed.) 1989: *God and Religion in the Postmodern World.* Albany: State University of New York Press.

Hall, Stuart 1968: *The Hippies: An American Movement.* University of Birmingham Press.

Harding, Douglas 1961: *On Having No Head: Zen and the Rediscovery of the Obvious.* London: Arkana.

Harvey, Andrew 1991: *Hidden Journey: A Spiritual Awakening.* London: Rider.

Hay, Louise 1991: *The Power is Within You.* London: Eden Grove.

Haule, John Ryan 1999: *Perils of the Soul: Ancient Wisdom and the New Age.* York Beach, ME: Samuel Weiser.

Heelas, Paul 1996: *The New Age Movement: The Celebration of the Self and the Sacralization of Modernity.* Oxford: Blackwell.

Heelas, Paul, Martin, David and Morris, Paul (eds) 1996: *Religion, Modernity and Postmodernity.* Oxford: Blackwell.

Hillman, James 1967: *Insearch.* New York: Charles Scribner's Sons.

—— 1972: *The Myth of Analysis.* Evanston: Northwestern University Press.

—— 1973: 'The Great Mother, Her Son, Her Hero, and the Puer', in Patricia Berry (ed.), *Fathers and Mothers*, 2nd edn. Dallas: Spring, 1990.

—— 1975: *Re-Visioning Psychology.* New York: Harper & Row.

—— 1979: *The Dream and the Underworld.* New York: Harper & Row.

—— 1983: *Archetypal Psychology.* Dallas: Spring.

—— 1992 'Preface: A Memoir from the Author for the 1992 Edition', in *Re-Visioning Psychology.* New York: HarperCollins.

—— 1995: *Kinds of Power: A Guide to Its Intelligent Uses.* New York: Currency Doubleday.

—— 1996: *The Soul's Code: In Search of Character and Calling.* New York: Random House.

—— 1999: *The Force of Character.* New York: Random House.

Hillman, James, and Ventura, Michael 1993: *We've Had a Hundred Years of Psychotherapy and the World's Getting Worse.* San Francisco: HarperCollins.

Hillman, James, Bly, Robert, and Meade, Michael 1994: *The Rag and Bone Shop of the Heart: An Anthology of Poems for Men.* New York: HarperCollins.

Hope, Deborah 2000: 'In good spirit', *The Weekend Australian*, 'Review', 8–9 January 2000.

Hughes, Robert 1987: 'The Geographical Unconscious', in *The Fatal Shore.* London: Pan.

Huxley, Aldous 1946: *The Perennial Philosophy.* London: Chatto & Windus.

Jacoby, Mario 1980: *The Longing for Paradise.* Boston: Sigo Press, 1985.

Johnson, Robert 1974: *He: Understanding Masculine Psychology.* New York: Harper & Row, 1977.

—— 1976: *She: Understanding Feminine Psychology.* New York: Harper & Row.

—— 1984: *The Psychology of Romantic Love*. London: Routledge & Kegan Paul.

—— 1989a: *Ecstasy: Understanding the Psychology of Joy*. San Francisco: Harper & Row.

—— 1989b: *Inner Work: Using Dreams and Active Imagination For Personal Growth*. San Francisco: Harper & Row.

—— 1991: *Transformation: Understanding the Three Levels of Masculine Consciousness*. San Francisco: HarperCollins.

—— 1993: *Owning Your Own Shadow: Understanding the Dark Side of the Psyche*. San Francisco: HarperCollins.

—— 1994: *Lying with the Heavenly Woman*. San Francisco: HarperCollins.

Jung, C.G. 1912/1952: *Symbols of Transformation*. CW 5, 1956.

—— 1916a: 'Seven Sermons to the Dead', in *Memories, Dreams, Reflections*. New York: Random House, 1973.

—— 1916b: 'The Transcendent Function'. *CW* 8, 1960.

—— 1919: 'Instinct and the Unconscious'. *CW* 8, 1960.

—— 1921: *Psychological Types*. *CW* 6, 1971.

—— 1927/1931: 'Mind and Earth'. *CW* 10, 1964.

—— 1928: 'The Relations between the Ego and the Unconscious'. *CW* 7, 1953.

—— 1928/1931: 'The Spiritual Problem of Modern Man'. *CW* 10, 1964.

—— 1929a: 'Commentary on "The Secret of the Golden Flower"'. *CW* 13, 1968.

—— 1929b: 'Freud and Jung: Contrasts'. *CW* 4, 1961.

—— 1930: 'Complications of American Psychology'. *CW* 10, 1964.

—— 1930/1931: 'The Stages of Life'. *CW* 8, 1960.

—— 1932: 'Psychotherapists or Clergy'. *CW* 11, 1958.

—— 1933a: 'The Meaning of Psychology for Modern Man'. *CW* 10, 1964.

—— 1933b: *Modern Man in Search of a Soul*. *CW* 10, 1964.

—— 1934: 'La Revolution Mondiale'. *CW* 10, 1964.

—— 1934/1950: 'A Study in the Process of Individuation'. *CW* 9, part 1, 1959.

—— 1935/1954: 'Archetypes of the Collective Unconscious'. *CW* 9, part 1, 1959.

—— 1936a: 'Wotan'. *CW* 10, 1964.

—— 1936b: 'Yoga and the West'. *CW* 11, 1958.

—— 1937: 'Psychological Factors Determining Human Behaviour'. *CW* 8, 1960.

—— 1938/1940: 'Psychology and Religion'. *CW* 11, 1958.

—— 1940: 'The Psychology of the Child Archetype'. *CW* 9, part 1, 1959.

—— 1944: *Psychology and Alchemy*. *CW* 12, 1953.

—— 1945: 'After the Catastrophe'. *CW* 10, 1964.

—— 1946: *Essays on Contemporary Events*. *CW* 10, 1964.

—— 1946/1948: 'The Phenomenology of the Spirit in Fairytales'. *CW* 9, part 1, 1959.

—— 1947/1954: 'On the Nature of the Psyche'. *CW* 8, 1960.

—— 1950: 'Concerning Mandala Symbolism'. *CW* 9, part 1, 1959.

—— 1951: *Aion. CW* 9, part 2, 1959.

—— 1952a: *Answer to Job. CW* 11, 1958.

—— 1952b: 'A Reply to Martin Buber'. *CW* 18, 1977.

—— 1957: 'The Undiscovered Self, Present and Future'. *CW* 10, 1964.

—— 1958: *Flying Saucers: A Modern Myth. CW* 10, 1964.

—— 1961: *Memories, Dreams, Reflections*. New York: Random House, 1973.

—— (ed.) 1964: *Man and His Symbols*. New York: Doubleday.

—— 1973: *Letters*, vol. 1. Princeton University Press.

—— 1975: *Letters*, vol. 2. Princeton University Press.

—— 1988: *Nietzsche's 'Zarathustra'*, 2 vols. Princeton University Press.

Kelly, Tony 1993: 'The New Age Movement', in *An Expanding Theology: Faith in a World of Connections*. Sydney: E.J. Dwyer.

Kohn, Rachael 1991: 'Radical Subjectivity in Self Religions and the Problem of Authority', in Allan Black (ed.), *Religion in Australia*. Sydney: Allen & Unwin.

Lasch, Christopher 1980: *The Culture of Narcissism*. London: Abacus.

—— 1985: *The Minimal Self: Psychic Survival in Troubled Times*. London: Picador.

Lau, Kimberly 2000: *New Age Capitalism: Making Money East of Eden*. University of Pennsylvania Press.

Lawrence, D.H. 1923: *Kangaroo*, The Corrected Edition. Sydney: Angus & Robertson, 1992.

—— 1924: 'Herman Melville's *Typee* and *Omoo*', in *Studies in Classic American Literature*. Harmondsworth: Penguin, 1977.

Lee, John 1991: *At My Father's Wedding*. New York: Bantam.

Lewis, C.S. 1946: 'The Decline of Religion', in *Compelling Reason: Essays on Ethics and Theology*. London: HarperCollins, 1998.

Lewis, James, and Melton, Gordon (eds) 1992: *Perspectives on the New Age*. Albany: State University of New York Press.

Lovelock, James 1988: *The Ages of Gaia: A Biography of Our Living Earth*. London: Norton.

MacLaine, Shirley 1990: *Going Within: A Guide for Inner Transformation*. London: Bantam.

May, Rollo 1991: *The Cry for Myth*. New York: Delta.

Miller, Thomas 1995: *How to Want What You Have*. New York: Henry Holt.

Moore, Robert, and Gillette, Douglas 1990: *King, Warrior, Magician, Lover*. San Francisco: HarperCollins.

Moore, Thomas 1992: *Care of the Soul: A Guide for Cultivating Depth and Sacredness in Everyday Life*. New York: HarperCollins.

—— 1994: *Soul Mates*. New York: HarperCollins.

—— 1995: *Meditations*. New York: HarperCollins.

—— 1996a: *The Education of the Heart*. New York: HarperCollins.

—— 1996b: *The Re-Enchantment of Everyday Life*. New York: HarperCollins.

—— 1998: *The Soul of Sex*. New York: HarperCollins.

Neumann, Erich 1949a: 'Mystical Man', in Joseph Campbell (ed.), *The Mystic Vision: Papers from the Eranos Yearbooks*. London: Routledge & Kegan Paul, 1969.

—— 1949b: *The Origins and History of Consciousness*. Princeton University Press, 1973.

—— 1955: *The Great Mother*. Princeton University Press, 1972.

Neville, Richard 1971: *Playpower*. London: Paladin.

Nietzsche, Friedrich 1872: *The Birth of Tragedy from the Spirit of Music*, in Walter Kaufmann (ed.) *The Birth of Tragedy and The Case of Wagner*. New York: Random, 1967.

—— 1885: *Thus Spoke Zarathustra*. Harmondsworth: Penguin, 1978.

—— 1886: *Beyond Good and Evil*. Harmondsworth: Penguin, 1973.

Noll, Richard 1994: *The Jung Cult: The Origins of a Charismatic Movement*. New York: HarperCollins.

—— 1997: *The Aryan Christ: The Secret Life of Carl Jung*. New York: Random House.

O'Connor, Peter 1986: *Dreams and the Search for Meaning*. Sydney: Methuen Haynes.

Pagels, Elaine 1979: *The Gnostic Gospels*. New York: Random House.

—— 1996: *The Origin of Satan*. New York: Vintage.

Palmer, Martin 1993: *Coming of Age: An Exploration of Christianity and the New Age*. London: Aquarian Press.

Papadopoulos, Renos 1992: 'Jung and the Concept of the Other', in Renos Papadopoulos (ed.), *Carl Jung: Critical Assessments*, vol. 1, London: Routledge.

Pearson, Carol 1989: *The Hero Within: Six Archetypes We Live By*. San Francisco: Harper & Row.

Possamai, Adam 1998: *In Search of New Age Spirituality*. Unpublished PhD thesis, School of Sociology and Anthropology, La Trobe University, Melbourne.

Plaskow, Judith, and Christ, Carol (eds) 1989: *Weaving the Visions: New Patterns of Feminist Spirituality*. New York: Harper & Row.

Raschke, Carl 1980: *The Interruption of Eternity: Modern Gnosticism and the Origins of the New Religious Consciousness*. Chicago: Nelson-Hall.

Ray, Michael, and Rinzler, Alan (eds) 1993: *The New Paradigm in Business*. New York: Jeremy Tarcher.

Raine, Kathleen 1979: *Blake and the New Age*. London: Allen & Unwin.

Redfield, James 1994: *The Celestine Prophecy*. London: Bantam.

Rhodes, Ron 1990: *The Counterfeit Christ of the New Age Movement*. Michigan: Baker.

Rieff, Philip 1987: *The Triumph of the Therapeutic*. London: Chatto and Windus.

Roszak, Theodore 1971: *The Making of a Counter Culture: Reflections on the Technocratic Society and Its Youthful Opposition*. London: Faber & Faber.

Samuels, Andrew 1985: *Jung and the Post-Jungians*. London: Routledge.

—— 1989: *The Plural Psyche*. London: Routledge.

—— 1993: *The Political Psyche*. London: Routledge.

—— 1996: 'Jung's Return from Banishment', *The Psychoanalytic Review* 83 (4), Special Issue: 'Symposium: Post-Jungian Thought'.

—— 1997: 'Introduction: Jung and the Post-Jungians', in Polly Young-Eisendrath and Terence Dawson (eds), *The Cambridge Companion to Jung*. Cambridge: Cambridge University Press.

—— 1998: 'Will the Post-Jungians Survive?' in Ann Casement (ed.), *Post-Jungians Today*. London: Routledge.

Spink, Peter 1991: *A Christian in the New Age*. London: Darton, Longman & Todd.

Spretnak, Charlene 1991: *States of Grace: The Recovery of Meaning in the Postmodern World*. San Francisco: Harper.

Tacey, David 1988: *Patrick White: Fiction and the Unconscious*. Melbourne: Oxford University Press.

—— 1995: *Edge of the Sacred: Transformation in Australia*. Melbourne: HarperCollins.

—— 1997: *Remaking Men: Jung, Spirituality, and Social Change*. London: Routledge. In Australia and New Zealand: *Remaking Men: The Revolution in Masculinity*. Melbourne: Viking Penguin.

—— 1998a: 'Jung and the New Age: A Study in Contrasts', *The Round Table Review of Contemporary Jungian Thought* 5(4), pp. 1–11.

—— 1998b: 'Twisting and Turning with James Hillman: From Anima to World Soul, From Academia to Pop', in Ann Casement (ed.), *Post-Jungians Today: Key Papers in Contemporary Analytical Psychology*. London: Routledge.

—— 1999: 'Why Jung would Doubt the New Age', in Susan Greenberg (ed.), *Therapy on the Couch: A Shrinking Future?*, The Mindfield Series, Issue 2. London: Camden Press.

—— 2000: *ReEnchantment: The New Australian Spirituality*. Sydney: HarperCollins.

Teilhard de Chardin, Pierre 1959: *The Phenomenon of Man*. London: Fontana.

Tillich, Paul 1949: *The Shaking of the Foundations*. Harmondsworth: Penguin.

Toolan, David 1987: *Facing West from California's Shores: A Jesuit's Journey into New Age Consciousness*. New York: Crossroad.

Vogt, Gregory Max 1991a: *Like Father, Like Son*. New York: Plenum.

—— 1991b: *Return to Father*. Dallas: Spring.

Von Franz, Marie-Louise 1970: *The Problem of the Puer Aeternus*. Santa Monica: Sigo, 1981.

—— 1973: *The Interpretation of Fairytales*. Zurich: Spring, 1978.

White, Patrick 1948: *The Aunt's Story*. Harmondsworth: Penguin, 1984.

Whitman, Walt 1855: *Leaves of Grass*, in Mark Van Doren (ed.), *The Portable Walt Whitman*. New York: Penguin, 1977.

—— 1860: 'Facing West from California's Shores', in Mark Van Doren (ed.), *The Portable Walt Whitman*. New York: Penguin, 1977.

—— 1888: 'A Backward Glance O'er Travel'd Roads', in Mark Van Doren (ed.), *The Portable Walt Whitman*. New York: Penguin, 1977.

Whitmont, Edward C. 1982: *Return of the Goddess*. New York: Crossroad.

Yeats, W.B. 1920: 'The Second Coming', in Timothy Webb (ed.), *W.B. Yeats: Selected Poetry*. Harmondsworth: Penguin, 1991.

Yoffe, Emily 1995: 'How the Soul is Sold: James Hillman and Thomas Moore', in *New York Times Magazine*, 23 April 1995, pp. 44–9.

Zukav, Gary 1980: *The Dancing Wu Li Masters: An Overview of the New Physics*. London: Fontana.

Index